Midwif

Returning to the Arms of the Ancient Mother

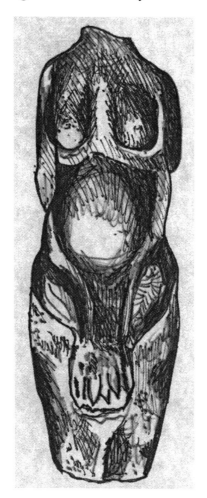

Leslene della-Madre

Plain View Press
P. O. 42255
Austin, TX 78704

plainviewpress.net
sbright1@austin.rr.com
1-512-441-2452

ISBN: 1-891386-42-5
Library of Congress Control Number: 2005903979

Front and back covers: Detail from *The Mothers: Moon, Sun, Earth/underworld, Monica Sjöö. 2000*
Title page: *Double Goddess figurine*, Grimaldi, Italy c. 28,000-20,000 BP, drawn by Melissa Meltzer

Acknowledgements

I wish to extend thanks and gratitude to all my "Ansisters" and to all the pioneering women in women's spirituality and all the women who work diligently to serve the Goddess. I thank my ongoing circle of friends who have supported me over the years and who have helped me with proof-reading and editing. I also give great thanks to everyone in my life who has given me opportunities to practice what I preach. And I give great thanks to the Mother for giving me life.

Contents

Leya's Farewell Circle

And the Faeries Danced in the Mist, Monica Sjöö, 1993

Providing a space for a dying person to meet with loved ones and receive blessings one last time can be incredibly magical. Such was the case for Leya. I did not know Leya, but when I met her, I felt like I had known her a long time. She suffered from liver and pancreatic cancer. Her swollen belly on her smallish frame made her look about six months pregnant. Her skin was orange. Her eyes, however, were shiny and clear. I was asked to facilitate a healing circle for her, and felt honored to do so. About twenty-five people gathered, some of whom had never sat in sacred circle before. Leya entered the room and was surprised to see all these loving faces there just for her. She went to lie in the special bed that was placed in the circle for her (she was not in the center of the circle, but was a part of the circle).

Creating sacred space is a cross-cultural spiritual practice. Placing a shared intention into the space creates an openness and allows for pristine aware-ness or presence to emerge. Reverence for ancestors and guiding energies of the universe can be invoked in many different ways. For Leya, we created the circle by calling to the four directions of the universe, praying aloud and asking for guidance. We used a cleansing smoke to clear any energies that didn't need to be there and we made unrehearsed sounds with our voices. They were the deep harmonic tones of the spirit/soul heartsong arising from within each being in the moment. We also drummed and rattled together-- an ancient practice that moves the collective energy into a deeply reverent place of being. People then went around the circle introducing themselves, saying how they were connected to Leya and something they appreciated about her. The love and compassion in the room was delicious. Leya's spirit was very strong. Her presence was vital and energetic. Next, we began a chant as people went one by one offering flowers and blessings to her at her bedside. Many knew it would be the last time to see her in body. Her graciousness, beauty, love and gratitude were a powerful teaching for all of us. Incredible peace radiated from her being — that eternal unencumbered place. Before the closing of the circle, Leya said it was time for her to take her leave. It felt prophetic, now that I look back on it. It was truly her time, for the next evening, she died.

I cannot think of a better way for someone to pass from this world. The circle was magical and healing, and Leya took all that energy in and made her transition in peace and love. Some said she was waiting for the circle to happen before she passed. So, she did, and then she died in a way showing all who were there how to go in love. One of the women who organized this circle for her called me up the day after she died and told me how beautiful she felt Leya's passage was. She felt inspired to make sure that she, at her time, if possible, could spend time like that with loved ones offering blessings and love. There was no fear present. I felt Leya had all the permission she needed to move on, and that she felt safe in the presence of so much love from the circle. I could see her being embraced by great loving arms, holding her to the breast, comforting her. It was a healing for all of us.

When something like this happens, the energy that ripples out from the center touches the world in profound ways. It transforms the deep-seated conditioning about fear of death, and makes it possible for us to find a more meaningful connection to our own lives, and to live our lives in more authentic ways. Something opens up and gives permission for us to be more loving and kind to ourselves and to one another. Perhaps we realize that life is short, and that what we do really does matter. Perhaps we come out of denial and addiction to wake up to what is real. Whatever it is, witnessing a peaceful, loving passage of someone in their death challenges us, at least in that moment, if we are paying attention, to face our fears and evaluate what is important in our lives.

Introduction

by Monica Sjöö

My Sons in the Spiritworld, Monica Sjöö, 1989.

People have in all times known that the ancestors, who are the dead, who are ourselves, always guide and teach us. The people in trance states listen to the voices of the spirits whispering and roaring in subterranean waters under red ochre crevices looking like vaginas. The closest I have come to this experience was spending time on my own whilst drawing within the subterranean temple/womb/tomb on Malta, the Hypogeum, where the Great Mother and Her spirits dwell. Yes, I believe that the figurines of the Goddess facilitated the entrance (through Her opening/Yoni) into the subterranean womb, assuring a place of regeneration. I believe that my own paintings are similar portals to and from other worlds. The sacred sites of the Goddess — such as the stone circles, standing stones, holy wells, mounds representing Earth's pregnant womb — are also places of trance-states and communications with other realms or the worlds of the Faerie/ancestors/the dead. There is at all times a telepathic communication, an umbilical cord, between us and the Mother Earth. We are, after all, her children, although we have forgotten.

Ever since a powerful initiation to the Goddess in the land at Avebury and Silbury in 1978 I have pilgrimaged to Her sacred sites. There are something like 900 stone circles, Lunar temples, on the British Isles.

My very first initiation to the Great Mother had been during the natural home birth of my second son in 1961. During that incredibly powerful birth I had seen in my mind's eye great radiant masses of darkness alternating with great masses of light, coming and going. Although I didn't know it then, this was the Goddess who is both Dark and Light, beyond all polarities. Did she show Herself to me in Her pure energy-body? This changed my life and set me on a life-long search for the ancient women-led cultures of the Goddess. I did my painting "God Giving Birth" in 1968. Ever since the sixties I experienced those ancient women — sisterhoods who co-exist with us now in another time-space, communicating with me, and speaking through me. I am their medium. Vicki Noble once wrote that the birthing woman is the original shaman as she hovers between the worlds open to the Spirit world from which she brings the child into this realm. This was my own experience. No wonder that the male priests of the disembodied godfather set about de-sacralizing women's life-giving powers and that the priestesses/wise women of the Goddess — who in all times were healers, midwives, astrologers, reckoners of lunar tides and the communicators with the Great Unknown — were vilified and persecuted and burnt at the stake as "witches" during the European witch hunts. Then the male priests claimed that their godhead, who doesn't indwell in creation, was the creator of life. This "God" carries on warfare against Earth and women.

Birth was a Sacrament in Goddess times and women gave birth in sacred enclosures by holy wells aided by The Mothers, triple wise women, who, like the Norns, wove, maintained and cut the web of life.

The ancient shaman women or Shamankas also acted as guides for the dying as they returned to the womb of the Mother; birth and death being the two sides of the same process, coming and going.

I thought that I knew all of this and had painted, written and done slide shows of my art while speaking of these mysteries during many years. But . . . in spite of everything, I was not prepared for the sudden and tragic death of my young son, Leify, on that fatal August full moon in 1985. I had already had many bereavements in my life . . . such as my beautiful artist mother who had suddenly died from stroke at home in Sweden (I am Swedish by birth and upbringing, but have lived in Britain for many years). She was only fifty-four years old and I was in my twenties. Young Swedish friends had committed suicide, and my musician-husband drank himself to death at thirty-six years old.

My young son, who was mixed race (his father African American), was only fifteen years old. We had been visiting friends in south of France. My son was run down by a car as he ran across a busy road. Oh, why, my son, did you run? I had spoken to him only five minutes before. There I saw him like a wounded animal bleeding to death on that road behind a car, not able to speak, unseeing eyes, blood in his mouth, a piece of his skull crushed by a car wheel, no oxygen reaching his brain, dead when the ambulance arrived. Never had I known such a pain as this, never had I known that this is possible . . . my life stopped there on that road, my heart torn out, darkness in my mind . . . all future cut off, sterility. The only reason I didn't lose my mind there and then is because I saw with my own eyes how his face was utterly peaceful and beautiful when the medics turned my son over. The thought that came to my mind was "you are innocent, Leify, you have nothing to fear."

I wanted to go with him into the Otherworld. I had experienced even before then that those who have gone before us want in some strange way to pull us along with them into that world. I do not feel that this is of any malignant intent but perhaps simply trying to spare us from things to come that they can clearly foresee.

A mother's sense of guilt when a child dies is total and overwhelming. I spent thirty hours at my son's brain-dead body, his heart still beating with the help of a machine, in the hospital in Bayonne. I wailed and cried and asked his forgiveness for all the ways I had failed him and had not been able to protect him . . . from racism, from patriarchal men, from his sense of not belonging anywhere.

I went with him in a kind of near-death experience, flying with him on great white wings, into a great light and presence of a great luminous being of no specific gender. I can see how Christians could interpret this as "the Christ," but this is not how I saw it. The words that came into my mind from my son were "the only thing that matters is love . . . ." Or was this the Goddess speaking to me?

Nothing of what I had ever thought I knew had prepared me for this and I realized that I know absolutely nothing.

Circumstances that had led up to my son's death made me fear my own work and even the Great Mother, who, after all, had taken him. I had to keep reminding myself that I was only his earthly mother while She is his greater Mother. I had to believe that there is a reason for why things happen the way they do. Everything that had sustained me during many years, such as pilgrimages to sacred sites, my paintings and writings became meaningless and like ashes, even dangerous. I felt that I had been punished for daring to oppose patriarchy and its deadly godhead. It felt as if on another level I was made to enact the mysteries of Inanna as She went into the Underworld being stripped of everything as She sought Her son/lover . . . or of Demeter, who having lost Her daughter Persephone, threatened to blight all of Nature. The mystery is that Persephone, as Kore, is the new corn, or Maiden of spring who returns to her mother, while as Persephone she is the Queen and ruler of the dead in the Underworld.

During some years I lived in a twilight world of shadows and pain.

In the meantime, a few months after my young son's death, my oldest son was diagnosed with lymphoma cancer. He lived another two years and during that time the only thing that mattered was to keep him alive and care for him through grueling chemotherapy and other treatments. He died twenty-eight years old, and like his brother, on a full moon. To carry the ashes of two sons in my arms is unspeakable . . .

I spent much time in a very negative headspace when I wanted every cell in my body to seize up, and didn't want to be in my body. I identified with disasters in the world and was tuned into all suffering. I couldn't bear beauty in nature or in summer because Leify had died in the south of France on a beautiful August day. I couldn't bear that people live on and age when my son wasn't allowed to grow up and to experience everything that he so intensely longed for. And, I was someone who had for many years celebrated our women's lunar menstrual cycles and loved our Mother Earth! I have now returned to life and want to spend the rest of mine working on Her behalf to protect our Mother and Earth's indigenous peoples and dark women everywhere from patriarchy's onslaught in the guise of the New World Order, the multinational corporations, the transnational corporatons, the World Trade Organization, etc.

I have come to understand through years of grief that not only was I the birthing Shaman woman bringing my sons to this realm, but I also was the Shamanka who had to witness their deaths. Women in all times aided the dying and those being born. There is a great similarity between the birth and the death process, such as traveling through the dark channel from the dark womb into the light of day, into the light of the Goddess Otherworld at death, coming and going. She is the great luminous Mother of the dead or ancestors who await us AND She is the great Dark Mother of the fertile Earth that gives us life. She who is both Dark and Light.

What Leslene della-Madre writes is so important and to retell my experience is also important because in the present day New Age movement there are now such superficial ways of looking at death. Some New Agers speak of physical immortality and deny the natural cycles of Mother Nature while others eagerly await ascendancy into a bodiless realm that they call the "Fifth Dimension." It is also becoming popular to see death as a happy adventure into a kind of virtual reality "Final Frontier." A lot of it is about wanting to escape Earth and biological/physical realities to escape our Mother.

In Scandinavian mythology one can see perfectly clearly how Hel, the Great Goddess of the Ancestors/the Dead who live on within Her magical realm within the mountains or under the lakes, was demoted over time. Ancient Northerners called themselves Hel's people. She was the Faerie Queen who dwelt within the uterine shrine or cave of rebirth. Her cauldron-womb was filled with creative and cleansing fires. Her Heaven-mountain was the source of all life-giving waters. During the time of Odin and his male priests, the time of warfare during the patriarchal Iron age, Hel's world became, however, a gloomy and miserable place of cold and shadows. Hel was now an ugly Hag of the giant race. Only the conquered and enslaved indigenous peoples went to Her realm while the heroic dead, Odin's warriors, went to Valhalla where they feasted and fought. Christians named Purgatory "Hell." To be born of a mother was an abomination to celibate monks and priests of the "Father." The creative forces of Hel's womb/cauldron became the fires of the damned, Her world a place of eternal sorrow, torture and pain. Hel's light-filled magical realm of the Blessed dead within the mountains became known to Christians as "hell-hole!"

I feel that we are now living in patriarchal end-times when both birth and death have become utterly desolate and alienated experiences — all of life medicalised, high-tech births and drugged and unconscious hospital deaths. Male medicine having taken over with a vengeance. Children born by totally unnecessary caesarians who become so alienated that they live on Ritalin and other tranquilizers at an early age while their mothers are on Prozac. Scientists speaking of mothers as "fetal environments" and "egg farms," advocating surrogate "motherhood" while they dream of cloning themselves, becoming "male mothers." These are anti-natural scenarios that wreak of hatred of the Earth who is treated as an indigenous redundant dark mother.

We must now return to the Mother. We must listen to Mother Earth and Her spirits as they speak to us at all times. If we turn away from Her into genetically engineered and virtual "realities" we will all die or we will no longer be human.

It has dawned on me while writing this that I didn't really believe in an afterlife in the past, even though I spoke of how the Blessed dead live on in the womb of the Great Mother awaiting rebirth. These were just words. It is only after my sons' deaths, lucid dreams in which they visit me, experiences when my young son went to the Otherworld — that I "know" in my bones that there is a life eternal and that She, the Mother, always transforms. This has been a great gift. I now do not fear death and look forward to being with my sons again.

"She changes everything she touches and everything She touches changes."

Thank you Leslene for writing this book from a Mother/Goddess perspective.

Blessed Be.
Monica Sjöö
April 2000

Dedicated to the Mother of All

Invocation

Summer Solstice at St. Non's Well, Monica Sjöö, **1997**

As I have worked with death and dying for several years now, I have become increasingly aware of a searching need in the human psyche to find solace and peace in the dying process — not just a wanting to be at home surrounded with loved ones, which can be truly wonderful, but a need that calls out to open to love and to shed fear in the face of death itself. In the teachings from the *Mahabharata*, an epic poem from India comprised between the fourth and tenth centuries BCE, we are told that only insight will help us at the moment of our death and that our loved ones, our possessions and our own bodies will be of no use to us as we face dissolution in the dying process. This is not to say that being surrounded by loving kindness will be of no use when we are dying. Of course it is. But what it does mean is that it is up to us to find our way in facing our own death, alone which is really "all one." If we have lived our lives in fear and suffering, we may not even be able to respond to a loved one who is devoted to being there for us in our dying process. If we have lived our lives in kindness and generosity, I am convinced this makes a difference in the way we meet our death. In witnessing this deep need in people I have had the honor and privilege to be with while they were dying, I began to question what we know in Western society about death and dying.

With the work of Elisabeth Kübler-Ross and the hospice movement, much light has been shed on the process, and yet, I still sense that something is missing — something in the spiritual realm that can reach deep into a person's being and hold them with love and tenderness as they approach death and as they pass through that gateway. It then occurred to me that we don't really know much about death in a positive sense — much of what we know, we fear. I wondered why we don't know, and began to wonder if some of the wisdom of our early ancestors could hold a key to informing our experience of how we currently see and embrace death and dying and preparation for death. I realized that if I were to delve into this, I would have to go back in time prior to the advent of the ruling dominant paradigm — often referred to as "patriarchy" or the dominator model, or the global ruling hierarchical structure of society, government and religion. Patriarchal society is based on "power-over," or domination, and has been in place for about 5,000 years, beginning with the Bronze Age. Because patriarchy is governed by androcentrism, all that emerges from this view is colored by this bias. In androcentrism, maleness and what I call the patriarchal male mind is prized and valued above anything else. I felt that if I wanted to write about the wisdom of our ancestors about death and dying, I would have to look beyond this bias.

This search is what inspired me to write this book. I could not accept teachings about death and dying that overlooked this insidious bias, because I feel this prejudice severely limits the truth and understanding about human existence. Looking into what is considered prehistory I have found a wealth of information regarding death, and its companions, regeneration and rebirth. This information I have researched comes from the Goddess-centered cultures of the Paleolithic and Neolithic time frames — mostly of Old Europe, with some reference to Middle Eastern cultures, based primarily on the work of the late Marija Gimbutas, the eminent archeomythologist, linguist, scientist and historian whose work is changing our view of world history, just in the nick of time, as we find ourselves propelling toward a collective near-death experience on this planet. I have come to the conclusion that this missing element in our death practices is the same missing element in our life practices — the absence of the presence of the Divine Feminine consciousness — the Cosmic or Universal Mother so appreciated and revered by our earliest ancestors. Comprehending the implications of this missing piece is not simple, for to truly understand this, one must realize the far-reaching effects this absence has had on humanity for millennia.

It is my belief that women's reality about life and death is a very different reality than what is offered by patriarchy. Since our current global religious traditions are ruled by the patriarchal mind, we are conditioned to accept what is offered as "the way" — and "the way" of patriarchy is characterized by denial, fear and control. Our tendency to place death in the hands of others is a common occurrence. People die in hospitals all the time, hooked up to machines and tubes or drugged into oblivion, attended by some local chaplain administering last rites, most likely male, or schooled in male thinking, and who most likely has no connection with the dying person. Because the medical system does not honor spiritual process, pain is often seen as something to get rid of or fix. Because people are terrified of pain, they do not find empowerment in being with what is — not that one has to suffer, but exploring the possibilities of healing while dying is more than being drugged for pain.

Others project their own pain onto the dying, and can't bear to see a loved one in the dying process. Because the chaplain is schooled in patriarchal thought, he or she may not really even know how to be present from the heart for the dying. Reading from a book is okay, but I would much prefer the loving look and touch of the Mother who knows what I'm feeling and can respond and act accordingly — not following some written protocol, but following the heart. An attentive mother knows what her child is feeling, and finds the way to comfort that child, to soothe her/his pain, and to hold that child in loving arms. Often pain is really fear of the unknown, and as Ondrea and Stephen Levine have observed, resistance frequently takes the form of pain. If the loving arms of the Mother can soothe that kind of pain, I feel that we would see less of a need for drugs. This is my idea of a conscious death.

This book is my offering to the Goddess of my own remembering of the ancient ones and their wisdom. It is my prayer that through changing our consciousness in how we live, we will remember how to die, and in changing our consciousness in how we die, we will remember how to live.

Creating a Beauty Field For the Dying

Creating a beauty field means taking care of the energy of the space and tending to it, simply making it beautiful and taking care that it is a safe container. You can place favorite things of the dying person in the space, and have some of those things in their view, if possible — pictures, sacred objects, candles, flowers, etc. As much as possible, involve the dying in the creating of the space — it is, after all, their space. Let them feel that you trust and love them, and respect their input. Help them to feel honored. Pay attention to the quality of energy in the space. Don't allow people to be insensitive. If necessary, gently ask them to be there for the person, and not to take up space by talking about themselves. People in the presence of the dying need to know how to be attentive and present. Instruct people in being mindful and sensitive to the needs of the dying person. That doesn't necessarily mean asking them every moment if they can do something for them. It simply means being there for whatever arises. Dying people need to feel safe and comforted and that dying is okay.

Make sure the person is comfortable. If they are taking medication, be sure you are informed. Hospice can help with this. Make sure that you are free from your own need to control as much as possible. If necessary, do a meditation that lets you open to outcome and surrender to the arms of the Mother. Let Her guide you. Pray for Her guidance and pray for healing for the greatest and highest good. What you want may not necessarily be what is needed. One cannot really know the path of the soul of another. We make many assumptions that we can, but we can't.

Remember that the dying person is in a state of losing everything they have known. Their life is coming to a relative end, and they are dealing with huge loss. They may feel frightened and angry, simultaneously. They also might vacillate from happy to sad and back again. Try not to take anything personally while at the same time not letting yourself be dumped on. It is important to not be co-dependent in any situation.

It is a good idea to give loved ones permission to die. Tell them that it is okay and that you will be okay and that those left behind will be okay too. Tell them that you will miss them but that it is okay to go, and that everyone dies. If they are in coma, you can still talk to them this way. Be mindful of what you say around people who are in coma. It is said that they hear everything. I think it is perfectly permissible to share grief with those who are dying. Grieve together, if you can.

As the person enters the active stage of dying, you can midwife them by holding their hand, singing to them, breathing with them, using the AHHHH practice (a breathing practice of relaxation of inhaling and exhaling slowly, with an extended AHH on the exhalation — the person dying can practice this as well as the people attending, in unison or individually), encouraging them that they are doing a good job, and guiding them into the arms of the Mother. The Tibetans say that if you guide someone into the light, you want to tell them to go into the blue light, as that is the realm of rebirth for humans. You can do the phowa practice. (See "Practices" page 203.) Phowa is a Tibetan Buddhist practice of working with consciousness at the time of death. If they are conscious, you can suggest doing phowa with them and tell them you will be right by their side. If you feel that they need to be alone, then tell them that you will come back. Let them know that what they are doing is perfectly natural. Whisper gently into their ear that letting go is okay and encourage them with loving words. My experience with the dying has taught me that most people just need to feel safe and that things are okay. They need to know that letting go is safe. They need to feel held in the process of surrender. They need to feel loved, so do your best to love them.

Make sure that the space is prayerful and that the activity surrounding the newly dead is respectful of their sacred space. Treat the space as if a new baby has just been born.

Gentle music may be appropriate during the letting go process and after. By paying attention to the energy, you will know what is needed. Move slowly and evenly, with calmness. Calmness works magic and allows for spacious presence.

Allow the sacred to fill you and the space like the fragrance of a delicate flower.

Crone-ology

The Mothers: Moon, Sun, Earth/Underworld, Monica Sjöö, 2000

Living in a patriarchal society has meant for all of us that we have not been given the whole truth about our humanity. We have, however, been constantly dosed in our educational process about our inhumanity, where the school curriculum requires that our children be taught about male domination, war, and violence without even blinking an eye. With the constant subjugation of our children to the study of war, conquerors, and pillaging male heroes we wonder why our society has become so violent. We brainwash our children from an early age about what history is, teach them about this abuse and domination, as if things have always been this way, and expect them to ingest this and not get sick.

Our schooling and education have left out entire pieces of the real truth, pieces that are essential to finding peace in ourselves and in the world. We have not been given the truth about history, mythology, religion and spirituality, evolution, the creation of civilization and culture, the arts, the sciences and whatever else we have been taught as "the truth." Women and women's culture have been essentially disregarded by those who tell history, i.e., his story. Feminist historian, Max Dashu, says:

> "Women of power are the women edited out of history books. Outstanding women are not necessarily famous women, though there are many examples of female achievers, some against tremendous odds. We are dealing with an information blockage, not a complete lack of knowledge about these women. We are simply not informed about societies which accord women powerful roles in government, religion, the arts, and economic management. These include national leaders, priestesses and shamans, clan elders, herbalists, educators, writers, musi-

cians, athletes, warriors, freedom fighters, inventors, craftswomen and farmers. Women did these things both in societies that afforded them a wide choice of roles and professions, and in male-dominated cultures that did not always succeed in limiting the scope of enterprising females." (Dashu, www.suppressedhistories.net/articles/women'spower/html).

Because of this absence of the truth about who we are, and who our ancestors were, humankind suffers. Patriarchal overlay obscuring the truth exists worldwide. The creation of patriarchy and its attendant dysfunction seems to have originated some 5,000 years ago, when the people known as the Indo-Europeans, identified by Marija Gimbutas as the Kurgans, invaded the peaceful, matrifocaled cultures of Old Europe, introducing weapons of battle, male dominance and the concept of a sky god. (I use 'matrifocal,' 'matriarchal' and 'matristic' throughout the book to describe woman-centered cultures. Feminist writers are currently engaged in discussion as to what accurately describes woman-centered cultures. Max Dashu uses 'matrix.' In any event, woman-centered cultures were not dominator societies, so they were not the opposite of patriarchy.)

Kurgan patriarchal philosophy has spread out over our globe, with different peoples and cultures becoming assimilated, finding survival through creating their own brands of patriarchy. From the first threat of the spear to the current threat of nuclear power, the paradigm remains the same - male superiority, in the name of "God," controlling and dominating nature, women and children. With the advent of the patriarchal mind, and its tendency towards self-centeredness and destruction, we have lived without benefit of the wisdom of the matriarchal mind. The matriarchal mind is not the opposite of the patriarchal mind. It is the mind that is reflected in the cultures of peace of pre-Bronze age antiquity — cultures that thrived longer on this planet than those based on domination, competition and war. The matriarchal mind is the one that births, cares for and loves life. It is the primordial ground of our being. It is that from which we emerge and it is that to which we return in our death. It is the mind, heart and womb-wisdom of our mothers. It is in this herstory that I have found answers to my inquiries about the possibility of experiencing peaceful and ecstatic death.

I have also realized that we are a society that does not practice ancestor worship. Without this deep honoring of the wisdom of those who have gone before, it is very difficult to feel any kind of continuity of life. We have long forgotten the wisdom of our foremothers, and when we forget, we find ourselves in deep spiritual, psychic, emotional, psychological and ecological trouble. It is self-evident that we are living in a time of great suffering. I feel this is directly due to the fact that we have denied the Mother — the Great Mother of antiquity so revered by our ancestors, for millennia upon millennia. There are Goddess figurines that are dated as far back as possibly 800,000 years — the Acheulian Goddess found in Israel in 1981 is such a figure. The image of her full-bodied shape remained in the imagination of humans across time for thousands of years as her descendent appeared in the form of the Goddess of Willendorf in Austria some 27,000 years ago bearing a remarkable resemblance to her foremother. There is evidence in Africa from circa 900,000 BCE revealing the presence of people who revered a female deity. How could we be so ignorant as to disrespect the wisdom of the earth and those who have gone before us who understood how to live in harmony with their environment and with each other? What were humans like before the coming of the dominator model? How did we live? And how did we die?

We have evidence from early matrifocaled societies that people lived a life based on the belief in regeneration. For instance, Marija Gimbutas tells us that egg-shaped graves found in Sardinia were the resting place of the dead awaiting rebirth. There seems to be a sense from ancient peoples that death was not feared the way we fear it today. There is evidence that death was seen as part of life, not its opposite. The concept of regeneration is the same as the scientific axiom that states, "energy is neither created nor destroyed." Energy changes form. So, we change form when we die. If early peoples were able to celebrate this, why can't we? We have become frightened of life's cyclical pattern as we have attempted to control nature. Controlling nature is impossible. It is terribly egocentric to think that nature is ours for the taking. What would our lives be like if we lived in the conscious psychic experience of this cyclical pattern? Would we be afraid of dying? Would we be able to accept death as a change of form rather than fear it as the end?

Early peoples experienced deity as female. The first humans on this planet felt, experienced and saw deity as a great mother — a goddess. I do not believe they revered the female form only without reverence for the male form. However, birth from the body of woman was seen as miraculous, as it should be regarded. Witnessing the emergence of both female and male babies from the body of woman was deeply inspiring. I also do not believe that early people were ignorant about procreation. They were not stupid. Images of a copulating couple are found within the Paleolithic cave site at Laussel in France, dated nearly 25,000 years ago. Their emphasis on the female form as deity was because She gave birth to all form — all was birthed through Her. And, as people celebrated their spiritual lives, there evolved an appreciation of the cycle of the Mother's great round of life. From this came the three-faced Goddess, the original trinity, the Maiden, Mother and Crone, later co-opted by Christianity. It has been shown to me through visioning, shamanic journeying and contact with the Grandmother ancestral wisdom which I identify as coming from the "realms of remembering," that we need to reclaim the Crone in our death process. She has been rendered nearly invisible in this patriarchal society. She has been demonized, as the snake-headed Medusa who had to be killed because she turned "men" to stone. She has been told in present time that she is not beautiful — that looking and staying young are more important, and that when women no longer bleed, and are no longer able to breed, our life is over — we are no longer useful. The wise grandmother of the matrifocaled cultures has been driven underground.

The problem with this is that the Crone is absolutely essential to the cycle of life — there is no way we can live without her. When we deny her, and relegate her to the shadowlands, she still demands our attention, through projections of what is denied and split off, dancing in the recesses of our minds. The preoccupation with death, violence and sex accompanied by violence, in patriarchy, is evidence of her shadowy presence. She simply cannot be done away with. And if we choose to live trying to deny her, then what our experience becomes is what it is now — a dissociated death urge — violence in many forms such as war and pornography perpetrated mostly by men towards women and children. We suffer from a tremendous denial of the Crone's power.

She is the face of the Goddess who stands at the crossroads of life and death, holding the secrets of sexuality and regeneration. It is interesting that the compulsions and obsessions of the patriarchal mind deal with death and sex, twisted and distorted, because the Crone's truth is not allowed. Most therapists will tell us that what we deny haunts us until we are ready to look at what we have been trying to hide from ourselves. And what we hide from ourselves has a life of its own — an energy that pushes us into often painful experiences in order for us to end our denial and find our truth.

I have been experiencing for quite some time now a deep kind of remembering that has been emerging from a profound connection with Goddess. I have been a spiritual seeker for over thirty years. After experiencing shamanic dismemberment during 1966-1969, with the aid of the sacred hallucinogens, I traveled and then settled down to live in community in Tennessee with about 1,000 hippies on The Farm. (Shamanic dismemberment is a process of delving into one's unconsciousness and coming out the other side, reborn.)

During that time I experienced another kind of shamanic opening through tribal living, and through natural childbirth. Experiencing natural childbirth was a peak shamanic experience (term borrowed from Vicki Noble) for me, as I was taken to the edge of life and death while bringing into this world from another, through my body, a precious soul. I went through this process twice, birthing two beautiful daughters. We also practiced Mahayana Buddhism and tried to live our lives in such a way that we looked at everything as a meditation — whether working, walking, sitting, talking, sharing and communicating. We were committed to truth telling, though sometimes we didn't always know how to practice. I left that community in 1984, after nearly eleven years.

Even though I went through hallucinogenic transformation, natural childbirth and shamanic dismemberment, I still did not have conscious knowledge of the Goddess. And, so, still the pilgrim, I finally matured enough to come into relationship with Her. The lap of the Great Mother and the arms of the Goddess have become my resting place, my home. It was the midwifing of my father's death that brought Her to me, though, still, at that time, seventeen years ago, I did not know where my path was going. I did not know of the Goddess of antiquity residing in my cells, of the early matri-focaled societies, or that women created true civilization. I only knew that something was stirring in me, and later came to discover that it was really old — that it was cellular memory of something hidden deep inside of me. It has only recently come into visible flowering, and was incredibly enhanced by midwifing my mother through her death.

Sharing the same process with my mother further expanded the shamanic opening that occurred for me during midwifing my father in his death. The ten years in-between their deaths were filled with amazing growth, and it is the Goddess who has taken my hand and shown me Her world. And what a world it is — full of ecstasy, love, intelligence, containment, kindness, wisdom, laughter, wildness, and freedom. It is the world of the non-patriarchal mind and heart, the original world of our ancestors, the world that reveals the Sacred Feminine at its core. It is the medicine-world of healing for body, mind and spirit. It is the presence of the absence of suffering. It is a world of peace.

The midwifery movement for natural and conscious childbirth placing birth back into the hands of women has been alive since the 1970's. The community in which I lived played an active role in bringing back spiritual midwifery — in fact, we wrote a book by that title. I had begun apprenticing in our community's midwifery program when I left, but attended enough births to become certified as a labor coach by the Farm School of Midwifery. Now, I see that my training there has served me in understanding the true nature of the midwife — one who helps another through certain life passages, including the passage of death. The spiritual midwifing of death is not a movement yet. But, just as the birthing process is returning to the hands of women, so does the deathing process need to be returned.

Women are the creators, sustainers and nurturers of life. It was only natural that human life was tended by women who, in addition to being the mothers, became the healers and first shamans — or "shemamas," a word I have coined to describe a totally female energy, without patriarchal overlay. These shemamas practiced the sacred arts of "shemoonism," another word I use, free from patriarchal overlay, to describe sacred spiritual womancraft. These women, guided by the rhythms of the moon, and the mysteries of blood, birth, life and death were attuned to lunar magic. Women everywhere are awakening to the call of the Goddess — to reclaim our lunar heritage — to reclaim our power in our menstrual blood, to guide each other in birth with love and wisdom, and to find and live from our power in our lives.

And so it is time to find our power in our dying. There are two kinds of people in the world: women and our children. Because this fact is not revered around the world, all of humankind suffers. It is imperative that women's power — a "power with," not a "power over" — be reinstated to its proper place. That place is the place of the giver, guardian, and caretaker of life. It is the place of she who guides and shapes the form and being of her children, just as the potter shapes her pots of clay. The artisan pays exquisite attention to her creation. She communes with beauty itself, and labors until she brings it into form. It is the same with she who births life. She who births life is uniquely bonded with the being that emerges from her being. It is only natural that women tend those in birth as well as in death, for in this tending, the circle of life is complete.

The Dark Mother

Spiderwoman, Monica Sjöö, **1999**

In the beginning of beginningless time was the Dark Mother. She is the cosmos — eternity itself. From the very depth of Her being all life arises. It is no wonder, then, that the first homo sapiens mother was African — she who embodied this numinous dark in her very skin. There is only one race of people, and that is African. All of the mitochondrial DNA in the cells of humans comes from our common ancestral African mother. This DNA is passed on from mother to child. Males do not pass it on. We are all children of the Dark Mother, biologically and spiritually. "Mitos" means "thread." Consonant with current astrophysics, this connection from mother to child reflects the Superstring Theory that contends that the physical universe is comprised of loops of vibrating strings all connected to and interacting with each other.

We are all fluid, vibratory beings dancing with each other at varying frequencies, the most primal of which connects us to our mothers. From the Motherland of Africa, people migrated from the sub-Sahara, the Rift Valley, first into West Asia. They carried with them their rituals and memories of the Mother, of the black Goddess, into other parts of the world, and so began the story of humans, not just homo sapiens, on this planet. From a 3.4 million year-old hominid named Lucy, found in Africa, to the establishment of the earliest religious sanctuary in the world at Har Karkom circa 70,000 BCE (currently known as Mt. Sinai) where megaliths are incised with 40,000 year-old African instruments, archeological and genetic evidence reveals that all people are of African descent. Peacefulness, justice, compassion and celebration characterized very early African cultures. Rock art found from the world's richest site south of the Sahara (from where modern humans emerged) depicts figures dancing, singing and playing musical instruments. (Birnbaum, **dark mother**, pp. xxvi, xxxix, 7, 43). At the center of these cultures was a female deity. It is this consciousness that gave rise to comprehension of the Goddess in her many forms around the world.

From early Paleolithic Goddess worship to the current re-awakening of Goddess spirituality, the Goddess is the primordial core of every world religion — even if she is denied. And she is African — brown as the earth and black as the night sky, transformed over time becoming white as the stars of the Milky Way, red as the color of sacred ochre and yellow as the sun. But black, first. Lucia Chiavola Birnbaum, author and feminist cultural historian, informs us in her book, **dark mother**, that the African Black Goddess Isis became the Middle Eastern Cybele, the Indian Kali, the Japanese Guan Yin, the Tibetan Tara.

The plethora of Black Madonnas in Europe and the Mediterranean, clothed in Christian garb, are remnants of the black African Goddess. I visited a church once in Malta housing one of these Madonna figures, Our Lady of Loreto, and I could feel her African blood beneath the layers of her robes, which actually looked to me as if the designs on them were woven with the threads of not-so-distant African memories. Another Black Madonna on Malta I was not able to visit, Our Lady of Mellieha, is sought by numerous pilgrims in search of healing. Willow LaMonte, Goddess scholar and editor of *Goddessing*, a spiritual feminist magazine, describes her grotto as a healing sanctuary "with people leaving milagros, small metal votives of various bodied parts healed by prayers to Our Lady, beside numerous gifts of crutches, protheses, photos, embroidery, collages, letters of thanks, baby clothes and folk art." (La Monte, *Goddessing*, issue #6, p. 35).

Lucia Chiavola Birnbaum has focused her writing on the African origins of the Goddess to help unite women in our pursuit of feminist spirituality. She asserts that Eurocentrism in Goddess spirituality has caused some real problems, and that with the understanding of the black African Goddess, homage will be paid to the original Goddess, which is essential for women of color to be recognized for who they are within the Goddess movement. "Women/people of color" are descriptions of people that have evolved in patriarchy as ways to identify non-whites. We could easily identify whites as people of no-color in order to identify dark-skinned peoples. According to Birnbaum, we are all peoples of color, so race is really not a reality, though we have believed it to be to the point of creating "other" from a white elitist view, which has caused great harm. Our sisters of brown and black skin and all the shades in-between need to be welcomed and embraced by those with white skin who have enjoyed privilege and entitlement at their expense.

The white sisters need to ask our earth-toned sisters for their stories and memories of their Goddess in order that a holistic remembrance of the wisdom of the Goddess can be expressed. Yoruba priestess, writer and performer, Luisah Teish, says "the Black Madonna is really Isis. Some academics choose to ignore what Merlin Stone made clear, which is that when the Ancients spoke of Ethiopia and Egypt, they were talking about an area that reached all the way down to Zimbabwe! When they face that they will have to deal with Africa's contribution to the world. And when they stop being scared of Africa and admit that She is their Mother, then they will have to deal with the guilt of matricide." (Teish, *Goddessing*, Issue #6, p.40).

It is of vital importance that recognition of the Dark Mother becomes an essential part of any reclaiming of Goddess spirituality. The memory in our cells of the Dark Mother carries information about early people and their way of life — a peaceful and joyful reality created by our antecedent culture creators, our African foremothers. I do not speak of the "Dark Mother" in this case as only the Goddess of Shadows — she is more than that. The original Dark Mother is the Great Grand Mother of humanity/luminosity — the cosmos herself. It is my belief that with an understanding and reverence of the truth of the Dark Mother, sexism and racism would not exist, nor would a fear of the natural life cycle, including death. The ideas of "Dark Mother" referring to the "terrible" or the "cast off" in current schools of psychology thereby emphasizing the Dark Mother as Negative Mother would change as well. The whole dualistic notion of light as good and dark as bad would also find transformation.

It is the Dark Mother who is our real mother. Residing in Her arms in life and returning to Her arms in death would be a welcome relief to the struggle and turmoil humans experience without Her. A nineteenth century Sicilian physician and historian, Raffaele Solarino, wrote about the African origins of Paleolithic burials of humans laid to rest in the fetal position in uterine-shaped grottoes, reflecting a belief in the return of humans to the mother in death. (Birnbaum, **dark mother**, pp. 85-86)

It is no mystery that it was the black "mammy" who nursed, nurtured and loved the white children of the elite during slavery, and whose image we have seen throughout Hollywood movies. She was the real giver of the true sustenance of life. I believe this portrayal comes from a deep memory of knowing her dark earth/womb/tomb as home. In my visit to a Nubian village, a young man was eager to have us see the bedroom as he explained to us that its rounded tomb shape reflected the womb. *Egyptians conceived of the earth as a sort of womb for all life, denoting it as the mother,* said Diodorus, a concept that the greeks appropriated in designating "the earth as Demeter, or earth mother." (Birnbaum, **dark mother**, p. 84) Our early ancestors seemed to have lived in an understanding of Her profound mysteries, continuously demonstrating for millennia a deep reverence for Her presence. It seems their understanding of Her mysteries was far more comprehensive than is ours at this point in time.

The very title of China Galland's book, **Longing for Darkness**, tells us something about a deep wish within the depths of our soul that longs for contact with that rich dark wisdom. It is the darkness of the womb that has fed all of us. Bestselling author Betty J. Eadie describes her near-death exprience in **Embraced by the Light:**

> "I could see nothing but the intense, almost tangible darkness. The darkness was more than a lack of light; it was dense blackness unlike anything I had known before. Common sense told me that I should be terrified, that all of the fears of my youth should have risen up, but within this black mass I felt a profoundly pleasant sense of well being and calmness...I felt a process of healing take place. Love filled this whirling, moving mass, and I sank more deeply into its warmth and blackness and rejoiced in my security and peace. I thought, 'This must be where the valley of the shadow of death is.' I had never felt greater tranquility in my life." (Betty J. Eadie, **Embraced by the Light** p. 38-39)

Our preoccupation with light/male/God/heaven and demonization of dark/earth/female/womb/blood has left us bereft of being grounded and rooted in the dark soil/soul of the Mother. We all know what happens to living things when they are not well rooted, when their roots have not spread and grown to absorb the moisture and nutrients of the earth. They shrivel and die. How would your life change if you totally accepted the Dark Mother as a divine nurturing presence? If you gained an understanding of this divinity as primordial and necessary in order to experience a truly peaceful life? A connection to the Dark Mother of our ancestors brings with it an acceptance of death and a return to her breast and womb. She is the bringer of light and life. Why have we allowed a terrible distorting fear of her — a fear of the dark — to enter our hearts, rendering them cold and hardened by denial?

One of the aspects of the Dark Mother is the Crone. She has been profoundly disparaged in patriarchy. Why? Because she is the face of death and regeneration — old, wrinkled and laughing. Her mysteries have been feared by the patriarchal mind for centuries. She has endured unspeakable pain and suffering at the hands of those who fear her power. It is time for her to return to us and melt our hearts.

Florence's Story

Florence lying in state, photo by Gregory Hayes

Florence came to see me upon the advice of her daughter-in-law. She was in her late sixties, and was seeking counsel on leaving her abusive husband of far too many years. It didn't take me long to support her in this decision. She was from an era of oppressed women (who isn't?), and didn't know if it was an okay thing to do, especially because her husband had been ill. I could see in her a woman who had "endured" life. Florence was a woman who had carried life on her back. I always feel a great sadness when I see the "wild woman" in any woman reduced to invisibility. There was nothing I could do but support her in her decision, and encourage her to follow her intuition. She was reaching out for some semblance of wholeness in her remaining years. I did not see her again in the context of spiritual guide/seeker, but heard from her daughter-in-law that she later left her abusive husband, and was enjoying life.

It was several years later when I met Florence again. I had heard she was diagnosed with cancer, and a friend of the family, a woman who had been studying with me and living with Florence's family, asked me questions about how to handle some difficulties in dealing with the situation. Florence was afraid; she was pushing her loved ones away. I had asked my friend if she thought it would be okay for me to write to Florence. She thought it would, and so I sent a letter to Florence just letting her know that she was approaching a time in her life when she was going to need her loved ones and that it was okay for her to let them help her. To my relief, Florence responded positively to my letter, and was touched by it. Her family brought her home where she could be surrounded by the love of her son, daughter-in-law, granddaughter, and her dear family friend. This is where she died   peacefully several weeks after moving in.

While she was alive, her son, daughter-in-law and close family friend asked me to come and spend some time with their family and with Florence. Florence agreed that it would be a good thing. I arrived, and wasn't sure exactly what I was going to do. I usually work best when I feel the energy of the moment and of the people involved. We gathered in circle, with Florence sitting on the edge of her bed. She hadn't done that in quite a while. We passed sage burning in a shell, and smudged. We called in guidance from the ancestors. It became apparent that the family needed help figuring out how to care for Florence with compassion. At the same time they didn't know how to help Florence to learn how to express gratitude.

When people are afraid, they sometimes become very constricted, controlling and demanding. I have learned that it is important to learn to serve, but not to become a slave in caring for the dying — or to anyone, for that matter. In council form, we passed a talking feather, and everyone spoke from their hearts. (Passing a talking object allows the person who is holding it to be heard without being interrupted. When that person is done, the object is passed on to the next person who wishes to speak.) Florence was assured that her family wanted to care for her, and she committed to being more gracious by noting the difference between asking and demanding. The circle was honest and authentic — a wonderful blessing to share with a family struggling to find their way with the dying process of a loved one.

Florence passed away several days later. I was not present for her crossing-over, though I was called in soon afterwards. When I arrived, I was greeted with warmth and loving kindness. Florence's family felt grounded and peaceful. I entered the bedroom where Florence was lying on the bed. She was beautiful. The lines in her face had relaxed, and placed above her was a photograph of her in her youth. I marveled at how much she again looked in her death like that photo. Robin, her daughter-in-law, Julia, a close family friend, and Nicolette, her twelve-year-old granddaughter, had all made flower wreaths for our heads. There was a bowl of chocolates on the table.

We gathered around Florence and held a prayer circle, feeling gently embraced by the golden, flickering candlelight. Those who felt moved to, spoke simple prayers. We sang a song or two and then shared the silence together, all bearing witness to Florence. I felt glad that Florence found this kind of peace in her short years of freedom after living in abuse for so long. I felt she deserved better, and hoped that in her next cycle, she would have that. Her family had obtained a simple pine box coffin from a company called "A Plain Pine Box." In peaceful acceptance, her grandaughter sat on the coffin lid and in delicate, innocent twelve-year-old artistry inscribed her grandmother's name. I thought how wonderful it was to have this lovely, budding young woman sitting on the coffin of her grandmother, painting it, and making it beautiful. There was a conspicuous absence of fear in Nicolette regarding the death of her grandmother, and I thought that was just as it ought to be. Florence rested in her coffin in the back yard for three days, surrounded by yard torches and flowers. The setting was exquisite. Large old oaks watched over her like ancient grandmothers while the gentle wind stirred and cleansed the constantly moving energy around her.

Robin recently told me on the third day when she went into the yard, she could sense that Florence was still breathing as she could see a rising and falling in her chest. Robin later learned about the outer and inner breath when she read Sogyal Rinpoche's **Tibetan Book of Living and Dying** which suggests leaving the body undisturbed for three days in order to allow time for the inner breath to cease. Robin had seen the cessation of the inner breath without knowing anything about it.

Nicolette drawing on her grandmother's coffin, photo by Gregory Hayes

Florence's family honoring her passage, photo by Gregory Hayes

Who is the Crone?

Bride's Well at Imbolc on Lewis, Monica Sjöö, **1989**

What does she have to do with death and dying? The Crone is the third face in the original trinity, the trinity of birth, life and death, or creation, preservation and dissolution. In her timeless ancient countenance we witness the map of life — her mountain wisdom etched across an expanse of her earth-face. She shows us the nature of dissolution as her steadfast gaze reveals a fierce compassion. It is the Crone who teaches us about egolessness; about endings and beginnings and the eternal moment.

If we look deep enough into her eyes we fall into the black well of her mysterious womb-cauldron from which all is born and to which all returns. To one who loves life, which by the very act excludes fear of the cyclical process of life, one reveres the Crone and her transformational powers. To one who fears life, and to one who pursues egoic immortality, she looms as a frightening presence — one who "turns men to stone." She must then be controlled, conquered and beheaded. And the one who accomplishes such an act is touted as a great hero. Unfortunately, acting out in this manner becomes a controlling, conquering and beheading of nature, which, of course, becomes a self-inflicted wounding, or a killing of the self, which we call suicide. So, denial of the Crone equals self-annihilation.

What good are our spiritual teachings if we refuse to understand right relationship with immanence? The Crone-Mother is the teacher of non-grasping, surrender, impermanence and non-duality. She is the "root guru," the original lineage-holder of the teachings of life, death, sexuality and regeneration. Her teaching is earth-based, not sky-based. It is into her arms we return in our death.

In Western society we have been instilled with a deep fear of death and dying. This is the only result of the legacy of the patriarchal mind set, or what I call PMS. The patriarchal mind-set is obsessed with youthfulness, large breasts and ego immortality. The obsession with youthfulness reveals fear of aging and the denial of the natural cycle of immanent wisdom that we cannot control, no matter how hard we may try. This mind's obsession with large breasts reveals the deep hunger of the soul to experience nurturing, tenderness, and a warm, soft safety.

Women and men alike experience this obsession. Since men rule in patriarchy, this mind has been created by men's cravings, due to their separation from the Mother-wisdom several millennia ago. And equally unfortunate, women have been controlled by these cravings for the same amount of time, and have learned to define ourselves by them. So, women pursue the knife of the plastic surgeon to give men large breasts, at the expense of self-mutilation and a great deal of suffering. Self-mutilation and self-annihilation go hand-in-hand, of course. In societies in which the Sacred Feminine is honored, male shamans will often dress as women, including wearing symbolic breasts, because they know the sacred truth of that which births them. They themselves don the symbolic breast in order to know their connection, from within, to the Goddess. What men have created in Western society with their desperate obsession with female body parts, is the shadow aspect of this connection, created by denying the truth of the primordial femaleness of all life — that which eighteenth century Bengali poet, Ramprasad, refers to as the "ungendered feminine."

This nurturing tenderness and safety are not found in the sky, with an angry, punishing sky-god. They are found in the earth herself, in the body of our mother and in the lap of our grandmother. The obsession with immortality reveals the deep fear of letting go, which then creates ultimate grasping and self-cherishing as well as ultimate aversion. These are thoroughly destructive behaviors.

Therapists and spiritual teachers instruct us that we must learn to break the patterns of old habits in order to heal, to find whole/holiness. Yes. But, we cannot break habit patterns if we do not know what they are. And if our guides along the path have not shed their own conditioning far enough and deep enough, then where are we? The habit patterns of the patriarchal mind-set cause much suffering. This suffering lives even in the face of profound spiritual revelation because the habit patterns of the patriarchal streams of thought run devastatingly deep. For instance, what is the unspoken teaching of a text or teacher that teaches us about psychological/spiritual purification written or spoken in a sexist context?

We have had 5,000 years of male spirituality and the world is getting worse. These deep underground currents have not been seen for millennia, until recently, with the emergence of Goddess spirituality and *thealogy*. It is through Her awareness that we will return to right relationship with ourselves, the earth, all of life and the natural cycle of life itself as a complete circle where death is not in opposition to life, but experienced as a part of it.

What does the Crone reveal?

When we think of recycling, we think of putting things back into a cycle of usefulness, after they have already been used. If we look at how our bodies recycle foodstuffs, for instance, we see that food substances in one form are used by the body and converted to many other forms of energy, and the unused portion is discarded as a brownish colored matter. Interestingly enough, feces are the same color as the earth. Some people devoted to recycling, as in Taos, New Mexico, have created ways to recycle human feces through the use of composting toilets that break down the feces into a kind of ash that can be used as compost.

If we recycle our table scraps and create compost piles, we see the transformation of these scraps into rich black earth. So that which gives rise to our sustenance, the rich black earth from which our food grows, the dark womb from which light emerges, is the dark Goddess — the original Mother, the black Mother, the earth Mother. Our food, which is light energy, emerges from the black earth, which is the dark womb of creation. This reflects the cosmos in which most matter in existence is called "dark matter" — the root of "matter" is "mater," or "mother."

This dark matter is not visible, but is detected by the speed at which stars move through space as well as by the intensity of their brightness. It is the gravity of dark matter that holds galaxies together. The dark gives birth to the light. And, in complete harmony with this is the knowledge that African mothers were the first human mothers, and that we are all descended from them.

The Crone shows us that everything is in a flow of transformation/transmutation, that we emerge from her, our sustenance emerges from her, and that we return to her in our death to merge once again with her to be reshaped and reused by her. The Crone is the wise shemama who stands at the gateway between life and death and points the way.

For priestess, author and teacher of women's spirituality, Shekhinah Mountainwater, "The Crone is a teacher or wise one, sometimes called the 'wayshower' as she shines the light of wisdom for all to see. She passes her learning on to the next generations, thereby giving roots and continuity to cultural tradition. She brings patience and seasoning to the raising of children, healing of the sick, and the deciding of community issues. Some of her names are Hecate, Cerridewen, Kali, Baba Yaga, Wind Woman, Morag, Hag o' the Mill, and Morrigan." (Mountainwater, **Ariadne's Thread**, p. 93)

She knows what we are doing at the time of our death. She is our guide into a new realm that we have perhaps forgotten about while embodied in flesh. She lights the way for the dissolution of the body and the journey of the soul once it has shed its body. She knows that there is both birth and death and neither birth nor death. She understands this paradox. Hers is a both/and universe. She tells us we must understand the paradox in order to have a peaceful death and in order to live in her immanent/transcendent mystery. To only focus on the teaching that "there is no birth and death," as in Buddhism, does not do justice to the women who labor and risk our lives to give birth. I wonder, indeed, what the men who engage in such teachings think about where they came from.

The transformative flow of life moves through the openings we call birth and death. Since energy is neither created nor destroyed, these openings are gateways for the impermanence of life to pass through. All is in flux, flowing in the river of change. But we do not say that the river does not exist. We value the experience we have in immanence as we flow into transcendence and back again into immanence. Immanence and transcendence are interwoven. It is the Crone who knows these secrets. She knows that this wisdom is to be celebrated in the body as well as out of the body.

This is why she holds the mystery of sexuality and regeneration. She shows us that as we shed the old, and pass through an opening from one realm to another, we are free to experience the Goddess in another form brought into being through sacred sexuality. She knows that sacred sexuality is the way in which the Goddess dances with herself, and loves herself as she creates life, in a never-ending rhythmic, ebb and flow of manifestation and dissolution.

The Crone reveals to us that creation and de-structuring are the same, and that one cannot be without the other. She stands at the crossroads asking us to let go, to enter her womb once again — to enter the mystery that we have never left except in our delusional condition, and urges us to do so with courage, grace and beauty.

The Crone reveals to us that aging is beautiful. It is the manner in which the creative life force spirals its way through ever-changing form. An acceptance of aging rather than denying it can give us a profound appreciation of the cyclic nature of life. If we can learn about non-attachment to form, that form is inherently empty, that is, with no permanent identity that lasts in that form forever, and that emptiness is form, then we can participate in this dance of life, surrender to the incredible intelligence of our universe and realize that we are the All, that we are the One forever moving and dancing about. The sparkle in the eye of the Crone glistens with this wisdom.

This emptiness is not nothingness. It is spacious, luminous clarity, "no thing ness." When the vase is broken, the space inside merges with the surrounding space. This Crone wisdom is Prajnaparamita, or "The Mother of the Buddhas," Kali and Shakti. Recognition of this Mother-wisdom is essential for Her devotees to be in conscious relationship with Her. If it is not named, then how is the experience of Her available to us? And why has She been purposefully unnamed in male-dominated religions?

The Crone reveals to us that her wisdom has been cast out, is absent from view and invisible in just about every major world religion — not only as Crone, but as the Mother, Herself, the primal creatrix of life. We rarely see images of the Crone Goddess; when we do she is often demonized. Somehow we are supposed to accept that this face of the Goddess is not alive — that it is she, in fact, who takes life away and with that, removes any hope of immortality. There could be nothing further from the truth. It is she who teaches about immortality — an immortality devoid of ego and narcissism. All succumb to her — all are returned to her waiting arms.

We cannot escape this, though we see current New Agers telling us that if we just think "right," we don't have to die, that our bodies can stay young, that it is our belief in death that makes us die. I wonder if dying leaves falling from a tree have a profound obsession with death, and this is why they die. Or babies who die from SIDS believe too much in an intellectual system that promotes death. Or if my cat died because she was too invested in believing in her own demise.

Ultimately, it is true that we do not really die; it just looks like we do, because our bodies do die — that is, the form we know so well that we refer to as "our body" ceases to remain in that form one day, and returns to the elements from which it has come. So why all the fuss about preserving the current body? We must take care of our body, nurture ourselves and one another, but what are the ramifications of holding onto a particular body in a particular point in time?

Instead of fearing and demonizing the Crone, we should be connecting with that glint in her eye and spending our lives preparing to meet her. It only follows that if the wisdom of the Goddess is covered over with patriarchal distortion, which it is, then we are going to be left with forms of "spiritual" systems that do not ultimately serve us while our souls continue to hunger.

When the truth about how we get to be here, in the flesh, experiencing this beautiful planet and her multiplicity and diversity and how we leave here to once again be with our "original face" before we were born is not told, taught, held, revered, protected, shared and nurtured, then we, as children of the divine, suffer greatly. When Buddha left his princely estate, and traveled about, he noticed disease, illness and death. I do not know if he noticed the absence of the Goddess, but it was She who came to him in the guise of a woman offering him milk curds in the midst of his self-imposed austerity, and is was She he touched when he called upon the earth to help him find stability.

When I travel about I notice the absence of the Goddess and the presence of profound suffering. And I see a direct connection. This absence is not Her abandonment of us. This is an absence that lives in the belief systems of Her children. Her children have abandoned Her. She is crying out — shaking us through any means possible — earth changes, new diseases, horrors of war, abuse of women and children, trying to get us to wake up. We are told that God gave his only "begotten" (whatever that means) son and sacrificed him so that we all could live.

The Mother is sacrificing Herself to get our attention, trying to tell us that we had better wake up, or it may be all over for our species. If the very heart of a people—women and children—is abused, then it is not long before those people will meet with their demise. When the very heart is beaten and raped, it is the Mother showing us that we are killing ourselves, that we are killing Her.

It is the Crone who is calling to us now — in all her fury, destroying and shattering ego structure, showing us our own self-hatred as it manifests in the very heart of our being.

Nothing could be more devastating to the soul, to the spirit, than living in a time when women and children are so tortured — nothing. And this can only come about when there has been a deep denial of the Mother, the Goddess in all Her aspects. The Goddess has no choice but to hold up the mirror to us. I believe that humankind has never seen such wanton destruction of mind, body and spirit as we are experiencing now.

This is the Mother's cry for us to feel this terrible pain and put an end to it. It is in Her ruthless compassion that She shows this to us, asking us to face our fears, our violence. So even in this unspeakable pain and horror, She lives, reminding us that our true nature does not really want to perpetuate this despicable behavior.

But if we don't listen, we will continue to kill ourselves, perhaps until there is no one left from our species. At this point, it seems that this could actually be beneficial to the planet. But the Mother loves us and wants Her children to "get it." She wants us to love ourselves and experience the bliss of Her being — to live in harmony and unity, dancing in ecstasy, dripping with the sweet sweat of love.

Meeting the Goddess of Death and Regeneration

Rites of Passage, Monica Sjöö, **1994**

In evidence that Marija Gimbutas gives us from Old Europe, we see that the Mother, the Goddess was life-giver and death-wielder.

> "The primordial deity for our Paleolithic and Neolithic ancestors was female, reflecting the sovereignty of motherhood. In fact, there are no images that have been found of a Father God throughout the prehistoric record. Paleolithic and Neolithic symbols and images cluster around a self-generating Goddess and her basic functions as Giver-of-Life, Wielder-of-Death, and as Regeneratrix. This symbolic system represents cyclical, nonlinear, mythical time." (Gimbutas, **Language of the Goddess**, p.x)

What were the beliefs of the people living during Paleolithic and Neolithic times in Old Europe regarding death? In truth, we can really only speculate from the trails of evidence left behind. There is a great deal of evidence to suggest that a belief system attributed the Great Goddess with the powers of creation that included the experience of death and regeneration. Life and death were (and are) not opposites.

Death served life in a cyclical pattern. This is a very different notion than a nihilistic or transcendent view of death. It is a view based in immanence — that life came from the Great Mother, and returned to Her, and that Her body was the earth. Author, archeologist and artist Cristina Biaggi writes in **Habitations of the Great Goddess,** a definitive work on the Goddess temples of Malta, and the Orkney and Shetland islands north of Scotland:

> "To enter Her habitations and to consider what they suggest and evoke is to open our minds and hearts to the reality of a long-lost world in which gynocentric values prevailed and in which a matristic society may have been the natural order. Recognition of the Goddess is the first step in an exploration and understanding of the Neolithic world. To enter Neolithic tombs, temples and even houses is to enter the habitations of the Goddess: it is to enter Her body." (Biaggi, **Habitations of the Great Goddess**, p.153)

In these early gynocentric matrifocaled cultures, there is no evidence of war or weaponry.

> "It is a gross misunderstanding to imagine warfare as endemic to the human condition. Widespread fighting and fortification building have indeed been the way of life for most of our ancestors from the Bronze Age up until now. However, this was not the case in the Paleolithic and Neolithic. There are no depictions of arms (weapons used against other humans) in Paleolithic cave paintings, nor are there remains of weapons used by man against man (sic) during the Neolithic of Old Europe.
>
> From some hundred and fifty paintings that survived at Çatal Hüyük, there is not one depicting a scene of conflict or fighting, or of war or torture." (Gimbutas, **Language of the Goddess,** p.x.)

It appears that our ancestors from these regions believed in a nurturing Goddess who provided them with sustenance. "Old European village sites are not remarkable for their defensive positions but were chosen for their convenient setting, good water and soil, and availability of animal pastures." (ibid.)

This is a very different notion and experience of deity in the daily lives of these people than what our experience is, living with an angry male sky-god. And it seems that in their death, they were returned to the Mother to await rebirth in another form. It seems to me that these early people had a simple beauty and a simple truth that imbued their daily life. The creative artistry from these cultures is astounding. From the Paleolithic stone carvings of the Goddess, to the exquisite examples of Neolithic pottery found throughout Old Europe to the murals on the temple walls in Çatal Hüyük in Turkey, we are given a glimpse of the deep sense of beauty embodied by our early ancestors.

The wall murals in Çatal Hüyük revolve primarily around the Goddess of Regeneration, portrayed as a frog-shaped woman giving birth. She is surrounded with figures of animals, including the vulture representing her death aspect, and the bull-head, representing regeneration. (ibid.) Daily life was sacred, as was the entire circle of life itself. All was sacred. From the earliest times, and prior to Greek, Roman and Christian civilizations, according to Sicilian physician and historian Raffaele Solarino, there was no separation of the spirit or the soul from the body. "This african holisitic belief, which is counter to christian canonical doctrine, has persisted throughout the christian epoch in subordinated cultures of the world." (Birnbaum, **dark mother**, p. 86)

If people were to live in a psychic environment where all is sacred, then perhaps fear as we know it would be virtually non-existent. It seems that there was a peaceful acceptance of life in its own flow, and they were a part of that flow.

How then would a Great Goddess be perceived in her death aspect? Would people who lived in peace, and as in Çatal Hüyük, where three different "races" of people lived for 1,000 years, come to fear death if they had lived their lives in peace, in matri-focaled societies in an absence of violence? Or would they be able to die with the same peacefulness and reverence they knew in their lives? And if they died in states of reverence and peace, did they know that dying this way would create auspicious rebirth? Or did they just trust that returning to the Mother was a total surrendering and a total trusting in Her divine authority? Perhaps what we know of some of their rituals regarding death and regeneration can help answer some of these questions.

Carol's Chronicle

I first met Carol and her husband Marty when a friend referred them to me. They were looking for some guidance in improving their relationship. Carol was pregnant with her second child and they were both committed to going deeper with each other and finding out how to love one another and how to bring more compassion and loving kindness into their lives. After the birth of her daughter, Rebecca, Carol was diagnosed with breast cancer.

Carol four days before her death ,
photo by Marty Rubin

As Carol began to breast feed less and less, she noticed that one breast was not changing as much in size as the other one. Carol was trained as an RN, and she intuitively knew that something was wrong. However, she was not acting in capacity as her own nurse, and so she relied on the advice of others. She later reflected on the fact that the "others" she listened to were males — her doctors as well as her doctor-husband and doctor-father.

This became a factor in her awakening to herself — that she had given her power away to others, and frequently, men. In her last month of life, she found it very important to state that she did not want to give her power away to anyone, anymore.

Her doctors told her not to worry about it, that it was probably a clogged milk duct. When the lump did not go away, she was biopsied, and found she had an aggressive, progressed form of breast cancer. From that point forwards, her life was completely changed. A young mother, with a new baby and a toddler, was facing the possibility of a premature death.

Carol was in a battle for her life for over two and a half years. She endured chemotherapy and radiation, a bone marrow transplant, experimental trial treatments with HERII, Japanese, German and Italian therapies, and diet and vitamin therapies. She received perhaps more gamma knife treatments to her brain than anyone in the world. She found a spiritual path and became committed to changing ingrained patterns of behavior that no longer served her. She found her voice and her power, and learned to set limits with difficult people in her life.

One month before Carol entered her dying process with grace, the hospice doctor told her family that she would probably die within hours to days. Carol surprised everyone, as she usually did, by not complying. She spent her last month processing unresolverd issues with her loved ones. Carol was one of the most courageous people I have ever known. I saw her do everything in her power to find healing, and as a mother, I know that her deepest concern was for her children. I cannot imagine the pain of knowing that one is leaving behind small children. I witnessed Carol grieve this reality, as she moved into a place of trust and surrender.

The relationship Carol and I cultivated together was based in love and trust. I served as her therapeia — in the original sense of the word — one who tends to the needs of the soul. These needs include the psychological, emotional, spiritual and physical. When Carol learned of the metastases to her liver, she called me and asked me, in tears, if I would be present at her death. I agreed to serve as midwife in her passage. For a month and a half, I was with Carol as much as possible. We talked extensively. I crawled into bed with her to hold her and massage her shoulders. We sang together songs that played on the radio. We cried together and laughed together. We shared many meals together, a favorite pastime of both of ours. And, we shared chocolate — one of her favorite "medicines."

When Carol ate chocolate, she talked. She talked about things that bothered her and she sought resolution. Marty and I offered her chocolate cake, doughnuts and brownies to keep her energy up long enough to finish important conversations.

It is said in spiritual teachings dying people can often come to a place of clarity and wisdom — that they access a deep inner knowing that is more readily seen as the masks of the personality fall away. Carol was a teacher to everyone around her. One time we were sitting on the deck with her wonderful female rabbi. Carol quietly remarked, "it's a teaching." I leaned over and asked her "what is a teaching?" And she replied, "What isn't?" Exactly. What isn't? I was sitting with a Zen master!

Once when I climbed into bed with her to rub her shoulders, she asked me to put on a tape called "Music to Disappear In." The music began to play, and we both enjoyed relaxing together. I was gently massaging her when she quietly remarked how good it felt. She began to surrender into a deeper state, and seemed like she was going to sleep. At this point, something changed. I was sitting behind her, holding her as she leaned against me, much the same way a partner in birth holds the birthing woman. Her bed faced a beautiful picture window that looked out on a magnificent natural setting.

I was looking out the window, and slowly the room began to fade away. Light began to fill the space. I felt myself, along with Carol, flying out the window, into the expansive blue sky. I felt our spirits were experiencing a oneness, and we were experiencing a oneness with the greater whole — what I call Mother, or Goddess. There was a profound sense of expansion, connection and merging. I couldn't feel any edges — of myself, of Carol or of the room. I was full of light and peace. I didn't feel any opposition — that this was the "saving" light that is opposite to the scary dark. It was light simply held by the dark. Carol was showing me what it was to die. There was such grace and beauty. I began to gently weep. There was no fear. There was a falling away of the limitations of the physical, and an opening into spaciousness—what I can only describe as the arms of the Mother.

I had a spiritual awakening in that moment. I felt deep in my soul a lack of fear about dying. I knew Carol and I were in some kind of altered state together, even if only for a few moments, where a deeper mystery was revealing itself. I felt profoundly privileged and honored to be in that moment with her. I thanked her telepathically and said I had learned from her in this experience not to fear death. Slowly the room began to take its familiar shape, and we were together again on the bed. I felt that somehow, with Carol resting against me between my legs, I was giving birth. Not necessarily to her — but to the experience we had just shared. I was reminded of shamans who take certain postures in order to access altered states of consciousness.

It didn't matter to me if Carol was "awake" or not. I believe there are many levels where one can be awake, and I felt, on a soul level, we were both awake and very much in sync with each other. In that moment limitless and esctatic love, our true nature, abounded. It has given me pause to reflect on the nature of death and dying and the patriarchal conditioning we hold in our collective unconscious, which in turn, holds us. With so much fear instilled in us as a result of the denial of death, how are we to come to a true understanding of the process? And with so much fear instilled in us in the name of religion, how are we to know how to meet this journey? Some Native Americans believe they go to the Spirit world in death — it is something they accept rather than fear. I know that the wisdom of this experience with Carol will stay with me for a very long time.

Where did the fear of death enter into our collective unconscious? It is my sense that this happened when we, as a species, began to experience a separation from the Great Mother. Without a deep psychic connection to the primal feminine, we now share a common fear instead of a common love. With the sense of isolation that the psyche experiences in this separation, it is no wonder that death looms as something to fear. Denial then becomes a tool for the ego to attempt to survive the fact of death, and the fear simmers undisturbed in the depths of our being. Under these circumstances, when death is upon a loved one, or oneself, we are at a loss as to how to behave.

Many people become very controlling, and unable to allow the dying person to have their own unique, mysterious reality. In Carol's case, her mother simply wanted her completely sedated — asleep. I feel it was because her mother could not tolerate her own pain. Carol's dying was too much for her mother, and her mother wanted it completely controlled, in the name of giving Carol peace. Her mother was not to blame. She just didn't understand. She was angry with Marty who chose not to sedate Carol to the point of oblivion so Carol could be as present as possible to experience her death. As Medical Power of Attorney, Marty's job was to decide.

But the issue of who was in control of Carol's death was difficult for her parents. It seemed to me her father was afraid he would lose his own immortality if Carol died. I could feel the internal conflicts and fear within each of her parents who were facing the death of their daughter. They had been divorced for many years, and the unresolved issues between them were also palpable. I feel they did their best to keep focused on Carol, and still, because of their own pain, controlling tendencies arose in the face of that which they couldn't control. I observed how this pain, unnoticed and unclaimed, created obstacles for each of them in being able to let go into presence. They loved their child, wanted her to not suffer and did not understand how their controlling energy caused more suffering. Carol told me in a particularly lucid moment that the conflict she felt between loved ones exacerbated her pain. As the midwife, I felt I needed to find a way to facilitate a gentle understanding that Carol was on her own journey, and that all of us present were there for her. During this process, I met in circle with many family members in another room adjacent to Carol and I listened to the voices of unrest and fear. Fear was hungry and looking to be fed. I knew Carol could feel this energy. I felt the need to cut through it. So, I rose up from my chair, and twirled in the middle of the circle like a purple whirling dervish. Her father blurted out, "You look like a goddess!" (He had not heard me talk of the Goddess prior to this, though he may have heard Carol talk of Her.) The energy shifted, and the truth of what was needed — presence for Carol — re-emerged.

Carol's Passing

I seemed to be in a timeless space for a long time after Carol died. Having been so close to her, and shared with her deep concerns and fears as well as deep love, I grieved the way a mother would grieve. Her own mother was unable to be present for her, even though she did the best she could. (Sadly, her mother committed suicide two years after Carol's death.) Carol stayed in her process of "working things out" until she couldn't really talk anymore. She told Marty, "I need your love now," shortly before entering a coma. Marty laid his head on her chest, sobbing, telling her she had all his love. I was there because I had been asked by Marty to help them work through some very difficult feelings Carol had been expressing. When she told him she needed his love, Marty seemed to come to a kind of surrender that he had not experienced before in their relationship. He fell more and more in love with Carol as she went deeper and deeper into her dying. The three of us together shared a deep bond that comes when authenticity is the only experience left to have. There is no controlling anything. There is only being present to what is.

I could feel Carol begin to enter what is known in Buddhism as the "great dissolution." At this time, the elements that constitute the body begin to dissolve, and flow into each other: earth into water, water into fire, fire into air. There is a presence of a deep internal process. I talked to Carol about this process as she was experiencing it, comforting her and letting her know that it was okay to die and let go. I trusted that she could still hear. When family and friends came to sit with her and hold vigil, everyone would gently tell her who they were as they came into the room.

At one point, her healing circle of women who had been her support group all gathered around her bed. I gently told her that her circle was with her, and she responded with a deep groan. We all knew she was acknowledging our presence, and could feel her great effort, in making that connection with us. We all talked to her individually, first saying our name and then sharing with her from our hearts. We then sang to her. Singing to her was something that I began to do a lot with her when she was in the dissolution state. Even her father, who was beside himself, asked me to sing to her when he was with her. He would join in. I could tell that he felt comforted by the gentle singing, and it allowed him to be more present for his daughter, rather than focused on his own grief. People would quietly come and go, and a rhythmic flow developed, creating safety and containment. It was truly amazing that such a varied group of people could all find their way to be with Carol in community.

Marty's parents commented that they never knew that death could be like that. They had taken care of their parents, and remarked that much of what went on around their experience was hidden and secret. Even her two children, three-year-old Rebecca and six-year-old Jeremy were involved from the time that Carol became bed-ridden. They would get into bed with her and talk with her, and in her coma state, her son wanted to lie next to her. He had avoided her somewhat previously, due to what I believe was his knowingness that his mother was dying, and so wanting to lie next to her was very important for him. He would kiss her and I felt that his love for his mother was beyond any fear. He said at one point, "she is the best mommy in the universe and I love her more than the trees and nature. If she passes tonight, she will be the best thing in the universe." Nothing can describe what I felt in that moment, hearing such precious jewel-words from this incredibly loving child.

Carol passed quietly around 1:15 in the morning on a day that is heralded in her tradition as a holy day — the "deathday" of Moses. In her tradition, it is said that when one passes shortly after midnight on such a holy day, that person is considered to be a great soul. Indeed she was. I believe that she has gone on to other worlds, spreading her love in other realms.

As a priestess-midwife attending Carol, I guided her immediately after her death into the unseen realms, drawing on the teachings of the Tibetan tradition that I accept, particularly the Mother/Child luminosity, which I consider to be actually older teachings from the matristic cultures in that part of the world. Carol never discussed with me exactly what she envisioned for her passing, so I did what I thought she would have liked. (Carol had accepted teachings about the Goddess tradition, and was finding ways to merge that with her Jewish heritage. She had also become a student of the mystical Quabbala and had been posing questions to several male rabbis about the sexism she saw within the tradition.) Marty, her parents, his parents, her brother, a good friend, two wonderful caregivers and I were present. The guiding was spontaneous — I did not read, but rather spoke from my heart and mind. I could feel her presence fill the room, as well as her sense of humor — which really surprised me. As the guidance was taking place, Carol's open mouth slowly began to close and a faint smile appeared on her lips.

Because she never really discussed her plans with Marty or her family about what she wanted following her death, Marty felt that he should follow the traditional Jewish burial practice. He carefully placed Carol's body on the floor of her bedroom, with her feet pointing towards the door. Marty had her children come in and see her. They were not afraid. He spent time with them looking at her and talking. I came into the room and the four of us stayed with her. Her sweet daughter picked up some flowers and began moving them over her body, making soft singing noises. I asked her if they were the singing flowers, and she said "yes." It felt natural and right for her children to be an integral part of her passing. It felt quite inappropriate, damaging even, to hide anything from them.

After a while, different family members and friends came in and out of the room to be with her body. In Jewish tradition, it is important to bury the body within twenty-four hours. Carol's healing circle of women came in to wash and ritually bathe her body, following the guidance of her wonderful female rabbi. I felt the ancient presence of women once again ushering life into a new passage. It felt very important that women were doing this — I felt that something was being restored in a deep way that is missing in our current patriarchal way of doing death.

It felt holy to have so many women's hands touching her — it was the touch of the Mother caring for Her child. Carol's body was laid to rest within fourteen hours of her passing. The memorial service occurred the same day. It all went very quickly — not something I would choose for myself. However, it was her tradition, and so it was.

As Carol's "shemama" and therapeia, I feel that my spiritual and emotional involvement with her was one of the most healing ways I could be there for her. I feel this is the Goddess-Way, the Mother-Way of being with people who need to feel safe and loved, which is what real healing is all about. Discussing issues was important, of course, but to be there, the way a mother would be, became much more important. There were no boundary problems because I chose to be there for her outside my "office" (which I refer to as my "healing space"). There were no boundary problems with Marty, who was also a client. What we experienced was a deep and profound trust and open-heartedness, which allowed for a beautiful peacefulness to pervade Carol's sanctuary, as we called it. We were humans sharing on the deepest level possible — being with life and death.

Regeneration and Karma

Crop Circle Goddess, Monica Sjöö, **1997**

It does not seem that early people had elaborately developed explanations of "karma" in the ways that many of us have become familiar with today. In fact Monica Sjöö in **Return of the Dark Light Mother** speaks of the origins of the doctrine of karma as "a Brahminic innovation and very useful politically since it taught that righteousness and justice are embodied in social and caste obligations. The Aryans originally had no concept of reincarnation; it is not mentioned in the Vedas." (Sjöö, **Return of the Dark Light Mother**, p.161) In this section I take a close look at how karma is regarded in the Tibetan Buddhist tradition, as that tradition is becoming very popular in the West, and so much information about karma and rebirth is available to the public now from Tibetan thought.

Though the doctrine of karma, at its core, is really about action and consequence, or one reaps what one sows, or what goes around comes around, it has become a twisted concept of complicated rationalizations in the service of hierarchy and dominance. Feminist writer Barbara Walker tells us that female-oriented religions were ruled by the cyclic patterns of karmic balance, "Every burgeoning was inevitably followed by corresponding decline. There could be no dawn without dusk, no spring without fall, no planting without harvest, no birth without death. The Goddess never wasted her substance without recycling. Every living form served as nourishment for other forms. Every blossom fed on organic rot. Everything had its day in the sun, then gave place to others, which made use of its dying." (Walker, **The Crone**, p.21) In this view, life is not opposed to itself in death. It is a never-ending cycle in which all things are interdependent rather than in opposition or dual. Did the ancients feel that to be born an animal is to become "less than," to be stupid, as some Tibetan teachings say? I think not. From the Paleolithic and Neolithic ages, the Goddess was embodied in many different animal forms.

It is well known that Ramana Maharshi, a Hindu saint, lived with a cow, Lakshmi, whom he considered to be enlightened. (The cow, of course, being the age-old symbol of the Goddess) Did the ancients feel that if they were "bad" they would take a "lesser rebirth?" In Buddhism we find the arrogant teaching that a female rebirth is simply inferior to a male one: "Milarepa constantly warns of the destructive powers of women, admonishing his followers to reject their seductive charms, and become meditative hermits. Even a demon, who is subdued by Milarepa after *she* (italics mine) emerges from a crack in a rock, is told that *she* is in an unfortunate rebirth, not because of her demonic form, or because of living in a rock, but that 'Because of your evil habit propensities formed in the past, and your vicious doings in the present . . . you were born as a lower form of woman.'" (Campbell, **Traveller In Space,** pp. 32-33)

This nonsense demeans the knowledge and wisdom of the ancients — those who worshipped the Goddess/Mother from their direct experience of the chthonic shamanic realms. What we do know from the archeological evidence is that for the ancients, death and regeneration went hand-in-hand; death signified a return to the Mother — "The Great Goddess was intimately involved in every manifestation of death as she was in those of life, which is why she had an 'emanation' for each fatal disease, such as Mari-Amma, Ankamma, Mutteryalamma, etc. Her priestesses supported and taught the dying. 'As among the gods, so among the mortals was death everywhere woman's business. A woman is said to have invented the wailing for the dead . . . Women cradle the infant and the corpse, each to its particular new life.'" (Walker, **The Women's Encyclopedia of Myths and Secrets,** p. 215)

It seems that this return to the Mother was something natural, expected. Egg-shaped graves found in Sardinia from the mid-fifth millenium BCE, for example, tell us that the idea of burying the loved one in a shape well-known to the Goddess and of the Goddess' domain was very important — perhaps more important than wondering where or what that soul would become in the afterlife, because the afterlife, after all, was still Her domain. Perhaps there was a natural trust that return to the Mother was, in itself, auspicious. When I visited some of these sacred sites, I was astonished to see the Neolithic Mother Goddess, or Dea Madre, as she is called to this day by Sardinians, carved into the rock, her timeless presence as guardian and protectress of all who rested within her sacred body/sanctuary gracing the natural beauty of the now.

It seems the emphasis in death was this return to the great womb of the Mother; that this returning was naturally to Her. It seems that the ancients didn't really think there was any other place to go in death — the place to return in death was to the place from where one was born. This idea is conspicuously absent in our spiritual teachings today. There is very little mentioned, if at all, about returning to the womb as something sacred, as something to look forward to, as something important for our experience in the afterlife, or "continued life."

The references I have found to the womb in patriarchal religions are debasing. Tibetan Buddhism teaches that when one dies and is searching for a place to be reborn, one is filled with immense suffering and worry. Where does this idea come from? When one finds the proper womb, the competition will be fierce to enter it, because "at the entrance of the womb there will be many beings waiting, hovering like flies on a piece of meat." (Nyima Rinpoche, **The Bardo Guidebook**, pp. 15-16) This guidebook goes on to say:

> "If one is going to be born as a male, one feels aggression toward the father and passion toward the mother; the opposite is true for a female. Through the power of this passion and aggression one immediately enters the womb.
>
> The consciousness is like a fly and the red and white elements from the father and mother are like glue; one's mind sticks to that glue. Once one has entered the womb, one lacks the ability to leave; the freedom to say 'I don't like this place.' It is said that our kind mother carries us for nine months and ten days. During this time the breath of mother and child is the same. When the mother is active there is much discomfort to the child. When she eats the child experiences the terror of being pressed under a big mountain . . . .During birth, one suffers pain that is similar to flesh being peeled from one's bones. The actual moment of birth is like falling from the sky and crashing down on the earth."(Nyima Rinpoche, **The Bardo Guidebook**, p. 16)

Does he remember all of this while in the womb, or did his male "lama-mothers" condition his thinking with their own accepted suppositions and fears handed down through their male hierarchy? With such apparent misogyny, it is no wonder, then, that the Tibetan male system of spirituality was in need of finding a way to be rid of the feminine, which it did, through the tulku system. We are being asked to accept that being in the womb is a failure — that we enter and re-enter womb-space because we failed to achieve "enlightenment" in the after-death out of womb state.

Why would Nyima Rinpoche's query into finding oneself in the womb take the form of immediately thinking that one would not be free to leave and not like it? In Tibetan Buddhism there is often reference to the "impurities of the womb," as if it is some undesirable place we all wind up in like fallen angels. Author and former Tibetan Buddhist translator to Kalu Rinpoche, June Campbell, informs us that such language appears frequently in Tibetan Buddhist philosophical texts.

"For example, the Mahayana Uttara Tantra on the 'Changeless Continuity of the True Nature,' describes Buddha nature in a series of metaphors concerning perfection situated within polluted images.

Buddha nature is a 'king . . . a future ruler of men in the womb of an unfortunate, ugly woman, and its emergence, the 'birth of the royal child' who escapes the 'impurities of the womb'. With the metaphor of enlightenment encoded in this way in gendered terms, the female body represents the imperfect or dangerous containment of the (male) Buddha nature, along with other polluted metaphors such as the 'decaying lotus', the bee-swarm, the husk, the filth, the ground, the fruitskin, the tattered rags . . . and the clay mould.'" (Campbell, **Traveller In Space**, p. 87)

Such a drastically different view of the female form is held in this tradition than the one of the ancients in pre-patriarchal times. What happened to honoring ancestral wisdom?

From a distinctly different perspective than the Buddhist view, Barbara Walker, in **The Crone** reflects: "Creation myths the world over begin with chaos, the condition of non-differentiation between self and other, with 'primordial element' suggesting the uterine environment: darkness, churning, the 'eternal flux', the maternal ocean of blood holding all future forms in formless potential. Often there was a reference to a lesser entity inside another, greater one, 'when darkness was enveloped in Darkness,' and the future cosmos was still united with the Formless Mother." (Walker, **The Crone,** p. 27) I find it interesting that men's spiritual traditions have negative references to the womb, not only in Tibetan Buddhism, and women's spiritual traditions have positive ones. What could this be about? Are you listening, Sigmund?

I suspect that this deep-seated misogyny is the same the world over. Men are afraid of women's creative, dark, uterine, bloody powers, the life that emerges from such mystery, and the non-negotiable terms of returning again to the womb/tomb in death. They have succeeded in demonizing women as well as our bodies and body parts in order to ensure some kind of immortality — as in the Tibetan Buddhist tulku system, where men have devised a system of becoming "self-born." Life itself is nothing to celebrate; purification of the soul (usually male) is encouraged so that it may reside in some heaven or "Pure Land" where male attributes abound.

The viewpoint that regards women and mothers as mere profane receptacles to be used to bring "the divine son" into the world rather than as sacred beings who give of ourselves, risking our lives to give birth, has become the universal patriarchal notion of motherhood, allowing men, in their various traditions to create "male motherhoods" that have then become the definition of "sacred and true motherhood." Female mothers are profane and worldly, while male motherhood is sacred and spiritual. The implication then is that one, meaning male, must get away from the female, the mother, the earth, as soon and as quickly as possible in order to find and experience the sacred. "The aim of a rebirth from the father is to undo or overcome the mortality implicit in the female, phenomenal world and achieve a timelessness or unchanging absolute quality, associated with maleness." (R.A Paul, **The Tibetan Symbolic World**, p. 279)

The domain of the Goddess is one of constant change. There is no way for an unchanging quality of maleness to exist separate from the Goddess. It is this split from the Mother that is the underlying universal karmic condition of suffering shared by all around the globe. The destruction that comes from this disconnection manifests the same way — domination, colonization, rape, torture, and on and on, which has not slowed down to this day. With such insidious misogyny what can these teachings offer when they, themselves, create negative karma and perpetuate suffering?

Another prominent feature of Tibetan Buddhist spiritual teachings on death, dying and karma is a kind of preoccupation with failure in the bardos — "bardo" means "gap" describing the gaps as death, in-between lives, and life itself. Sogyal Rinpoche refers to "failure" often in **The Tibetan Book of Living and Dying** — "If again you fail to recognize and gain stability, the next phase unfolds, called 'union dissolving into wisdom'" . . . and "So, for example, if you fail to recognize the red, ruby light of the wisdom discernment, it arises as fire . . . if you fail to recognize the pure nature of the golden radiance of the equalizing wisdom . . . . . . and so on." (Sogyal Rinpoche, **Tibetan Book of Living and Dying**, pp. 277, 281) Chokyi Nyima Rinpoche also advises us, "If we fail to recognize the ground luminosity we again commence the creation of karma through dualistic fixation." (Nyima Rinpoche, **The Bardo Guidebook**, p. 118)

The implication of a teaching such as this is that as long as one incarnates, one has failed to do it right in the bardos, and one will always be bound by passion and aggression in rebirth, (unless one has chosen to return as a bodhisattva) unable to be "free" from being held hostage by an impure womb. In this way, dualistic thinking is the only experience of incarnation, with built-in deluding passions and aggressions towards one's parents. I wonder if Freud, father of psychoanalysis, and Padmasambhava, father of Tibetan Buddhism, were co-horts in a past life. Or, maybe they were the same person, reincarnated.

I can accept that life does not die, that is, energy does not die with the body and that there are streams of consciousness that continue to evolve. If a person dies in a state of fear and anxiety, or anger, then the energy that is released into the great cosmic flow from that being will have to find a way to transform. If we had a way to prepare for this while alive, which is what world religions attempt to teach, but are really unsuccessful without the Mother teachings, we will be ready to accept the after-death states without fear of punishment or failure. We could accept that we have work to do, and will find new incarnations to continue our work, while being held in the arms of the Mother — beneficent, loving, fair, merciful and fierce — but not punishing.

If we can allow mothers to be true mothers, free from the oppression of patriarchy, then we will be taught by our mothers how to love, through their loving us. And if this is our experience in life, why should it be any different in death? If patriarchal privileged men, through their distorted, fearful need to control, would stop their interference with the mother/child bond, and simply allow women who choose to birth children to be ourselves, then we will see much healing in all realms of the global human family.

If patriarchal men could let themselves be supportive of women who mother, and women in general, and serve the greater good of the Goddess, and let go of the competition and jealousy they engender because they don't bleed and give birth, and learn to truly love women, then a new spirituality will be born. The grief I have witnessed of some of the mothers who have surrendered their boy children to the various monasteries because they are the supposed incarnations of so-and-so goes unnoticed by the very system that espouses compassion. I wonder if these monks have ever considered what the karma is of creating such an ocean of grief?

It appears to me that there are vestigal teachings from the Goddess cultures that inhabited the land prior to the twelfth century when Padmasambhava brought Buddhism to Tibet. One of these teachings about death and dying is called "path luminosity and ground luminosity." Beings, such as you and I, are the path luminosity, also called the child luminosity. In death, we are given an opportunity, (which most "fail" to achieve according to several sources on this subject, as it only arises for a very short time, and if you miss it, then you have failed to achieve union), to merge with the ground luminosity, or the Mother luminosity. Chokyi Nyima Rinpoche refers to this merging in **The Bardo Guidebook** as a meeting of mother and child much in the same way a happy child jumps into the lap of his (sic) mother. (Nyima Rinpoche, **The Bardo Guidebook**, p. 115)

I believe this to be one of the most profound references to the feminine in Tibetan teachings on dying. I find this particular teaching quite beautiful. I also find it very odd indeed that a system that found a way to divest itself of female wisdom, with the exception of certain androcentric views of Tantric union and the doctrine of emptiness, relies so completely on this essential merging experience of Mother and Child luminosity in death. Nyima Rinpoche goes as far as to say that all of the Buddha's teachings converge into understanding path and ground luminosity. Ground luminosity, the Mother, is the true essence of mind — non-conceptual wakefulness. This is the Mother luminosity. This is Mother. This is Goddess. This is Prajmaparamita, the Mother of all the Buddhas.

But it is not taught this way. In an all-male system, how could the concept of Mother be truly respected? In an all-male system that removes little boys from their mothers, the children are removed from the true Mother luminosity to learn about it from men, who then give teachings to the world on Mother/Child luminosity. The absent feminine in Tibetan Buddhism is the same "feminine famine" we can witness in other major world religions, and I think this famine has had a profound influence on every aspect of our lives, including the way we birth and the way we die. I should think it confusing to spiritual practitioners in Tibetan Buddhism particularly, to learn about a teaching that is available about death, the Mother/Child luminosity, and not be trained in it from their own mothers.

I wonder what practitioners would experience in the after-death states if they were introduced to teachings of the Mother/Child luminosity that included practices of connecting to the Divine Feminine, or Goddess, as source while alive. Respecting one's mother as Goddess and honoring the selfless love that a mother practices on a daily basis would be a good place to start. Jumping into the Mother's lap while alive is very comforting and joyous, as any child who experiences this will express through giggles, nuzzling, sighing, etc.

The sense a child feels in this moment is one of complete safety and joy. If a child is raised with this, and taught that on the other side of death one meets with the same experience, only much bigger, how could anyone "fail" in this? If a person does not fully awaken to the Mother in her/his lifetime, because energy does not die, it would seem that in the after-death states, which is Her domain anyway, we would still be held by Her, while still needing to learn about the truth of awakening, or, liberation. If we could learn to trust that our journey is profoundly mystical, and that it is Her love that holds us in all aspects of our travels, no matter where we may find ourselves, we can surrender to Her, and find peace and joy — while alive, while dead, here on earth or in some other dimension.

June Campbell's brave look at the hierarchical tulku system in Tibetan Buddhism in her book, **Traveller in Space**, reveals a very deep-seated misogyny living in the secrecy maintained by lamas engaging in sexual "Tantric" practice. She informs us that as a secret sexual consort of Kalu Rinpoche, who espoused celibacy to the public, she would be subjected to a terrible karmic misfortune, as other women had been, if she did not participate in the secrecy.

She was frightened into submission. So, what are we to believe regarding teachings from such "masters" on karma and rebirth, death and dying?

With the publication of **Traveller in Space**, we are shown that there existed an underlying awareness in Tibetan Buddhism of the male practitioner that he knew he must connect with the female principle to achieve liberation. So, this awareness belies some kind of idea that connection with the female is essential to wholeness. Of course it is essential. Why separate any child from the female, from Mother, in the first place? Without this separation, I don't see the need for elaborate teachings that say we must do it just right in death or we will find ourselves back in some womb at whose entrance the spirit flies have congregated.

This kind of teaching can only be found in a patriarchal world that suffers from the absence of Sacred Female Authority. In this patriarchal view, both Eastern and Western, the female body is debased — regarded as sinful and dirty and symbolic of the earth which must be left behind in the pursuit of the patriarchal mind's obsessive focus on the light and compulsion to render the body immaterial, disregarding sacred sexuality and its primacy in rebirth and regeneration. I think the teachings are quite different in a world embracing this Sacred Female Authority. These are the teachings that are needed now, which include enlightenment and endarkenment as well as the celebration of mind and body, earth and spirit and women's awesome power of creation.

In the videos available to the public on the **Tibetan Book of the Dead**, the procedures and process are seen from male viewpoints only, with the future lamas, as boys, learning at the side of the adult male lamas. In these videos, there is no presence of anyone cradling, touching, singing to, or generally, just loving the dying. The lamas ask the people not to cry, for it disturbs the journey of the dying. Perhaps. But why be told not to cry at all? Why not just suggest that grieving could take place in another room? Where is the wisdom from women who created wailing for the dying? And why is it left out in this tradition?

In one scene, a boy asks his mentor about birth, and the lama tells him it is nothing to celebrate, nor is death. With this grim, nihilistic teaching, this boy, who, as a child is open to the wonders of the universe, is taught to shut down. Life is not worth celebrating because it is empty. This motherless, female-absent tradition has given us probably some of the most available teachings on death, dying and karma in the West. While there seems to be much wisdom in these teachings, I feel that they are interwoven with androcentric ignorance. What would Padmasambhava, credited with the origination of **The Bardo Thödol,** the Tibetan manual on death and dying, have taught about death and dying and karma if he had not been conditioned by patriarchal influences, which went unrecognized as such back then, as well as now? What would these teachings become if the Goddess was remembered, recognized and included?

Perhaps it would be something like what Anne Brener shares with us in **Mourning and Mitzvah:**

"The El Malai Rakhamim calls upon God to embrace the soul of the deceased with compassion as it is bound up with all the other souls, under the nurturing wings of the Shekhinah, often described as the feminine face of god. The Shekhinah portrays God as being present, close, personal and nurturing. Rakhamim refers to God's compassion. Its root, rekhem, means 'womb.' It alludes to God's maternal attributes and to the nurturing, loving quality of the ever-present Shekhinah." (Brener, **Mourning and Mitzvah**, p.80)

Or, what is truly is as described by my Maori friend, Mary Mem Joe:

"...it is only the women who can and must be the bridge between the world of the living and the world of the dead. So, they go before the body chanting ritual karakia/prayer. They surround the body as it is carried out, because it is the sacredness of our wombs and the birth passage that can and will negate any invisible evil and they must also walk behind because it is the women who help the spirit leave the place to travel to its final resting place." (personal conversation)

Diane Stein, author and feminist healer, in her **Psychic Healing with Spirits and Angels,** extensively quotes the Tibetan system as the path of truth on death and dying. She says concurrently that rebirth is the outcome of karma, and once we figure out that we can purify our karma, we will not need to incarnate again, but also says that being in body on the Earth is good, and so rebirth is not all bad. I regard this as a conflicted viewpoint over transcendence and immanence. What is so bad about incarnation at all? Apparently, if we don't "get it" in the bardos, then we are just too ignorant, and have to be reborn to live on this planet. Is this planet not our home? Are we just to be here and live as linearly and efficiently as possible so that we can be done with rebirth, as if rebirth is a kind of shaming, lower-level experience for stupid and ignorant people? The ancients totally celebrated rebirth and regeneration before the idea of bardos even existed.

I had a very difficult time reading some of Sogyal Rinpoche's book to my mother when she was dying. I eventually had to stop. I felt that if I continued to read to her, she would become afraid of "failing" in the bardos. And I felt that causing her to be fearful was not creating good karma, for her or for myself. I preferred to talk to her in loving kindness, to guide her with reassurance, to direct her into the light and arms of a loving Mother who was waiting for her. My mother called out "Mom" when she was deep in her dying process, and "rooted" into her pillow the way a newborn child does, looking for the breast. My mother felt safe surrounded by love, tenderness, and reassuring touch. She responded to heart-inspired encouragement. I felt that since the first language of humans is touch, there could be nothing harmful in offering that to her in her dying. Being sensitive and aware of her psychic and spiritual needs was essential. It was important to be mindful of not touching her in a way that would have interfered with her process. I also played inspiring music for her. My intention was to create a place of safety and beauty that would make it as beautiful an experience as possible for all involved. I felt the presence of such profound mystery and beauty, that I felt she couldn't help but be okay in her after-death experience. Failure felt like a foreign concept.

Since we are not solely/souly our physical bodies, and since streams of consciousness live beyond the body (which is why I don't believe in the death penalty), we do need to purify our consciousness — transform anger, fear and ignorance, in order to create peace and harmony. If one is controlled by the reactive nature, and lives in ignorance, then karma does accrue, and that karma continues until it is transformed. I perceive this as "getting off the wheel" — when we are no longer controlled by reaction. Why does this imply that we are then done with incarnation? Is incarnating only about purifying one's karma? Is the earth only for purification purposes?

Billions of years in the making, this blue-green jewel glistening in space, in the exact temperate zone, not too far and not too close to the sun, a work of unspeakably beautiful living art, is merely a weigh-station for unclean souls to get smart enough to advance to somewhere else? Somewhere we can't really see while we are here because we are too impure? Barbara Walker posits:

> "The naturalistic world vision was pushed aside by rising patriarchal religions, which were basically anti-nature, viewing all flesh as sinful and all death as punishment rather than a universal recycling process. To such as the Jain Buddhists, Zoroastrians, Essenes, Manichaeans, and early orthodox Christian sects, earthly life was not an end in itself. It was only a testing ground for the soul, which could theoretically conquer death and attain a permanent, static Nirvana, or paradise, or possibly an eternity of torture. They said the only real purpose of living was to decide one's status in the afterworld. This was supposed to give meaning to an otherwise meaningless existence." (Walker, **The Crone**, p. 21)

Perhaps the earth herself is really the diamond jewel in the lotus. And women, endowed with the only organ in existence created exclusively for the sake of experiencing ecstasy, the clitoris, are the microcosm of the macrocosm, as the clitoris becomes the diamond jewel in the vulva-lotus. How interesting that the Buddhist chant chanted by monks too numerous to count, "Om Mane Padme Om," popularly translated as "hail to the jewel in the lotus" is most likely an invocation to the "essential sexuality of the female, i.e the deity of the clitoris-vagina," not so popularly known. (Campbell, **Traveller In Space**, p.64)

We can be in the body and be purified of our negative karma, and enjoy life. Buddhists say that when this happens, then one can choose to come back into body as a bodhisattva, to help others. Is that the only choice, once one has purified one's karma? Naturally, in a world full of pain and anguish, a purified soul would tend to create healing wherever s/he happened to be. However, there is an implication in Buddhism that says that if one has purified, there would be no reason to come back to the earth other than to be a bodhisattva. What if one just really loved to be here? Is the earth not a Pure Land? Why wouldn't one want to be here, in the lush garden of the Goddess, and enjoy it? Are the only Pure Lands in the other dimensions? Who says so? If the human body is precious, as is taught in Buddhism, because it is hard to obtain one, then why wouldn't where the human body lives be as precious?

Stein equates Buddha mind with the Goddess. In some ways, I perceive this to be true. But in other ways, Buddha mind was interpreted by the male mind for primarily males at the time, and all that comes from this teaching is colored with this androcentric bias. It is surprising to me that Stein, a known feminist and teacher of women's spirituality and the Goddess, does not seem to notice this. The Goddess was not present for men at the time Buddhism was on the rise, and in many ways, still is not present for the men who espouse profound spiritual teachings from this tradition. On the contrary, male tantric practitioners are encouraged to envision imaginary consorts in some kind of disassociated practice of connecting to the feminine.

The Dalai Lama has spoken of the need for a new spirituality in the world, noting the fundamental close relationship between mother and child as essential to true intimacy and well being. In his book, **Illuminating the Path to Enlightment**, he says:

> "The key factor in developing and increasing basic human values — the sense of caring for and sharing with one another — is human affection, a feeling of closeness with one another . . . . According to some medical scientists, the uborrn child can recognize its mother's voice. This indicates that even then, the child feels close to and dear towards its mother. Once the child is born, he or she spontaneously sucks it's mother's milk. The mother also experiences a feeling of closeness to her child. Because of this her milk flows freely. If either side lacked that feeling of intimacy, the child would not survive." (The Dalai Lama, **Illuminating the Path to Enlightment**, p. IX)

This is interesting commentary from a man, who as a boy, was taken away from his mother to be put into an all male environment to learn about "motherly love" from men who somehow wound up with the title "lama" which means "la," soul and "ma," mother. I wonder what the karma is of co-opting motherly love, putting it in the hands of men, and conditioning boys to regard their relationships with their male mentors as the mother-child relationship?

Because we do not honor loving kindness, tenderness, compassion, gentleness, softness, sensitivity, and egalitarianism, as well as who women really are and what women really do, it is no wonder, then, that we have much fear about death and dying in this patriarchal culture. Where are the concepts of nurturing in our death process? In our beliefs about karma? Where is the Mother — She who births us, and waits for us at the end of a life, to take us to another shore? If we do not know from whence we come, how can we possibly know where we are going?

Much of what we know about karma comes to us from Eastern religions. In my study of Tibetan Buddhist dying practices, I have read about the bardo states. Tibetan Buddhists feel that one's rebirth is determined by how one lives one's current life. I can accept this. I can also accept that rebirth into the six lokas — the god realm, the demi-god realm, the animal realm, the human realm, the hungry-ghost realm and the hell-being realm is about rebirth into experiences of psychological states.

Karma does not need to be a system of rewards and punishments. As I earlier cited from Monica Sjöö, some traditions used the concept in this fashion. In Buddhism, men teaching women that a female rebirth is inferior is a very useful tool for an established male hierarchy to oppress women, which is further perpetuated by the removal of boy children from their mothers. In pagan philosophy, "do what you will and harm none" and "what you do to another will return to you threefold" are two laws that reflect an understanding of karma. It only makes sense that karma is a system of accountability and responsibility. We teach our children to take responsibility for their actions. Living by the law of karma does not mean that we should not want change.

The world is suffering from karma generated by ignorance perpetuated by patriarchy — from the actions set into motion by poor choices that cause suffering for all of Gaia's children. As long as misogyny exists in our thinking, we will be creating karma while we are at the same time attempting to create healing, harmony and peace. We cannot simultaneously create peace while perpetuating separation from the Sacred Feminine, as is encouraged in certain male-centered spiritual teachings. Karma reflects a universal law of the dance between action and consequence. There is also group karma, in which individual karma is part of the group's karma. In patriarchy, when women are oppressed and abused by the controlling patriarchal male mind, hatred and violence are perpetuated. When women internalize this hatred and violence, women then contribute to the continuation of the group karma of this suffering.

The group karma of women's suffering affects the whole globe and all of her delicate structures and ecosystems. How did we get from the matrifocaled, Goddess-loving cultures to what we have now? I don't know that anyone can really say why this happened, but we can say that it certainly did, as Marija Gimbutas has so painstakingly tracked. Why does anything happen? Is there a great cosmic plan for everything that happens? A violent mindset appearing on the peaceful scene in Old Europe, for instance, introduced new thoughts and thought forms, and they gathered momentum over time, leaving a wake of destruction which we are still experiencing. I do not think we need to believe that women did something "wrong" to "deserve" the karma of current abuse and misogyny, as some New Age writers and some religious credos purport. This would be far too simplistic.

I think that when dominating, violent forces suppress, oppress, depress, repress and compress the life force, devastating consequences will occur. Women are the heart and womb of this life force. It only makes sense that disrespect for life would be reflected in disrespect for women, and all that comes from our wombs. This is the group karma all humans suffer. It is this disrespect for life that causes the suffering — not that women did something "wrong" in the past to deserve what is happening now. What we are experiencing now is a collective consequence of the misogynist actions set in motion 5,000 years ago. I see a colliding of forces, not accidental, but as part of the experience possible within the Goddess, subject to freewill.

If someone could have subdued that first spear-thrower, and taught him the value and meaning of life; if that first male did not sell that first female into slavery and explained to both of them that subjugation of the other was not allowed; if the violent thought forms were not allowed to take root; then the karma of today would not be what it is. We are still at the psychic juncture of those first events — desperately needing to change and transform our actions before we annihilate ourselves. So, all of the karma created since that time has served to bring us to an edge of a collective near-death experience.

If misogyny stops, then so will sexism, racism, abuse, hate, war and violence. All the karma created from such ignorance will be transformed by what takes the place in the absence of this misogyny, which is love, which is what women know how to do quite well. How can we have teachings that harbor misogyny telling us at the same time to love one another? They become an oxymoron. We need the same medicine now as we needed when patriarchy first reared its ugly head. If enough people knew how to keep humanity from coming to this current edge, and I suspect there were those who could "see" the effects of the consequences set in motion at that time, we would be having a very different experience. Karma is not written in stone. It relies on choices and actions in the moment.

That is why it is necessary to purify ourselves — to purify our thoughts and to become as conscious as we can, so that we can make wise choices and understand the effects of karma and consequence on our children's children's children. Without this vision, we kill ourselves. Now, we are at a point of desperation, and it might possibly be too late to turn things around. In this scenario, things are returned to the great cauldron of the Goddess, to be stirred yet again into the Mystery of the great round. Regardless of outcome, the process is still the same — birth, life, death and regeneration.

Paleolithic and Neolithic Burial Practices of Old Europe

Triangular-yonic stone at grave chamber. Wildeshausen, district of Oldenburg, Schleswig-Holstein, drawn by Melissa Meltzer

As far back as the Neanderthal, some 200,000 years BCE, there is evidence that people lived in relationship with the earth and had a concept of deity. Perhaps it wasn't a concept the way we know concepts, with our brain, but rather a body concept based on witnessing and feeling. Perhaps it would be more accurate to call it a sensing, or a psychic attunement to the cosmos that didn't require thinking as we know thinking, but rather a kind of animal-wisdom feeling.

This sensing was so great that they buried their dead by placing them in the fetal position, washing them with red ochre, anointing them with the life-color of blood. Why the fetal position, and why red ochre? Just think on this a moment. What would this mean to you today if this was your burial practice? Remember, our stereotypes of Neanderthals are that they were not all that intelligent and rather brutish. I think we can surmise just from knowing about their burial practices that our thinking about these beings has been prejudicial and erroneous for a very long time. Scientist Jonathan Leake writes that Neanderthals were not the unintelligent, ape-like creatures we have been taught they were. He contends they were deeply emotional beings with high-pitched voices who may have communicated in song, which he likens to a "living opera." Two new studies of the voice boxes of Neanderthals show that their voices were "womanly" and "melodic." Archeologist Stephen Mithen says they probaby communicated with each other in "part language and part song." From his studies of the Neanderthal, Mithen says," They must have been able to communicate complex ideas and even spirituality." (**Britain Sunday Times**, January 30, 2005)

In **The Great Cosmic Mother** by Monica Sjöö and Barbara Mor we are given a most vivid view of Neanderthal burial practices:

> ". . .during the Neanderthaloid period (dating from at least 200,000 BCE) evidence shows that great magical power was attributed to the earth as Mother of Life and Death. Neanderthals buried their dead curled in fetal position, painted red; bones were painted with red ochre. Analogically, the dead were to reenter the earth (the tomb, the womb) to be reborn again.
>
> A Neanderthal corpse found in Shanidar Cave in northern Iraq had been laid to rest on pine boughs and strewn with wild flowers. Even earlier than this, a remarkable find at La Ferrassie, in the French limestone country, shows the beautiful resonance that was felt in the minds and hearts of these earliest people between life, death, and the Mother. In a rock shelter, a child's grave was found covered with a large stone slab. On the underside of this slab small cupules had been scooped out — these were all in pairs, to symbolize the mother's breasts. These breast-shaped cupule markings were made throughout preshistory; they are found over great areas of outcropped rocks in Europe. But on this stone slab in France, covering a Neanderthal child's grave, is where they first appear." (Sjöö and Mor, **The Great Cosmic Mother**, pp. 46-47)

These breast-like cupules surrounding the dead are symbolic of not only nourishment, but also regeneration of the dead and are found throughout the millennia into the Neolithic. While Sjöö and Mor refer to these cupmarks as symbolic of the breasts of the Goddess, Gimbutas also connects them with the eyes of the Goddess, "Not infrequently they are surrounded by single, double, or multiple circles and are clearly metaphor — i.e., eyes that are simultaneously the source of divine liquid, the water of life itself, and its receptacles when it falls." (Gimbutas, **Language of the Goddess**, p. 61) Because many cupule markings retain the sacred rainwaters of the Goddess, Gimbutas contends that they are actually miniature wells — the precursor of the Holy wells of more recent times.

Also significant at this gravesite was the fact that this large limestone block in which these cupule markings were engraved was triangular in shape. The triangle, a sacred symbol of the Goddess representing the vulva, is found in many different sizes and shapes depicted in numerous forms — on iconography as well as in etchings on stone and in temple and megalithic tomb construction throughout Old Europe. Near Carnac, France, a dolmen — a chamber made of stones with a stone slab laying horizontally atop two or more vertical stones, symbolizing the yoni — captures the sun's rays at the moment of the autumnal equinox, displaying a magnificent triangular yoni. A Goddess figure from the Lower Paleolithic, believed to be from the Heidelbergian cultures, stands as a triangle sculpture, revealing intentional flint-knapped markings defining the head, breasts, and vulva of the Goddess. From its association with tools, this figure is dated roughly circa 500,000 BP.

From our very early ancestors we see a deep sensitivity and awareness of the earth and of Mother. There is an understanding of return to the womb/tomb — a returning to something greater than oneself. There is in these burial practices a deep honoring of the very primal essence from which we all emerge. The cupule markings symbolic of the Goddess' breasts and eyes marked on the grave of a child reveal an extremely tender relationship to death itself — that of return and re-nourishing. Imagine today if we painted our departed loved ones with red ochre and marked our caskets with paintings of breasts, or with carvings of breasts. Many people would regard such carvings as possibly pornographic, or at the very least, "indecent." How strange that we have strayed so far away from the simple connection to a nourishing source — to that connection of the Cosmic Mother that our earliest ancestors, who androcentric archeology has held as ignorant, understood.

We can appreciate that the use of red ochre was symbolic of the blood of life. And it was not only the Neanderthal that used it in their burial practices. "We see it in the trail of red ochre that colors the dead with the hue of life, from the caves of the Dordogne in 30,000 B.C. to the burial sites beneath the sleeping platforms of the living in Çatal Hüyük twelve millennia later. Three thousand years later, ocher still covers the dead at the great necropolis, the Hal Saflieni Hypogeum in Malta. Red ocher and other pigments color the Goddess too in her life-giving aspects: the pregnant, red-stained Venus of Laussel; figurines stained red from the Cucuteni culture; the red painted bulls' horns of Sardinia." (Streep, **Sanctuaries of the Goddess**, p. 15)

This use of red ochre throughout time — this red trail of life (menstrual blood) — reveals a thread of continuity in the imaginary realm of early humanity regarding life and death. A belief, or perhaps a "knowing" of rebirth seems to have been a part of many cultures across time, prior to patriarchy. In addition to the use of ochre, sacred objects have been found in graves in the Upper Paleolithic including shells, ivory and bone ornaments. "E. O. James suggests that in addition to the ocher tinted symbolic blood, shells, cowries among them, accompanied the dead precisely because they resemble the shape of the female labia, and thus figured in a 'life-giving rite' for the dead, a birth after death. Like the cupmark, the shell would not only be part of the burial of the dead for millennia, it also would serve, in Minoan Crete and elsewhere, to invoke the Goddess." (Streep, **Sanctuaries of the Goddess**, p. 30)

This connection in burial practices with blood and shells, symbolic of the Goddess and cyclical return to Her, of the sacred vulva from which all emerges, including the blood of life in menstruation as well as in giving birth, this returning to the primordial feminine ground of being and knowledge of regeneration, was known by the ancients — not intellectually, but somatically. The ancients had knowledge of life after life, or life after death, or life as a never-ending continuous cycle — whatever we choose to call it, they knew it. Artist and writer Buffie Johnson observes, "the image came first, and seeing remains the most natural mode of apprehension." (Johnson, **Lady of the Beasts**, p. 2) So if the first image of deity was that of a Mother Goddess, what does this mean?

The word "image" has cognates such as "magic," "imagination," "mage," "magician," etc. Since it appears that early people lived in awe of the mystery of nature, and understood the magical whole, every aspect of daily living was considered sacred and rooted in ritual intent. (ibid, p. 3) Therefore, the experience of this first image of deity of our ancestors, of the Great Mother, becomes an archetype in cellular memory for the individual. The magic of the Mother was visible and experiential, and is re-emerging now, for all of us, in this eleventh hour of need — in this time of our collective near-death experience.

Because early matristic people lived in sacred unity with nature and harmony on a daily basis, it is no surprise that they embraced the dead as the "living dead." Monica Sjöö and Barbara Mor have termed this "the cult of the dead, a very exact ancient science of spiritual invocation and conscious direction of natural forces." (Sjöö and Mor, The Great Cosmic Mother, p. 131) They say that the religious ideas of humans regarding death and resurrection go back at least as far as the Neanderthal and Cro-Magnon. They also point out that the first human religious rites of rebirth-resurrection-reincarnation were believed to occur in the body of the Mother as people saw mirrored around them the cycles of birth, death and rebirth in nature. (ibid., p. 77) Today the foundation of the living matrilineal Minangkabau culture of Sumatra is completely based on nature as teacher, "Matrilineal adat (custom) is in accordance with the flora and fauna of nature in which it can be seen that it is the mother who bears the next generation and it is the mother who suckles the young and raises the child. In nature all that is born into the world is born from the mother, not from the father . . . we must protect women and their offspring." (Sanday, **Women at the Center**, p. 24)

Embracing the dead continued through the millennia — even as people left the caves and began to live in constructed housing, this reverence for the dead prevailed. In Middle-Neolithic Çatal Hüyük, the bones of loved ones were placed under the floors and beneath sleeping platforms. In this way, they were included in the lives of the people they left behind in the realm of the living. If we were to place the bones of our loved ones under our floors or beds now, surely we would be regarded as someone "needing professional help."

This practice would scare the neighbors; we would be considered sinister and macabre and our children would have nightmares. Today, only deviants and psychopathic murderers practice such things in our patriarchal society. Of course, what they engage in is not at all what I am talking about as sacred. But, it is the only time we hear of bones buried around one's home — in the shadows of ignorance. If we were closer with the experience of life and death as a continuum, closer with the sacredness of the whole, we would not have the experience of fearing death, and therefore denying its existence; we would have the experience of embracing the mystery of life, of which death is an integral part.

When the bones of the ancestors are cared for as sacred, when people regard their dead loved ones as sources for accessing magic and mystery for healing, the experience of human beings as living beings is greatly enhanced. What we become with this connectedness is far different from who we are today, with our technology that keeps us isolated and rushed, and with our male-dominated "spiritual," psychological, "educational," and governing systems that control our wildness.

Communication with the dead is an ancient shamanic practice, still alive in hunting and gathering tribes. In going into the cave to trance, dance and partake of ritual, the shaman enters into relationship with the spirit world and retrieves information, often from communion with the dead. The dead are close with/to the Goddess. They have been returned to Her womb to await rebirth, and so inhabit Her sacred realms between incarnations. They live in Her sacred Dark. If we acknowledge this, and invoke them, they can be of service to us.

In Tibetan Buddhist practices, as in the **Bardo Thödöl**, people are instructed to pray for their recently deceased loved one for forty-nine days — the time they say it takes for a rebirth. This belief in powerful prayer seems to have been with humans for a very long time. It is my observation that we have lost some of the wisdom inherent in this knowledge, and that it is crucial for us to find it again.

The current celebration of Halloween is based in an ancient tradition of honoring the dead, when the veil between the worlds is considered to be thin and communication with dead loved ones is invoked. The Day of the Dead in Spanish traditions celebrates this same ancient remembering. In my community, I have offered an annual celebration of the "dark" and of the Crone, for women — just so we can be together and remember our ancient ways, and so that we can access the wisdom of the ancestors. We use prayer, ecstatic drumming and dancing and trance to enter an altered state — the reality that appears when the veils between worlds are thin. I am told repeatedly by women who have attended the event that the experience was very special for them — they actually connected with a loved one who had information, a gift or a message for them from beyond the veil.

Or they simply experienced being with a dead loved one who they hadn't had connections with, or thought to be "somewhere" else, unavailable. I hear that lives are changed from participating in this ritual. It is not my doing that brings this experience for others. I simply become a vessel for Her presence, and create a space where others can experience Her directly. She is the Goddess. She is the One who is making Her voice heard now, in these perilous times.

Neolithic rock tombs of Old Europe, as in Sardinia, were cut into egg or oven shapes into the rock face or into the ground. Marija Gimbutas has shown us that these egg and oven-shaped tombs were symbolic of regeneration. In the tomb of Cuccuru S'Arriu, a Goddess figure was placed before a body that was arranged in the fetal position and covered with red ochre. Echoing back to the Paleolithic, two halves of a shell filled with red ochre were also found. There is strong evidence indicating that these tombs were also sacred sites for ritual. What sort of ritual? Why would people do ritual around and within burial sites?

Perhaps because they knew, just as the peoples of the Paleolithic, that life is a continuum, and enacting ritual around and with the dead was integral to their spiritual wholeness. A dish from the later Neolithic Ozieri culture of Sardinia found at the stone monument site of Monte d'Accoddi depicts dancing women. The familiar Old European hourglass figurines have feet resembling bird claws — perhaps those of the bird goddess. Perhaps the five women holding hands might be portraying a ritual dance celebrating the reunion of the loved one with the ancestors as well as regeneration. How do you feel about dancing at a loved one's death ceremony? Would you like loved ones to dance at yours?

A particular type of artifact and iconographic figurine art found from the Upper Paleolithic through the Neolithic in Old Europe has been identified by Marija Gimbutas as the "stiff nude." These are carved female figures of bone, alabaster, amber, marble, antler, ivory and light-colored stone, with folded arms across the breast or extended at the sides, a long neck, and large pubic triangle. Some are depicted with full figures and some are thin-figured, more bone-like — all symbolic of the Death Goddess.

Death was associated with the color of white bone, not the color black that death is associated with today, with all of its attendant fear and horror. It is Gimbutas' speculation that the placement of the stiff nude Goddess into the graves of the deceased perhaps created an opening into the entrance of the subterranean womb, assuring a place in cyclical regeneration. It appears that the ancients of matrifocaled cultures were not concerned about burying loved ones with a plethora of possessions to ensure wealth in the after-life. Their connection to and honoring of the Goddess seemed to be the most important element in life and in death. To bury loved ones with the magic of the bones of the Goddess seems to me to reflect a deep and profound understanding of a chthonic psycho-spiritual-biological-mythological experience carried in the hearts, bodies and minds of these spiritually sophisticated human beings. It is my belief that we all carry the memory of this wisdom deep in our cells.

Today, it is women who are awakening to the call of the ancients, learning to listen to the womb-wisdom from within our own bodies, learning to give voice to what we know is true in our hearts, uncovering the over-grown well of the Goddess to restore the life-giving waters of Her love to this patriarchally parched, drought-stricken land. I pray it is in time.

Suicide — Yana's story

Firedancing Dakini, Monica Sjöö, **1998**

During the writing of this book a good friend of mine suicided two days before her fifty-fourth birthday. She knew I was writing this book, and I feel that it is her suicide and the impact of her death on her loved ones that are compelling me to include this topic. I had not intended to include anything about suicide — it hadn't occurred to me. I haven't come across information regarding how the ancients regarded this choice. I feel, however, that the death urge we experience in patriarchy today was for the most part non-existent in matrifocal society. This is my own conjecture based on what I feel to be true in my bones. Because the ancients experienced deity as female and cyclical, perhaps it was held that anyone who may have suicided back then was still thought to return to the Mother.

I had known Yana for nearly ten years during which time she suffered from chronic fatigue. We met when she was looking for a ride to a shamanic workshop at Esalen, a retreat center known for its beauty and serenity along the Carmel coast in California. I quickly learned that she was a sister with similar interests and over time we developed a friendship. She moved away to Santa Fe, which gave me an excuse to travel. During our years of friendship we spent time together sharing our lives as well as in ceremony — sweat lodge, sacred pipe, women's ritual, and shamanic healings. She introduced me to wonderful people at Hopi and we were privileged to witness some special Kachina dances together. We were some of the only white people there. We also shared the trials and tribulations of motherhood, as she was a single mother raising a beautiful daughter alone.

I knew Yana suffered from depression, but I did not know how deep her depression was. She managed to hide it from me. Other friends of hers knew her in a different way than I did and had dealt with her depression. But even they did not know how deep it ran. I am convinced that this depression — what I call "women's depression" — was the cause of her suicide.

Information regarding suicide seems to indicate that it is not a good idea. Someone told me that when a person commits suicide they remove the skeletons from their closet and hang them in yours. I am also aware that non-Western cultures, like the Iglulik Eskimo, believe that suicide is not a problem, and in some instances, is believed to be a purification. (Kalweit, **Dreamtine and Inner Space**, p. 23) Perhaps this kind of suicide is a very different one than that of a desperate, grieving soul who wants "out" of something which has no way "out" — only a way through. Barbara Walker reports that exercising control over one's own life in making a decision regarding one's own death was outlawed in the Inquisition. Medium James Van Praagh in **Talking to Heaven** indicates from the information he has garnered from his alleged connection to people who have committed suicide that they are usually filled with regret and remorse when they realize what they have done.

Whatever the philosophy, my experience with Yana's suicide was relentlessly painful and disturbing. I had to deal with a range of emotions including anger, fear, outrage and forgiveness as well as delving deeply into my own thoughts on the matter regarding women and patriarchy and why women decide to suicide. This has appeared to be the gift of her death — as I felt her to be a victim of how the oppression women suffer in patriarchy causes a deep and profound depression unnamed by current so-called therapeutic male-defined modalities. In other words, depression caused by oppression killed her. I know full well that patriarchy wants women dead. As in the movie with Meryl Streep, **One True Thing**, the narcissistic husband considers the wife courageous for choosing suicide.

Meryl Streep's character is considered to be brave when she kills herself. It is not the mother's legacy of truth and beauty that is transmitted to the daughter. It is the legacy of the patriarchal mind that thinks it of course knows best what constitutes women's reality. The daughter, who has stirrings of consciousness about the submissiveness of her mother and even manages to confront her father, acquiesces, and the movie ends with her instructing her father in the best way to plant bulbs in her mother's grave. The despair of the mother is passed on to her daughter. And in this despair, women are still expected to caretake men, as the daughter did in the end.

Yana's death has been symbolic to me of all women who feel the same way as she did and who suicide. Women and children are the casualities of the cultural battleground of patriarchy. Suicide in teens is definitely on the rise. As in **One True Thing** many women become the agents of patriarchy and kill themselves — doing the work of the demonic mind-set that hates them. As I became more of a radical feminist — one who loves the principals of truly feminist living, including such values as loving kindness, compassion, cooperation, power-with, peace, ecstasy and erotic creativity, which meant coming to terms with my deep-seated rage towards male domination and control (not men per se, but the patriarchal male mind) — Yana and I began to drift apart.

She could not fully tolerate my outspokenness — it was threatening to her internalized patriarch and she struggled with seeing me either as a wise woman or just "another angry woman," though shortly before she died, she told me she had begun to understand my view on this rage after listening to a tape I had recorded and produced and given to her. She had spent much time and money pursuing her healing with male practitioners, looking for validation from them. I could see that she was unwilling to confront her male-identification, her colonization.

As time went on, she began to grow weaker physically, but I also began to see this as a weakening of her psyche. Her own rage was unknown to her, and it began to grow into a deeper depression characterized by an apparent narcissism that had remained rather well disguised in the previous years of our friendship. She began to find ways to cut herself off from years-long friendships with women who had supported and helped her, blaming them for whatever she could. She became gradually more isolated and frightened, referring to herself as "an old woman." I could see and feel the self-hatred all women experience, that she had so desperately tried to keep in her closet, begin to break down the door and peek out through her eyes. She had been a good daughter of the patriarchy and had done everything "right," and now as she approached her cronedom, and had experienced menopause, she was being stalked by this ever-present demon of self-hate and rage.

Only her daughter knew this presence, as she was in the position of caretaker for her mother from very early on in her tender life. This narcissistic wound demanded constant attention from her daughter — and in the end, from Yana's journals, her anger at her daughter for "not being there enough" was quite apparent. But of course, it really wasn't anger at her daughter at all — it was the anger at the oppressive dominating force that took her soul and turned her against herself, turning her against her own divine female nature. But she could never name it, as the sense of betrayal of all she knew in naming it was too great. She could only feel its gnawing presence. She could only run from it. Eventually, however, she ran out of breath. She tried to kill herself twice within a few weeks. The first time, her house was neat and tidy and she was bedecked in her finery. Friends found her in time to have her hospitalized.

The second time, she was completely disheveled and her house was torn apart. I feel she was desperately looking for herself in those last moments, turning everything upside down. As the demon was unleashed from the closet, she frantically peered into the empty space of her cupboards to see if she could find herself. The telephone was still in her hands as she lay on the floor, the Maalox she had taken to keep the pills in her stomach, streaming from her mouth. Her friends did not find her in time. She died isolated and alone.

It is my belief that this was the true face of the demon that finally took her life — the misogynist demon of cruelty and destruction. I think chronic fatigue is a condition of many women who feel the despairing hopelessness of not ever having had their true identity and of being treated less-than by a society that supports the hatred of more than half of the human race. I also feel that the lack of present mothering contributes to this grievous loss and sorrow. Yana's own mother was deeply narcissistic and unable to find her locked-away love to give to her daughter. And how did that happen?

This is not a mystery. It is the lineage of women who live in, endure and survive in but rarely thrive in a male-dominated society. The absence and loss of this mother-love is beyond a personal experience — it is global. Traditionally, women's reaction to loss is depression. Loss of self, or grief of the loss of self one never had due to oppression, causes severe trauma to the psyche of women. Who notices this? Feminist psychologist, Phyllis Chesler, tells us in **Women and Madness** that women are in a continual state of mourning. (Chesler, **Women and Madness**, p. 44)

Nothing could be truer. If our mothers do not know their power, and most of them have not for about 5,000 years, how can we expect the children of these mothers to be any different? We are the suffering children of these mothers. Without the Mother, The Goddess, our lives are filled with pain — women and men alike. We have many descriptions of this pain, but it is all the same pain — the loss of the Mother, and hence, the loss of self. Men's outward aggression in the world is their sanctified reaction to this loss. Women react in not-so-sanctified depression. And, in Yana's case, suicide. Chesler states unequivocally and courageously, "Women who succeed at suicide are, tragically, outwitting or rejecting their 'feminine' role, and at the only price possible: their death." (Chesler, **Women and Madness,** p. 49)

While Chesler is talking about the binding and proscribed roles for women in patriarchy that have defined femininity, I also feel that there is another side to this statement. I feel women who are afraid of their own female power, due to colonization by the patriarchal mind, can turn against themselves to the point where sometimes the internal conflict, split and suffering feel unbearable. If their allegiance to the patriarchal mind (demon) is strong, and their owning of their female power would dethrone this demon, which they secretly would love to do in order to have an authentic sense of sovereignty, the terrible angst and pain of this split can cause a woman to spiral downwards in confusion, despair, depression and suicide.

All of Yana's male healers couldn't help her with this. They didn't recognize it. Nor did she. And her allegiance to the patriarchal mind was riveting — after all, she had survived and raised a child in a society that hated her. It was all she knew. She had to protect it — with her life, if need be. Who would she become if she confronted this demon? She was too afraid to know. She had contributed to her own oppression, and had thought she was healing her life.

I did not find out right away. It was several months later when I learned of her death and I am still reeling from the shock and pain. I was numb and angry with her for abandoning her daughter and for leaving me and her other friends in such a way. I grieved for her loss and for her suffering. I also lost sleep. I had never lost anyone close to me in this manner. I cannot put into words everything I experienced. Yana's spiritual group (Muslim-Sufi) speaks of her being with Allah and that all is well. I don't know.

If anything, I think she would be with Allah's predecessor, Al-Lat, the Arabian Goddess who was co-opted and made male by the Muslims. I do not accept that Yana's grotesque death is good and fine. After meeting her "spiritual father" in her chosen spiritual path, I was unimpressed. In fact, I felt that his supplications of "needing to create peace and love" were in direct contradiction to his using women to serve him. I felt nauseous in his presence. And then I began to think that Yana, in her vulnerability, was open to being used in this way — and was.

I actually feel it might have hastened her death to be subservient in this manner, thinking she had found the daddy who was going to save her, while she was quietly giving away whatever power she had left. I witnessed him embrace Yana's good friend after her memorial, who was completely vulnerable and sobbing in grief, whisper something in her ear. As a witness, I felt the energy to be really weird — seductive and manipulative. Gwenn told me later that while she was sobbing, he said to her that she was his spiritual daughter, and that he was waiting for her. I shared with her what I felt watching him with her and she said she left her body when he whispered in her ear.

She said she realized that it reminded her of her father who had sexually abused her — that same kind of seduction. So, "spiritual" male seduction is no different. I noticed he didn't come near me. And I also noticed that he could seemingly give something to Gwenn if he felt he could get something in return — her energy. He saw the possibility of her becoming like the other women who surrounded and served him, including Yana's daughter, for whom he thought he just might arrange a marriage. He saw Gwenn's vulnerability and zeroed in. At Yana's memorial, I looked deep into his eyes and summoned Al-Lat, and said that peace and love will not be experienced until women are fully loved and respected. I do not know if he heard me, though he bobbed his head up and down in agreement.

If he truly agreed, he would tell the women in his "harem" (I am not saying he sleeps with these women, as he is an elderly man, though, one never knows) that veils were no longer needed to hide their beauty and that he no longer needed to be served. I seriously doubt that this has happened, but perhaps a seed was planted.

I do feel that in her journey, Yana will know the truth. I have learned something deeply profound from Yana's death — that the suffering of women in a patriarchal society goes mostly unnoticed and unnamed. I have known this, as I work extensively with women, but the depths of this sorrow and pain are unfathomable.

Women's "depression from oppression" and lack of creative and wild expression is a condition that causes a contortion in a woman's ability to love herself, for she is constantly trying to find her place in the world of men in order to feel accepted, to feel at home. My grandmother committed suicide — in the early fifties, after years of struggle in a mental institution. (I did not know her.) She was the same age as Yana, and like Yana, left the same legacy to her only child, my mother, who was the same age then as Yana's daughter is now. And she told my mother "it was a man's world." To have been a woman aware of this kind of pain in that era was excruciating — especially when most Western women were busy being submissive and conceding that "father knows best." I do know that my grandmother's suicide did not end her suffering.

I had profound psychic contact with her in my early adult years and worked with her to help her in her healing — even though it was many years after her suicide. Yana also had a friend, Kate, who committed suicide several months before Yana decided to take her own life. Like Yana, Kate suffered from chronic fatigue and depression. I am convinced she suffered in a very similar way as Yana. Kate's suicide gave Yana a kind of dangerous, contagious permission to suicide also.

I have received what I believe to be messages from Yana, supported by some amazing synchronicities, in which she has expressed her remorse and her realization that her choice to suicide was wrong. This communication has inspired me to think on the nature of this kind of action women sometimes feel helpless to avoid. While I feel it is a spiritual task to find one's power, it is easier said than done. I have talked with some women who have contemplated suicide, and they have told me that in the face of living with perpetrators, suicide seemed to be an option — that in fact, it gave them comfort to think that they could find safety in taking their own lives. My friend and spiritual sister, Kim, writes, "I must have been somewhere between the ages of five and six years old and lived in the shadow lands of family secrets that included incest and daily psychological abuse that seemed to be without end. Once discovered, the idea of suicide represented safety for me. Finally, I realized that there was a way out and for the first time in my short life I felt a sense of control in an intolerable out-of-control situation. Although I did not make an attempt on my life until many years later, the thought was always there residing somewhere in the back of my mind. Oddly, as long as I had my

72

escape route available, I could manage." Kim, as a small child who should have been playing and laughing and held in safety by loving parents, had to instead contemplate the idea of ending her life as a way to be safe. She held onto this possibility until she began to find healing in her adult life.

When she was introduced to Goddess spirituality, she began to open to a deep recognition that the Goddess had always been there for her, in the form of the natural beauty of the desert where she grew up. Her connectedness to nature fed her soul, and Kim realized that this to her was the Goddess. The desert was her true mother. Many women are not so fortunate as she was. She once told me that she learned despite her own family life that familial love existed in the world by watching how the prairie dogs cared for one another.

For me, life is a gift from the Goddess, and is ours to regard as sacred. Because life emerges from the Great Womb, an individual is a part of that, not the creatrix of that. Life does grow in our wombs, and women do give birth to it — it is a privilege to do so. But it is so much larger than ourselves — which is why life itself is so mysterious. The Eskimos believe life to be a continuous stream, as did the ancients. While we can choose to dispose of our bodies, I do not think that the suffering we experience while in the body ends in suicide.

It seems that the Eskimos thought of suicide as acceptable when elders would decide it was time to die and would go out in the wild and do so. This is a different fate than killing oneself, trying to escape the jaws of torture. Therefore, it makes sense to me to work through our difficulties while we are in the body. Again, easier said than done when you are female and live in an environment that constantly mirrors hatred of you because you are female. It is my belief that in a truly loving environment, suicide would not loom as a way out of suffering the way it does today.

Women and mothers would simply not want to leave their children and loved ones. The thought of that would far outweigh one's own pain — seeing as how there would probably be very little psychic pain in an environment where women are loved and respected and where the creative life force is celebrated and honored, as it once was.

I do not know what the answers are about suicide. I only know what my experience with Yana has been, and I would not want anyone to go through this. I do believe it is her message regarding women's depression that needs to be heard. If depression from oppression for women is so great that a mother will kill herself and leave that legacy to her daughter, something is indeed very wrong. It is this that needs attending to regardless of the theories and spiritual beliefs people hold about suicide.

Several days after Yana's memorial, Gwenn, Yana's best friend, called me and was disturbed that she hadn't been sleeping and had been dreaming of Yana and hearing her voice speaking from an echo-like space saying "help me, help me." Gwenn said it was scary and she was feeling crazy. I could completely relate. We both felt very grateful to have one another to talk to, as what we were both experiencing was not something we could look up in any book or just openly discuss with anyone.

We both felt this frantic energy from our friend on the other side of the veil, and we were both deeply disturbed. We both felt haunted, though our experiences were at different times. Mine was before the memorial, Gwenn's was after. We both had to contemplate taking sleeping aids. We talked at length and realized that because we are not taught anything about death in this culture, we are not well prepared to deal with psychic phenomenon regarding the abrupt severing of ties that occurs in suicide. It has felt like "placenta abrupto" to me — the tearing away of the bond of love that leaves behind a bleeding wound. Gwenn felt that Yana was still pulling on her in death the way she had at times in life. We both realized then that her energy was still alive the way it had been while she was in body and this confirmed for me even more that killing the body does not really change the energy stream one thinks one is escaping in choosing to suicide. We talked about a ritual Gwenn could do, and then I realized that I could work again with Yana.

Gwenn's ritual was to release Yana so that she was not holding on to her in any way — either through anger, fear or attachment. Compassion was the key. We both felt that it was necessary to send her on her way in compassion, asking for blessings for her soul, spirit or whatever we call the energy of a being that does not die. I reminded Gwenn of the following teaching I received, and it helped to relieve and comfort her.

Following Yana's memorial, I went to the beach and sprawled on the sand, where I was serenaded by the ocean and bathed in the cooling rays of sunset from what had been an intense hot summer sun earlier in the day. I was at a favorite spot visiting with my "rock people" tribe — many large rocks, protruding from the sand like wise ancestors, resting in eternal patience, greeting the constant ebb and flow of the ocean — each with a different face and posture. I prayed that once her ashes had been placed in the ground, Yana would be able to find rest. And I was praying I would also. As I lay there, I had a vision. A great yoni appeared before me — beautiful and awesome. I watched with anticipation and wonder.

Out of the yoni came a black, four-armed dakini, dancing ecstatically, energized by the Shakti creative life force. She said to me "Yana was wrong. She made a mistake. But she will find healing. All humans make mistakes." Just then my dog showered my head with a rain of sand as she ran across my blanket. The vision was gone. But the message was clear. I felt graced by the love of the Goddess, and felt a sense of a loving kindness quite different than an eternal punishing anger for wrongdoing. Instead, I felt a kind of eternal, maternal forgiveness that allowed me to breathe easier. I felt from that vision that the Goddess, the divine female authority in the universe, does not hate, does not rule by inducing fear, is not eternally angry and is aware of the frailties of human beings, particularly in these times.

The compassion from the dakini was overwhelming. It washed over me like a waterfall and strengthened my ability to open to love — even in the hardest of times. The blessing was two-fold. Not only was she blessing me with divine cosmic love, which in and of itself was unspeakably beautiful, she was also blessing me with teaching about the after-death state — that there is healing available for those who make seemingly fatal mistakes. When I shared this vision with a friend of mine, she said she felt that when one dies, whether by suicide or not, the Mystery embraces us with unconditional love like a mother who welcomes the return of her children to her breast no matter what choices they make in life. Being a mother, I knew exactly what she meant. If we can welcome this deep truth — this woman's way of looking at life and death, which is vastly different than the masculinized versions we have been conditioned by and plagued with, how much gentler our lives and our dying would be.

Megalithic Tombs

West Kennet Long Barrow-Abode of the Dark/Light Mother, Monica Sjöö, **1989**

As people began to live in constructed housing, village settlements emerged. From there, these settlements slowly grew into city centers, as in the Near East. In the High Neolithic, circa 5,000- 4,000 BCE, archeological evidence from diggings shows that burial practices changed as the lifestyles of people changed. People were no longer buried in cave floors, or under the floors of homes, nor in cut-out oven shapes in rocks, but in larger habitations in rock chambers or stone structures built on the ground, mounded up and covered with earth. (Sjöö and Mor, **The Great Cosmic Mother**, p. 96)

These became the megalithic tombs, dolmens, passage and gallery graves. Megalithic graves are often found in the shape of vagina and uterus, signifying the shape of the anthropomorphic body of the Goddess. Sjöö and Mor write that the top stones of dolmens were charged with healing energy. The dolmen itself was associated with birth, rebirth and the beyond — the yoni/gate of life and death. The idea of creating such a tomb came from the early human perception of returning the loved one to the womb of the Mother to await rebirth.

The dead continued to be placed in the fetal position. Ancient primordial symbols found new expression in the imaginations of women — the life givers, nourishers and sustainers of life, as they began to become agriculturists. Later, as women spent time growing and caring for the plants and grain, they buried their dead in large egg-shaped urns underground, called *pithoi*. It is possible to sense the closeness that women had with the cycles of life, as menstruants, birth-givers, care-givers, and sucklers of new life. It is possible to understand that as they experienced the cycles of the Great Mother, placing the dead back into Her, into the earth, returning loved ones to the earth was a form of planting seeds.

The Goddess' womb was the tomb. The sacred pubic triangle was symbolic of the place from which life emerged as well as the place to which it returned at the end. If life emerging from the womb was sacred, then so must it be in returning to the tomb. The sacredness of the womb/tomb was not diminished in death. Living and dying were expressions of the sacred circle of beginingless and endless life, always changing form.

Some of the most magnificent megalithic tomb and temple structures in the world, built to honor the Goddess, can be found on the Maltese Islands, dotting the Mediterranean Sea, sixty miles from Sicily. They are the oldest free-standing structures in the world, predating the Great Pyramid by 1,000 years. Some of these architecturally grand structures, built in the shape and form of the body of the Goddess, maintain a distinct link with the past when humans first entered caves to honor the Cosmic Mother, and where entering the earth was entering Her body. These more than forty sacred structures were unrivaled in structure and artistry for a thousand years. (Streep, **Sanctuaries of the Goddess**, p. 83) Many of them were built as "twin" temples — perhaps inferring mother/daughter, and/or sister/sister and/or two women sharing power relationships, revealing the importance of the Double Goddess — She of life and death.

As these temples are known to be the most complete survival of the Neolithic vision of rebirth and regeneration within the body of the Goddess, they remain the oldest and earliest known megalithic structures in the world. The oldest sacred site on the islands, Ghar Dalam ("Cave of Darkness" in Maltese) dated around 5,000 BCE, is a cave sanctuary, serving both as a place for burial and habitation. Human bones, dusted with red ochre found at this site reveal a sense of the return of the dead to the regenerative womb of the Goddess. The rock-cut tombs at Xemxja, five in all and hewn by human hands, also emanate this same sense. (ibid., p. 85)

The Ggantija, on the island of Gozo, is a configuration of two megalithic temples joined by a common wall built from huge stone slabs, some weighing many tons. The rounded chambers on the inside of this sacred temple are built off a square inner court, with walls smoothed by mortar, reflecting a red hue. Peg Streep speculates, "What took place in the Ggantija's inner chambers can only be guessed at, but surely the ritual, ringed with the reflection of red from the walls in the light cast by hand-held lamps, concerned the eternal cycle of life and death symbolized in and controlled by the Goddess. The enclosed round space of the Ggantija must have felt like both a womb and a tomb, all-enveloping, dwarfing the humans within it, part of the earth yet rising out of it . . . . It is tantalizing to think that perhaps the earth itself holds the secret to the rites of the Ggantija." (ibid., p. 90)

Another magnificent structure on Malta is the Hal Saflieni Hypogeum. With construction beginning in the fourth millennium and finding completion hundreds of years later, this mysterious rock-cut city of the dead extended thirty feet below the surface of the hill into which it was cut. In all, it was three stories high, with the first story, the catacombs, extending into the earth. "Over the course of eleven hundred years, the bones of some seven thousand people were interred here . . . the ancient practice of burial with red ocher continued; when the Hypogeum was excavated and water from a modern structure above spilled into the sanctuary, the bones seemed afloat in a sea of blood." (ibid.) Because it took hundreds of years to complete this structure, with the persistent use of horn picks and stone mallets, the people seemed to maintain their unceasing connection with/to the Goddess.

There is an existent pattern in these Maltese structures of burial sites below ground and the sacred sites for ritual above. "The deliberate repetition and exchange of details illumines a key aspect of the spirituality of Malta: the circularity, the connectiveness, between life and death reinforced again and again . . . .That the Goddess of Malta reigns in both places is shown by the artifice of humanity." (ibid., p. 91) Says Gertrude Levy, "Here the sacred character of a familiar temple construction is artificially imposed to intensify the sanctity of the cave, just as cave sanctity is invoked by the structural forms above ground." (Levy, **Religious Conceptions of the Stone Age,** p. 135)

An exquisite find within the Hal Saflieni Hypogeum in egg-shaped subterranean rooms were two different forms of the "Sleeping Lady," one carved statue lying on a low couch, on her side and the other face down, appearing to be sleeping or dreaming. Her ample round body and egg-shaped buttocks are suggestive of regeneration. The mysteries of sleep, dreams and death seem to unite within her. Perhaps she is symbolic of the Goddess who dreams life into form, takes life back into herself only to incubate and dream again. Would you like to be buried in a womb space surrounded by the symbols of the regenerating Goddess? How would you face death knowing that you would be returning to the body of the Great Mother, uniting with a cosmic consciousness in which the cycles of life are never ending, where your bones would be placed next to those of your ancestors?

Looking at some of the ways in which people of the Neolithic in Malta buried their dead, as well as exploring their sense of spirituality, reveal that the construction of these mysterious and imposing structures centered around a cult of the dead with the regenerating Goddess at its core. In some of the other structures, an architectural pattern of rounded chambers and recesses centering on a central "spine" of courts and corridors hints at reproduction of earlier rock-cut tombs.

The sense about death through time remains the same, whether it be reflected in the ritual use of caves, catacombs, or megalithic structures — that regeneration in the womb of the Goddess was a perceived reality — so much so, that great effort was made in the building of these awesome structures to respectfully ensure a deeply sacred passage from life to death, and back again. The spiral motif, known in the Neolithic to represent cosmic renewal, rebirth and transformation, frequents the entrance walls and altars of these sanctuaries.

Megalithic structures abounded in other parts of the European continent as well. From Sicily and Sardinia, through France and Spain, to Brittany, Ireland and West Scotland, including the Shetland and Orkney Islands, the preponderance of the these structures reveals the widespread devotion to the Goddess, in many cultures, in many places. Marija Gimbutas tells us that there are approximately 10,000 such structures throughout Europe.

The British Isles, Brittany and Ireland are rich with monuments and tombs including passage barrows, standing stones and stone circles dedicated to the Goddess. The great standing stones or menhirs at Carnac, for instance, "were long believed by the local people to have mysterious powers, a trace memory perhaps of the sacred rites in which these stones once played a part." (Streep, **Sanctuaries of the Goddess**, p. 106) The passage graves of New Grange, Dowth and Knowth in Ireland built roughly around 3,500 BCE, breathtaking in construction, reveal a profound spiritual dedication to the Goddess. Many of the ancient symbols of the Goddess, such as chevrons, spirals, lozenges, dots and triangles are found etched and carved into the stones of these structures.

This symbolism is found throughout Old Europe, signifying the life-giving powers of the Goddess in birth and regeneration. The passageways into the main chambers are quite narrow and low in some places, indicating that it was probably necessary to crawl some of the time in order to reach the main chamber. It would appear that this crawling through an elongated passage was symbolic of rebirth — finding one's way back into the womb of the Mother. Some entranceways of these megalithic structures, such as Norn's Tump and Windmill Tump in England, are vulva-shaped with holes in the center stones or with openings created by the careful placing of stone slabs. New Grange appears to be both a habitation for the dead as well as a place of rebirth. It was constructed in such a way as to catch the rays of the midwinter solstice sun at the entrance of the tomb, where the passageway and innermost chamber recesses along with the bones of the dead would be illumined by the sun's life-giving radiance.

Other tombs, such as Gavrinis in Brittany and Maes Howe on the Orkney Islands, were built in much the same way where the midwinter solstice sunlight would penetrate the passageways and chambers creating a relationship with the processes of the natural world, the rituals of the people and their own life journeys, including the passage into death. It is also interesting to note the alignment of some tomb entrances with the position of the moon at the time of winter solstice suggesting the importance of lunar influences on burial practices.

Megalithic art was celebratory of the cosmic cycles of life and death as well as the patterns of sun and moon. The apprehension of the universe as the body of the Goddess by the ancients seems apparent. The illuminating light of the winter solstice sun penetrating the womb-chamber of the dead is a metaphor for the quickening of life — the warmth and light of the sun fertilizes the womb of the Goddess' tomb, enabling new life to arise directly out of the place of death.

England's sacred sites of Silbury, Avebury and Stonehenge tell mysterious stories of the Goddess' cyclical nature. Author Elinore Gadon tells us, "Avebury was a religious center and may have drawn worshippers from the whole of Britain. The monuments here are the most important Neolithic group in the British Isles and included England's tallest artificial hill and largest prehistoric tomb, the foundations of a monumental stone circle much like that at Stonehenge and the remnant of two stone avenues, each a mile and a half long.

"These mighty forms lie on the rolling chalk downs of the beautiful, ever green countryside of southwestern England. The waters of the landscape — two rivers, the underground streams, and springs — were also part of the ritual structure." (Gadon, **Once and Future Goddess**, p. 69) With awesome devotion, Neolithic people built Silbury Hill over a period of four hundred years using digging tools made of antler, creating an earth mound that rises up like a great pregnant belly. The geography of Avebury reveals the form of the pregnant Goddess Herself. Much like the Maltese, who built their monuments in the shape of Her body, the Neolithic inhabitants of these lands, of similar consciousness and spiritual devotion, built their own unique representations of Her as well. For millennia, an unceasing reverence for the Goddess inspired our ancestors to build and construct great temples, monuments and tombs to Her, showing their deep and profound experience of Her mystery.

How does this kind of devotion, mystical experience and connection to the Great Mother of these Neolithic peoples differ from what we experience today in our "deathing" practices? How would this kind of involvement with life, death and regeneration of a community of people, over hundreds of years, psychically and spiritually shape them? What did they know that we have forgotten? Today, most people are afraid of "getting dirty." We have elaborate caskets that shield the beloved from return to the earth and the elements. We have concrete structures that keep the ashes and bones from ever being reunited with the earth. And we certainly don't seem to have much reverence for the blood of life, as evidenced by how we treat menstrual blood — i.e., we "sanitize" ourselves, "deodorize" ourselves, and make everything white and sparkling "clean." In essence, we try to separate ourselves from the elements and the life-giving blood as much as possible. How do these practices shape us psychically and spiritually — in life and in death?

Death and Regeneration

Rebirth From the Motherpot, Monica Sjöö, 1986

In our busy, Westernized, patriarchal life-style that is consuming the earth, our thinking has become very linear, and what some would call "left-brained." This way of thinking perpetuates a malignant materialism that infuses many aspects of our lives, from the physical to the spiritual. Physical materialism and lack of understanding of regeneration is reflected in our "throw-away" consciousness and blatant disregard of the earth and the natural world. We are consumed by the demon of consumption. More is better. We must accrue more in order to be better than our neighbor. If we have more stuff, then we will have more respect and esteem by those that value stuff. If people like our stuff, then maybe they will like us. If our stuff breaks, we will just go out and get more. In spiritual materialism, we find people thinking it is important to be recognized as those who "know."

We have a plethora of books on spirituality that we must buy in order to find out how to be spiritual. We value our intellectual knowledge about how to do spiritual practice. If we are someone who can write about how to be spiritual, then maybe those who value the written word will respect us. If we don't walk our talk, that doesn't matter. There are countless stories of spiritual people writing great things, and not living them. In the entanglement of this distorted, linear thinking, we suffer from a form of amnesia. We have forgotten that life is to be lived in humility with intention and consciousness, with regard to all of our relations.

The word "humility" comes from "humus," meaning "earth." We have forgotten that we are all connected in this sacred web of life, and that what we do to one we do to all. We have forgotten that life is circular. In circularity, we live in a daily awareness of the rhythm of the universe, the ebb and flow of the tides of life, and the connection to the great vast heartbeat of the One. We have forgotten that it is Her heartbeat that sustains us, that we are contained within it, in just the same way that a child is sustained in the womb, attached by the umbilicus to the nourishing placenta, soothed by the constancy of Her drumming heartbeat. And the circle continues once we emerge from that womb-space when we are held and suckled at our mother's breast, nestled against warm soft flesh, uniquely scented, cradled by the familiar gentle drumming of that same heartbeat. With this amnesia and focus on living in a materialistic society — both physical and spiritual — that says we should throw broken things away, and just replace them, that we need to compete, or that it is okay to take what we want without giving back, we sow the seeds of our own demise.

In linear thinking, we think that things go from A to B, period. We think that life ends with death, period. We think that death is the enemy of life, and something to be feared. In circularity consciousness, we remember that life and death are integral to the Whole; they are not opposites. Life does not die. So, really, there is no death. However, from a relative point of view, there is the experience of the cessation of the body that we call death. And because we have been conditioned to invest our identity with our physicality, our body, in our linear thinking, we fear that the end comes with the death of the body. And we are terrified. We are so terrified that we just don't think about this ending we call death while we live. We live in denial, haunted by a lingering fear of our own mortality. Our image of death, the grim reaper, waits for us in the shadows of our unconscious. When one close to us dies, we don't know what to do, but we are glad it is not us who has died. We give the body to someone else to "prepare" for burial. Death is neat and tidy — all taken care of, out of our sight. We don't have to see it, or feel it. We just deny it.

When we find out we have an illness for which there is no known cure, we become desperate to live, afraid to die, afraid to even think about it for fear that it will bring it closer, afraid to prepare, afraid to accept the natural circularity and mystery of life. We have been so busy identifying ourselves with our bodies, our linear thinking and our stuff, that we have forgotten to notice that we don't control outcome, and the experience of living means to embrace the unknown. In this amnesia, we therefore try to control our daily lives, and each other, in living and in dying. I have witnessed how a person's death process can bring up deep control issues for family members, as well as for the dying person.

At this time in one's life, if there is the choice, wouldn't it be nice if things were taken care of ahead of time, so that one could die in peace with the family supporting such an event? Wouldn't it be nice if there were consciousness and awareness about the cycle of life, that we could participate in helping one another make a smooth transition, with our own personal fears and attendant worries absent? Wouldn't it be revolutionary to prepare, discuss and learn from each other about this whole process, prior to it happening? We certainly prepare for large events in our lives — rehearse them even.

But somehow we forget about this one. This is the legacy of left-brained, linear patriarchal thinking. It leaves us cold and isolated, in death as well as in life. To change this, we need the warmth and love of the Goddess. We need Her wisdom to awaken in all our hearts, to remember how to nourish, feed, support, guide and cherish each other — in all experiences in our lives. I much prefer an image of death that someone gave to me when my father died. My friend told me she was inspired by the reflection in a poem that painted a picture of life and death as experiences at the breast of the Mother. In life, we are nurtured at one breast, and in death we are nurtured at the other. This image is much more life-affirming than the one of a man nailed to a cross bleeding in agony and in pain.

I much prefer to think that we could experience an ecstatic death, rather than a grim and fearful one. If it is true that our endings become new beginnings, why wouldn't we want to end our lives in peace and beauty, knowing that ending to be the first cause of a new beginning? Why wouldn't we want to lovingly gaze on a kind face we know to be capable of giving tenderness and loving spiritual instruction in our dying moment? Why wouldn't we want to orchestrate exactly what we want for our death — complete with creating a beautiful environment, and discussing the details with loved ones prior to our passing? And why wouldn't we include in our spiritual teachings, how to prepare to die? And teach and empower our children about death so they can help us pass as well as be prepared for their own.

Why were death and regeneration paired together in the beliefs of our ancestors? What did they witness that allowed them to celebrate this truth? Death for them was not something isolated from life, but a contribution to it. Death and regeneration went hand-in-hand. Why would our ancestors have thought this? Was it merely a "primitive" belief based in fear? I think we can safely say that there was nothing "primitive" or unsophisticated about their perception of the cyclical nature of life's flow. Primal, but not primitive. Their fundamental primal awareness of the life cycles of the Goddess inspired them to revere Her in ways that are hard for us to comprehend. Humans living in peace for millennia? We teach our kids that humans have always engaged in war.

We give to our children fear-based teachings everywhere they can turn their heads. What do you think a child would think, without any propaganda, looking at an image of Jesus nailed up on the cross, dripping with blood from his "crown" of thorns and the nails in his hands and feet? Do you think that child would be inspired about death? If we told that child mean men put nails in him while he was still alive, and asked that child to wear this symbol around her/his neck, as a symbol of love, would that child feel good about it? Would that child feel good about the dying process? What if we showed an image to that child of a dying person, held in the arms of someone clearly loving that person? What would a child internalize from such an image about death? Many of us are taught to hide death from children. So, they learn that death is something to fear and that it is not part of life. How does this make for a sane society?

When my mother died, I had her at home, and the whole family participated in her dying. My daughters (then aged twelve and sixteen), at first, were scared, and didn't want her at home. But, when they were around her, they could feel she was at peace, and could feel the sanctity of the process. My mother could find peace because she felt safe and was surrounded by family and love. She was not a particularly religious woman. She suffered from unhealed wounds that caused habit patterns of anger and fear in her life. But in her deathing, she was able to find peace because she was midwifed with tenderness and compassion. My children had a chance to give her their love. It was a profound teaching for them. Death of a loved one, their grandmother, was in their home, in view. Nothing was hidden from them. They had all of their feelings, without shame and fear.

Because most of us in western society have not been taught the wisdom of our ancestors about life, death and the Goddess, we live in ignorance. As long as our religions do not embrace the wisdom of the Sacred Feminine, we will not understand who we are and what we are doing here. While there are many good and useful teachings, from many different traditions, I firmly believe that until we embrace and name the Goddess Mother wisdom, we are not able to experience uncompromised bliss. There is a specific energy that is felt and perceived when She is invoked. It is entirely different than invoking God, "he." This really cannot be intellectualized or conceptualized. It must be experienced in order to be understood. As John Rowan says in **The Horned God**, "So finding the Goddess was also like coming home. It was like something being restored which had been there before, and had been taken away. It was like finding a long-lost mother." (Rowan, **The Horned God**, p. 83)

A very extraordinary discovery regarding the Goddess, death and re-generation was the unearthing of the 8,000 year old community of Çatal Hüyük in Anatolia, Turkey, by James Mellaart in the 1960's. Though only one-twentieth of the thirty-two acre site has been thus far excavated, with new excavations just recently opening up, the evidence of a matrifocaled society, dwelling for nearly 1,000 years in peace, gives us much to ponder. "At Çatal Hüyük, the earliest known culture documenting the Goddess religion displays the full range of her iconography. The mood is joyful, the dominant themes celebrating the renewal of life. Religious practice was intimate, personal, integrated into rhythms of ordinary life. The shrines were next to the dwellings, sharing the same courtyard, with the same structure and the same furniture. The priestesses and their families were part of the community, sharing common space, common tasks, like ritual bread making."(Gadon, **Once and Future Goddess**, p. 36)

Some of these shrines were devoted to funerary rituals, just as others were devoted to birthing rituals. In the funerary shrines, the vulture is a prominent figure associated with death, as it is a non-aggressive carrion bird. "The human legs of the vulture in the Level VII, 21 shrine imply that it is not simply a bird but rather the Goddess in the guise of a vulture. She is Death — She Who Takes Away Life — ominous in flight on great, outspread wings. Despite the incarnate presence of Death, the vulture scenes of Çatal Hüyük do not convey death's mournful triumph over life. Rather, they symbolize that death and resurrection are inseparably linked." (Gimbutas, **Language of the Goddess**, p. 187) Gimbutas says the Goddess of Death and Regeneration is also the Bird Goddess, "the nocturnal aspect of the Life-giver," and that in her study of Goddess cultures, regeneration is more amply symbolized in the iconography than is death itself. (ibid., p. 165)

It is clear, then, that in order to be fully whole, healed/holy human beings, we must come to an understanding of the cyclical nature of life. Without this understanding, cyclical becomes "sicklical" — we get sick from living in fear and not knowing who we are. Why would regeneration be more important to symbolize to the ancients than death itself? It seems to me that the answer lies in how they lived their lives. With a love of the Goddess, and an acceptance of Her visible process as it was reflected in the natural world, they could feel and see the truth of regeneration — they didn't think or theorize about it. Nor did they have to measure it or scientifically prove it. What they did do was celebrate it and honor it. The Vulture Goddess in Çatal Hüyük, and the Crow and Owl Goddess in other cultures, is simultaneously the harbinger of death as well as the Goddess with breasts and life-creating labyrinths in Her abdomen and moist uterus, represented by fish, frog, turtle, and in Çatal Hüyük, the head of a bull. Plaster breasts placed on walls were formed over vulture skulls, allowing the beak to peek through the nipple showing the oneness of life and death. In other places she is represented by the triangle or vulva, or a double triangle in an hourglass shape with vulture's feet, signifying the life cycle of birth, death and regeneration.

It is She who controls the length of the life cycle. As Death Wielder, she does not punish; She simply fulfills her necessary duty. (ibid., p. 317) In the murals of Çatal Hüyük, a profound respect of the entire process of death and regeneration is visually displayed on walls of entire rooms — rooms that were not separated from the dwelling places of family life, but rather included in the layout of the home. What would your family think if you were to devote a room in your home to death and regeneration? Perhaps it would be the place where loved-ones would come to die — where rituals of passage would be enacted. Maybe the walls would be painted with cross-cultural Goddess symbols of life, death and regeneration. Perhaps this would be the true "living room."

Menstruation and Regeneration

The Cauldron of Cerridwen, Monica Sjöö, 1990.

We have seen how early people dusted and painted their dead loved ones with red ochre to symbolize the return of the soul/spirit to the earth, to the womb of the Goddess for rebirth. This was a cross-cultural practice shared by many peoples for a very long time. This red ochre was symbolic of the blood of life — the menstrual blood. Many artifacts, such as the Paleolithic "calendar bones" and the Goddess of Laussel who holds a crescent-shaped horn, marked with thirteen notches reflecting lunar cycles, the menstrual cycle and periods of gestation, point to an early understanding of the cycles and transformations of woman's body. We know that our first calendars were menstrual calendars — in Gaelic the words for "menstruation" and "calendar" are identical.

We also know that the first blood on the altars of our ancestors was menstrual blood — given freely and without sacrifice — given to show honor and respect for life. Menstrual blood was and is a rich, nourishing substance, considered by some to be the most sacred substance on the planet. Our ancestors knew this. We have forgotten, consequently living with the pain of "the curse." Can you sense how far we have strayed from the connection to the deep knowledge and wisdom of the blood of life? How do you regard your own blood? If you are male, how do you feel about menstrual blood and menstruating women?

Ancient women used to bleed together, finding their collective wisdom-time in menstrual huts where they would meditate, vision and find healing knowledge for the community. The original shaman was the female group — not the individual. The wisdom of the female group came directly from women's menstrual mysteries. Women's shared experience of the female moon-mind gave rise to ecstatic trance, ecstatic dance, dream-wisdom, oracular vision and all-around "lunatic" behavior — behavior profoundly connected to the magnetism of the moon. Interesting that the word "men" in Indo-European relates to moon, mind and wise blood, and "man" in Sanskrit means "moon" and "wisdom." Barbara Walker tells us "in the original Old Norse, 'man' meant 'woman.' The word for 'man' was not man but 'wer,' from the Sanskrit root 'vir.' The name Man meant the Moon, creatress of all creatures according to Scandanavian and other tribes throughout Europe. Even in imperial Rome, Man or Mana was the mother of all manes, or ancestral spirits." (Walker, **The Women's Encyclopedia of Myths and Secrets**, p. 574)

How and why do you suppose this naming came to be associated with those born with penises? Doesn't this somehow undermine that very famous myth we have in patriarchy that claims women are envious of penises? I think so. I think the real truth about envy between the genders concerns womb and menstrual envy.

There are many practices world-wide, such as circumcision, subincision, which is an incision of the penis to reflect a bleeding vulva, and couvade, a male birthing ritual (both practiced by aboriginal peoples in Australia) to emulate the menstruation and birthing powers of women. And there are other practices, like female genital mutilation in which the clitoris is removed, to suppress the ecstatic, creative power in women. We do not find rituals in which women imitate "penis-power."

Because menstrual blood was the sacred thread of life, matrilineal societies were bonded through the blood of kinship — the very word itself a derivative of the Great Goddess of the orient — Cunti or Kunda, meaning "yoni of the uni-verse." Author Judy Grahn states, "My broadest (and ultimately unprovable) premise is that all metaphor, all measurement, and all cultural norms, could they be traced back far enough, would lead us to menstruation and menstrual rite." (Grahn, **Blood, Bread and Roses**, p. 20) It seems, then, that regeneration is closely associated with the flowing water-blood of women's bodies — and the life-giving waters of the body of the Great Goddess. A bleeding woman is given the opportunity to experience, on a monthly basis, shamanic death and renewal.

The shedding of blood is a reminder of the possibility of the manifestation of life that does not take form. With that letting go, the cycle moves towards renewal, opening once again to possibility. With the consciousness of connectedness to the Goddess ruling their lives, our early ancestors understood menstrual blood to be holy. In more recent times, various indigenous peoples celebrate the first menarche of a girl as her initiation into womanhood, welcoming her into the circle of women who bring life into form. It is not difficult to understand what happens to a world when the respect of blood connection is interrupted and replaced by a purely controlling mechanism of ownership. These two conditions in the history of humanity are vastly different, resulting in very different consequences, the latter being extremely dangerous and destructive, as we currently experience.

In order for us as a people to be a viable species on this planet, we need to come into right relationship with this sacred blood of life once again. Understanding its wisdom will regenerate within us a remembrance of our connection to all life and to our own death. The menstrual cycle reflects a continuous movement of life itself through the body of woman, timed to the rhythms of the moon. As the Maiden becomes the Mother, the young woman begins her bleeding time and is honored by her elders as she enters the domain of the wise-woman mother creatrix. The truth is, without menstrual blood, none of us would be here.

Now, with male warblood, we are seeing that none of us will be here, either — but for very different reasons. Women's blood is the blood of life, and men's warblood is the blood of a disempowered death. This is not to say that this is the sole character of men — that they are just violent, always have been, and always will be. Not so. But, they have forgotten how they got here, and how to be here. If women are closer to remembering these things, then what is the big deal about speaking the truth of this forgetfulness, and its horribly damaging effects? Eckhart Tolle in **The Power of Now** states:

"Generally speaking, it is easier for a woman to feel and be in her body, so she is naturally closer to Being and potentially closer to enlightenment than a man. This is why many ancient cultures instinctively chose female figures or analogies to represent or describe the formless and transcendental reality. It was often seen as a womb that gives birth to everything in creation and sustains and nourishes it during its life as form. In the **Tao Te Ching**, one of the most ancient and profound books ever written, the Tao, which could be translated as Being, is described as 'infinite, eternally present, the mother of the universe.' Naturally women are closer to it than men since they virtually 'embody' the Unmanifested. What is more, all creatures and all things must eventually return to the Source. 'All things vanish into the Tao. It alone endures.' Since the Source is seen as female, this is represented as the light and dark sides as the archetypal feminine in psychology and mythology. The Goddess or Divine Mother has two aspects: She gives life and she takes life. When the mind took over and humans lost touch with the reality of their divine essence, they started to think of God as a male figure. Society became male dominated, and the female was made subordinate to the male." (Tolle, **Power of Now**, p. 137)

It is absolutely imperative that we reverse our thinking and embrace the truth about our very existence. Unfortunately, there are those who find the speaking of such truths to be very threatening.

At the first menstruation, the possibility of life to renew itself is created. Can you imagine how a young woman would feel if her entire community celebrated her first menstruation? As it is now in western society, this event is heralded by fear, and is therefore, something that can incite shame and self-hatred, certainly not the kind of insight of the matriarchal mind. Women are frightened to take our power from the blood mysteries, and often live in fear of the dreaded substance staining, seeping through, and showing up in an untimely or inconvenient manner, revealing once and for all that we do indeed bleed.

I have had the experience of knowing mothers who have wanted to give their daughters a ceremony to welcome them into the circle of sisterhood and their daughters are too embarrassed and shamed to allow themselves this gift. Things are slowly changing, of course, as there are those mothers and daughters who share in a ritual of honoring, and I think this practice is becoming more widespread. The magic of a bleeding woman who cycles with the moon is completely awesome — miraculous — and teaching this to our daughters has a direct effect on global consciousness.

A girl, who is welcomed into womanhood from elders, who can teach her truth, lives an entirely different life from one who lives in shame. When girls grow up loving themselves, they are able to pass on to future generations the sacredness of the truth from which life emerges — from the menstrual blood of woman. The virgin, the maiden, grows into she who bleeds life into form, she who creates life from her womb and she who moves like the earth during birth.

This closeness with the Earth makes woman a shaman, a she-mama, a witch (meaning "wise woman"), by becoming the vessel through which life passes. She does not have to have children to embody this wisdom. She is the Earth, creating Herself, as Her blood flows from her body, forming life, ideas, art and beauty. She is the Earth-witch, moving in rhythm to the heavenly moon-body, undulating, heaving, opening, and birthing creation. The bleeding woman as Goddess is She who gives from Her own body this magic magenta flow of life — this flow of dark, nurturing concentrated energy that is given without sacrifice and death. She embodies the numinous Dark. Her nurturing life blood flowing from Her body is the same as the dark, sweet Earth that nurtures seedlings to life.

The celebratory time of the first bleeding is the time when the girl-virgin becomes the mother-virgin. "Virgin" means "she who is whole unto herself." It has nothing to do with sexual behavior and chastity. To honor girls when menses begins is to honor all life. It is to show respect and reverence, to teach girls how to embody and nurture this energy within themselves.

In doing so, girls then learn how to impart the sacred teachings of being fully and completely female, instead of living in fear with the scared teachings of shame, self-hate, and betrayal of the self, which often manifests as girls grow into male-identified women. I remember when my daughters were about fifteen and I used to take them to school, I saw girls of the same age hanging out on the corners with boys, cigarettes dangling from their mouths, trying to be like the boys, trying to be liked by the boys. And I saw the boys not seeing the girls, but seeing only their own "superiority," their own conditioned consciousness that tells them they are "better" than the girls. I saw these girls struggle with being female, and I saw how the self-hatred grows. I know if they were honored for BEING female, the street-corner scenario would be very different indeed. The boys as well would benefit greatly from learning to respect the life cycle from which they are birthed.

Our boy children suffer greatly in their own way in a patriarchal culture. The taboo about vulnerability handed down to boys is crippling. If they were taught how and why to respect menstruation, and were given rites of passage that allowed them to open to their own mystery (not emulating women's mysteries, but truly celebrating their own connection to the Goddess, and their place in the whole picture), our boy-children would become strong, loving sons of the Goddess, free of shame, anger and hatred. I am reminded of the Kogi people in Columbia whose spiritual tradition of worship of the Mother has remained intact. The men, longhaired and of gentle demeanor, (shown in a one-time video they allowed to be made about them to inform the world that things need to change) carried, tied to their waist, a sacred object symbolic of the womb. I interpreted this to mean that they maintained their connection to their source, the Mother Goddess, in their everyday life. What would our society be like if men acted from this place of knowledge and love?

It is my belief that when menstruating women return the blood of life from our bodies back to the earth, as our ancestors did, we will see a psychic shift in the bloodthirsty patriarchal mind. Giving our menstrual blood back to the earth, as an offering of our gratitude, reconnects us with the ancestral memory of the eternal cycle of life, restoring us to healed wholeness. Barbara Walker shares, "As any flower mysteriously contained its future fruit, so uterine blood was the moon-flower supposed to contain the soul of future generations. This was a central idea in the matrilineal concept of the clan." (Walker, **The Women's Encyclopedia of Myths and Secrets**, p. 638)

When women feel this "ansister" connection in our bodies, we become wiser, and when we are wiser, we are more able to free ourselves from the insidious internalized patriarch. We can raise stronger healthier children, instilling in them true values of the matriarchal mind. We can give birth to ideas, philosophies, art and teachings that are life affirming. Through women reclaiming, celebrating and renewing this blood-wisdom, and passing it on to our daughters, life on this planet can be restored to health and sanity. This is the power of menstruation and regeneration — empowering future generations through the blood of life carried in women's bodies, creating life in our wombs, birthing that life through our living, breathing life-forms of the Goddess, and sustaining and nurturing that life, in whatever form our creativity births, with the milk of our breasts.

Menopause and Regeneration

Sheela na Gig/Creation, Monica Sjöö, **1978**

Menopause, or "moon pause" is the time when woman becomes the crone, or is "crowned" with her wisdom. It is the time when the moonblood is held in her body — informing her of new expressions of her creativity, since childbearing (keeping in mind not only children of flesh and blood) has come to an end. A woman in this stage of her life is given the opportunity to enter into a deep relationship with herself and the Goddess. The Mystery of the Dark Goddess unfolds within her very body. She becomes the "hag," or "holy woman." She becomes the mountain. In our society, this passage is feared, belittled, and disrespected. As we have seen earlier, the crone embodies the mysteries of death and regeneration. She is the doorway into life after death. I do not think that we need to perpetuate images of scary "wicked" old women, or the proverbial "evil mother-in-law" or anything else that maligns elder women. These images belie the patriarchal cultural fear of women's power.

What I think we do need to perpetuate are images of wise elder women in their power, full of stories and wisdom that guide the community, like the painting of the Great Goddess, Ayyyhyt of the Yakut in Siberia by freelance teacher of feminist studies and artist, Max Dashu. White-maned Ayyyhyt sits under a great, blessed tree and is said to sit atop the World Mountain at the center of the Earth. She is seen as the "gentle Creatrix", the "Birth-giving, Nourishing Mother" who inscribes the fate of all living beings on the leaves of the tree and provides all beings with life and a "ceaseless breathing." (Dashu, **Streams of Wisdom**, p. 2)

While the Goddess is the double aspect of nurturing and dissolution/regeneration, in which the face of death reflects non-sentimentality and does perhaps provoke fear in the uninitiated, nevertheless, She remains the source of our being and the primordial ground of our true nature. She is the All, and the All is not either/or. She is both/and. She is reflected in the Earth herself — from verdant lush valleys to parched desolate sun-scorched lands to cold and icy terrain. Life, however, finds its form in all of these places and She is everywhere, simultaneously. She is the turning of the seasons. Her inaccessibility has a reason. It is clear that the cycle of life must be regarded with deep respect. Her youthfulness and Her old age and decay must be held equally — both seen as beautiful by one who understands the cycle of birth, life, death and regeneration.

Even though our floundering/founding fathers borrowed heavily from the Iroquois (Haudenosaunee) Federation in creating the Constitution, they "forgot" to include the most important part — the circle of grandmothers as the real governing body of the people. Why did they leave this out? Because they feared women's power. And look what has happened because of this destructive fear. Cross-culturally, aboriginal peoples have known that the thriving of their communities depended on women's wisdom and guidance. Many have known the value of the menopausal woman as guide, teacher, prophetess, seer, visionary, healer, dreamer, artist, midwife, shamaness, psychopomp and creatrix of community. The Iroquois (Haudenosaunee) knew this, and were the first educators of the early suffragists Matilda Josyln Gage, Elizabeth Cady Stanton, and Lucretia Mott.

The menopausal and post-menopausal woman is the way-shower — the third face of the Goddess. Because women's bodies are in exquisite tune with the natural forces of nature, more so than men's bodies, it only follows that the wise women elders would be the matrix of the community. A woman does it all — she comes into bleeding in tune with the rhythms of the moon, she swells with the growth of life within her (whether she is ever pregnant with child or not, all women experience all phases of womanhood), risking her life, she gives birth from her own body, nurtures that new life from her own body and tends to it for many years. When the blood stops flowing from her sacred vulva/gateway she begins a new phase of life in which she should be sought for her wisdom and teachings about life and death. The menopausal woman becomes the living, breathing symbol of she who, with outstretched arms, accepts back unto herself that which she has birthed from her womb.

If we could reintegrate/regenerate the ancients' knowledge about death and rebirth as it is embodied by elder wise women, we would be able to experience a gentler, kinder reality that would serve as a container for the community and tribe. We would experience a sense of safety and comfort, knowing that our wise grandmothers see us and understand our journeys. It would be like having the sense that we are always unconditionally loved by a presence that has always been. It would be like being wrapped in a sweet-smelling soft warm blanket that was all yours. This reality is part of women's culture.

Many women today are uncovering the obscured truth about our culture and are remembering. Croning circles are becoming a part of many women's lives as we pass from Mother to Crone, where we are celebrated and honored by our sisters, and sometimes by caring and loving men. For women to be seen as wise elders crowned with our wisdom from having lived life would change the world. I am not intending to idealize elder people who have not found their freedom and liberation, as I am aware that age doesn't necessarily mean wisdom. What I am talking about is a vision of Goddess-loving women who age steeped in the magic, mystery, knowledge and wisdom of the Earth and who embody these truths. These are the wise women yearning and longing for freedom living inside all women.

Perhaps you might think of an elder woman to visit who has many stories to share. You might want to ask her about her views on death and dying and see what secrets she has locked away in her heart of wisdom. You might be pleasantly surprised at what is revealed when asked for.

The Double Goddess and the Power of Two

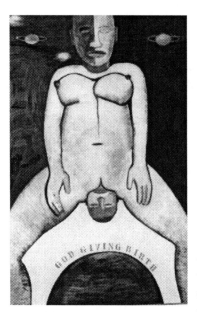

God Giving Birth, Mother Universe,
Monica Sjöö, 1968

It is important to include here the "double" aspect of the Goddess found represented as early as the Upper Paleolithic. As we begin to understand what our ancestors might have known about the cosmos, we can trace this sense of the "power of two" as a significant experience in their lives. Because early people seemed to enjoy a holistic approach to life, the concept of opposites does not seem to be so prevalent. What appears to be more present is an idea of continuity and connectedness and the creation of spirals and circles as symbols of the flow of the energy of life. As I reflected on the material I was researching for the writing of this book, I began to think about "doubling" from the point of view of being a mother of daughters. I thought about the concepts of "pairing" and "re-pairing." In the idea of "pairing" in my own experience, I have realized that the continuation of life is preserved by my daughters — the tribe continues because I have birthed she who gives birth. In that connectedness, we are paired — one gives rise to two. And we are not only mother and daughter, but sisters as well.

As my daughters come into their maturity we experience a "re-pairing" of sisterhood — we are able to share our uniquely female magic and mystery that is all but forgotten in the current male-dominated culture. In a culture not oppressed by male control, this experience between mother and daughter must have been profoundly sacred, as the whole community would have known that their continuance depends on women. At the biological level, we are literally paired with our mothers and grandmothers since all the eggs a woman will ever have in her lifetime are formed within the four-month old fetus growing inside her mother's womb. Our life literally begins with the growing fetus of our mother growing inside her mother, our grandmother.

Many stories are told of the double Goddess in early iconography and pottery, cave painting as well as in construction of temples, as in Malta and Gozo, where temples are actually formed in the shape of a large-bodied woman, often with a smaller temple adjoining the larger one. The ancient tradition of the Queen Mother and Queen Sister can be found in African mythology, giving rise to double Goddesses such as Isis and Nepthys and the "Two Ladies," the Vulture Goddess (Nekhbet) of southern Egypt and the Cobra Goddess

(Wadjet) of northern Egypt. After viewing the representation of the so-called "hermaphrodite" Hapi, considered to be the "god" (with breasts?) as the source of the Nile in the Egyptian museum in Cairo , I was convinced I was actually seeing an image of a double Goddess as source of the Nile. (The explanation given to us by our male guide was that even though Hapi had obvious breasts, his leg was masculine, therefore "he" was a hermaphrodite. I couldn't help but feel that this androcentric explanation was really covering up an inability to accept the primal powers of woman and creation — after all, birth of the Nile was a very important occurrence for the Egyptians, so from the patriarchal view, how could it possibly be of female origin?) The two identical images faced each other and the waters of the river flowed between them. Vicki Noble has commented that Isis symbolizes the ovulation pole of the female cycle and Nepthys, the menstruation pole, and that "together they were understood to represent the female's magical lunar alternating-twin wholeness." (Noble, unpublished manuscript.) Perhaps Hapi in her double form represents a similar authority of creation governed by the mystical powers of the moon.

The hourglass symbol of the Goddess, perhaps most commonly recognized as the Cretan Double Axe, is found in the sixth millennium BCE in Hungary on pottery. The Double Axe is also found in wall paintings of Çatal Hüyük, and also in Bronze Age Anatolia as well as in Thrace, and Africa. In Egypt, the word for "axe" is the same as that for "Goddess." (Noble, unpublished manuscript) Marija Gimbutas associates this shape with the Goddess of Death and Regeneration, a "supernatural doubling" of two triangles (vulvas) joined together. She also emphasized that the hourglass shape is symbolic of a butterfly, signifying transformation, metamorphosis and change. The doubling aspect of the Goddess is complex — symbolic of women in relationship with one another as well as the primal power of the birth-giving and death-wielding powers of the Goddess in her cosmic dance of manifestation and dissolution.

Marija Gimbutas states "to express intensification, the cultures of Old Europe used images of doubles to indicate progressive duplication, and hence, potency or abundance." (Gimbutas, **Language of the Goddess**, p.181) A marvelous example of this is the extraordinary mammoth-ivory carved Goddess of Lespugue, France, 21,000 BCE. Her exaggerated breasts and buttocks are reminiscent of large eggs, all centered around her womb area. Many figurines with emphasized egg-shaped buttocks, representing fertility and regeneration, are found throughout pre-historic Old Europe. Gimbutas states that, in her opinion, the steatopygia-type (extreme accumulation of fat on the buttocks) figures from the Upper Paleolithic are a metaphor for the double egg, the pregnant belly and intensified fertility. Lucia Chiavola Birnbaum states that this body type originated in Africa and was important in child-bearing, as seen in the current African San people.

It is not difficult to see how the sight of the smooth round curves of the body of a pregnant women, also reflected in the curves of the landscape, would inspire in the minds and hearts of early people the sensitive artistic expression of the sacred, mysterious, creative powers of the Goddess. Eggs were obviously a natural symbol of rebirth, as was seen in the natural world, and the "power of two" was visibly seen in the pregnant body of a woman.

When people perceive their environment as a connected web of life of wholeness, the numinous mystery of "becoming" is regarded with a deep reverence and awe. There is a sense of connection beyond the physical. The artistic expression of this reality spirals its way through the consciousness of the people as they emerge as the dancers of life — celebrating Her mystery through love, art, dance, song and sound, as evidenced by perhaps the oldest rock art found in Africa where most of the figures appear to be dancing and playing musical instruments. (Birnbaum, **dark mother**, p. 7) It is not hard to see why the honoring of the mysterious life force, as it is uniquely embodied by women, is an essential practice to ensure the well-being of the entire community, including the planetary community.

Woman is at the center of the mandala of life. The threads of continuity exist in the mitochondrial DNA passed on to us by our mothers. Past, present and future are merged as one in the reality of woman's ability to create and give life; anything that befalls woman befalls the entire community. In celebrating the power of women, the community thrived and lived in peace. In the degradation of women, the community suffers and lives in unspeakable horror and ignorance.

The mystery of "becoming" is no longer held in reverence. Women are brainwashed into having babies as quickly and as un-inspiringly as possible, with men still defining the "correct" ways to give birth. Even though we had a revolution in the ways of birth-giving in the seventies, I have noticed that more and more women are choosing the hospital and male medicine over home birth and women's homespun wisdom. Life is now often born into mediocrity. Our children become restless and bored. And then, they act out. This is not the vision of our ancestors. This is the monstrous creation of the dominator mind that sees itself as all-powerful without the connectedness to the Sacred Feminine. This mind has no concept of birth and continuity from the sacred realms of the Goddess — rather it believes its existence arises from some far-off vague sky place that is believed to be separate from the womb of the Mother, which is impossible. After all, what we refer to as the sky was itself created by the Earthmother.

The power of two has become distorted — the sense of strength from the double Goddess in Her creative authority of birth, dissolution and regeneration has been driven underground and replaced by the so-called power of the one "almighty god" who somehow gives "birth" from his ribs and forehead. Now really, how weird is that? Things have got to change!

Vessels of Renewal

Engravings of ceremonial ships have been found on the inner walls of megalithic tombs from Brittany, Ireland, Malta and the Cycladic Islands dating from the middle of the third millennium BCE. Though much of the engravings are abstract, there is a significant theme suggested by these images — that of regeneration. These ships are marked with the symbols of the Goddess — spirals, bird's feet, the vulva triangle, snake, serpent and fish motifs.

A prominent feature of some ships of renewal is the snake or serpent, found placed at the keel or winding along the whole length of the vessel. It is thought that these ships are "serpent ships," where ship and serpent are interchangeable symbols of renewed life. It is as if the Goddess Herself, in Her guise of the Bird Goddess, the Fish Goddess, or the Snake Goddess pulls the boat or the serpentine vulva-vessel of transformation across the waters of life. Marija Gimbutas writes, "The ship portrayals from north and south Europe are witness to very rich ritual practices connected with the idea of the renewal of nature at the winter solstice or at the crisis of human death." (Gimbutas, **Language of the Goddess**, p. 249)

The idea of a spirit vessel, or spirit boat has found its way into the shamanic practices of various tribal people who use the boat as a way to retrieve power for an individual in need of healing. In a description by Michael Harner we can see this idea of snake and serpent vessel has maintained a place deep in the psyche of some tribal people, "The use of some kind of spirit or soul boat in the shamanic journey is widespread in the primitive world. It occurs in Siberia as well as in Malaysia and Indonesia, where it is related to the 'boat of the dead.' Often the spirit canoe is in the form of a serpent, as in aboriginal Australia, or as in the 'Snake-Canoe' of the Desana Indians of the South American tropical forest." (Harner, **The Way of the Shaman**, p. 71)

In shamanic tradition the journeys undertaken in non-ordinary realities are regarded as ecstatic trances. I feel the sense of ecstasy describing such journeys comes from the fact that the original shaman was the female group — the collective, ecstatic body of women acting together as one unified healing presence. I believe that this body of women was a precursor to current

Scandinavian rock carving: female figure on "vessel of renewal", Fardal, Denmark, Bronze Age, drawn by Melissa Meltzer

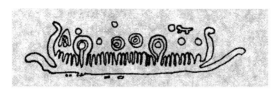

"Ship of Renewal" rock art, Bronze Age Sweden, Lokerberget, Foss, showing serpent,
drawn by Melissa Meltzer

systems theory in which "I" is not separate from "you" or "it." Joanna Macy writes, "As the systems theorists see it, our consciousness illuminates a small arc in the wider currents and loops of knowing that interconnect us." (Macy, **World as Lover, World as Self**, p. 189) The whole body was comprised of the individual women, and the wisdom of this body depended on the integration, diversity and collective illumination of the women, acting together.

I have experienced the power and truth of this myself with a group of women journeying together, to the constant beat of a drum, accessing knowledge and wisdom from the unseen realms of the Goddess, held in a profound sense of ecstasy and awe. Upon returning to "ordinary reality" we share our stories and learn that our experiences are very often similar and synchronous — finding ourselves in the same places hearing the same teachings. Mircea Eliade reports, "But we must remember that the shaman, too, everywhere conducts the souls of the dead to the underworld; and, as we have seen throughout

the Indonesian area the 'boat of the dead' — which is constantly referred to in the funerary recitals that we have just summarized — is pre-eminently a shamanic means of journeying into ecstasy." (Eliade, **Shamanism**, p.360)

It is interesting to note that funerary ritual, the boat of the dead and journeying into ecstasy are all connected. Marija Gimbutas informs us, "It was thought that the afterworld was in the West, and that a barrier of water existed between this world and the next that was crossed by ships, themselves symbols of regeneration." (Gimbutas, **Civilization of the Goddess**, p.400) If we could embrace that perhaps the journey we take in death to the waiting arms of the Mother is an opening into ecstasy, a dissolution into the All, we would be much less afraid of dying. With less fear about dying there is no doubt that we would have less fear about living. In Tibetan Buddhism the Goddess Tara carries souls across the ocean of existence to the shore of liberation and is called upon in life-threatening crises as the Savioress.

"Ship of Renewal" rock art, Bronze Age Sweden, Lokerberget, Foss, showing trees of life,
drawn by Melissa Meltzer

These waters are the uterine waters of the Goddess, from whence all creation emerges and returns. One travels these waters into creation as well as into the netherworld where the ancestors reside. Current pagan rituals involve visualization of a spirit boat imagined by a group of people to visit the Isle of Apples across the great ocean to the land where the dead and the not-yet-born meet the living.

Remnants of a connection to the female origins of life and the boat of regeneration can be seen in the current rituals of canoe-making among the Cacandon people in the village of Naha in Mexico. Here, the sacred mahogany trees are felled only by men whose wives are pregnant, ensuring the proper respect for the tree that has given itself to the people. As felling a tree is likened to giving birth, it is thought that only those men in relationship with a pregnant woman will understand how to give the proper care and attention to the difficult task.

While this boat reference is not specific to carrying souls in death, it is significant of the reverence of the female in the act of creating the boat itself, which remains a connection to life, as the tree is considered to be alive in boat form, and must be continued to be nourished by the connection to the new life, the renewed life in the womb of the pregnant woman.

The Warao people of Venezuela maintain a profound connection to the femaleness of life in their boat-building. Canoes are made from the red cachicamo trees, known as the Daurani, Mother of the Forest. I do not think it is an accident that the tree is red. She is the guardian of the forest, and any man who wishes to become a master canoe builder must be invited by Daruani herself. Rituals are enacted whereby a tree-maiden is approached by the canoe-maker initiate and a shaman who sings his assurance of the tender and loving reverence necessary to proceed.

The boat itself is shaped like a vagina, and whenever a man enters the vessel, he enters the daughter (the tree) of the Mother of the Forest, and the Mother herself. As the vagina of the Mother of the Forest, "the bounty or cargo that issues from her womb supports the canoe maker's family and his community." (Halifax, **Fruitful Darkness**, p. 145) Again, this is not a reference to the vulva-boat in death, but rather a reference to the vulva-boat in life. In truth, there is no difference. In death, the boat carries the seeds of new life. In life, the boat carries the sustenance necessary to life — all regenerative activities of the Goddess.

In patriarchal myths there are many references to souls crossing various waters in the underworld as well as seeking immersion in them in order to find renewal. The river Styx, known as Alpha, "the Beginning" was the red menstrual blood of the Goddess, emanating from her yonic source in a mountain by the city of Clitor. In her **Women's Encyclopedia of Myths and Secrets**, Barbara Walker writes of several stories and myths involving this concept:

"Greek mystics were considered 'born again' out of the Styx. Olympian gods swore their absolutely binding oaths by the waters of Styx, as men on earth swore by the blood of their mothers. Symbolic death and rebirth were linked with baptism in the waters of Styx, as in many other sacred rivers the world over.

Jesus himself was baptized in Palestine's version of the Styx, the river Jordan. When a man bathed seven times in this river 'his flesh came again like unto the flesh of a little child' (2 Kings 5:14). In Greek tradition the journey to the land of death meant crossing the Styx; in Judeo-Christian tradition it was crossing the Jordan." (Walker, **Women's Encyclopedia of Myths and Secrets**, p. 639, 640) In Norse mythology, Thor was said to have found the magic land of enlightenment and eternal life by bathing in a river of menstrual blood of "giantesses." (Ibid. p. 636) The Semitic word for "ark" from the Hindu "argha" means "great ship" and is metaphorically the Great Yoni: "a female-sexual vessel bearing seeds of life through the sea of chaos between destruction of one cosmos and creation of the next."(Ibid., p. 57)

Another meaning of "argha" is crescent, as in the moon as well as the crescent of the circle. These meanings refer to the Moon Goddess found in many early mythologies. "For the Moon Goddess is the Many-Breasted Mother of All, creator of all life on the earth." (Harding, **Women's Mysteries**, p. 128)

In Hinduism, the moon boat is said to carry the souls of the dead to the new world, or to new incarnations. It is probable that Noah came from the Babylonian moon goddess Nuah. M. Esther Harding writes, "Whatever may be the truth in regard to the deluge, it is clear that the story of the moon boat refers to psychological events." (ibid., p. 127) Are these psychological events death and rebirth? In the Vedas there is a parallel Noah named Manu, who also rode out a great flood in an ark with assistance from Vasuki, the

Art, page 100, top: *Vulva symbols shown on prow of ship, Aegean anthropomorphic platter, early Cycladic II, Syros, mid-third mill BCE, drawn by Melissa Meltzer*
Art, page 100, bottom: *Vulva flanked by branches, ship with fish and bird's feet sailing across a spiral sea, anthropomorphic platter, early Cycladic II, Syros, mid-third mill BCE, drawn by Leslene della-Madre.*

Great Serpent. This ark was seeded with plants and animals. "Manu's ark was the cosmic seed-vessel, in pre-Vedic myth the womb of the Goddess, which preserved the spark of life through cycles of destruction and renewal. It seems Manu was a masculinized form of Ma-Nu or Mother Night, the name she bore in Egypt, as the spirit of the primordial abyss that gave birth to the cosmos. Sumerians knew her as Nammu, 'the primeval ocean, the mother of the gods.'" (Walker, **Women's Encyclopedia of Myths and Secrets**, p. 580) It is no accident that the names Mary, mother of Jesus and Maya, mother of Buddha, are derived from Mari, the goddess of the primordial sea.

And, of course, no writing on the Goddess mythology of death and the afterlife would be complete without mentioning that patriarchy did indeed co-opt the powers of the Goddess' ships of renewal and vessels of life and placed them in the hands of male heroes. In Greek mythology, for example, it is Hermes, known to embody feminine traits, who becomes the psycho-pomp, ferrying souls across the waters to the land of the dead. It is said about Hermes that he found a reincarnation in Hermes Trismegistus, whose Hermetic vessel was described in a sixteenth century treatise as "a uterus for the spiritual renewal or rebirth of the individual . . . more to be sought than scripture." (ibid., p. 397) Why Hermes thought he could be the captain of a uterine vessel is beyond me, but then again, so are many patriarchal claims. The Egyptian Osiris known as the Moon God "ferried the dead man who had been initiated into his rites, over the waters to the Isle of the Blest, and so gave him immortality." (Harding, **Woman's Mysteries**, p.127) Since Osiris doesn't give birth, it is not exactly clear to me how he bestows immortality. And, of course, the well-known story of Noah and the Ark reveals a similar replacement of the original Goddess by the male consciousness that longs to be the carrier of new life and the guide of regeneration. Alas, it is not to be — never has been, and never will.

The idea of the Goddess as the one who ferries us across the waters in her vulva boat to her shore of regeneration is a comforting and soothing image — especially when we think about our own death. It is no wonder today that boats are referred to as "she," often named after women, and prows are often adorned with female figureheads. We have also seen where boats are considered to be the Goddess, the Mother, herself. It is a very old idea indeed that the Mother reaches for us in death and carries us across the waters of life into rebirth.

The Ending of the Goddess Cultures in Old Europe

Mother Earth in Pain: Her trees cut down, Her seas polluted, Monica Sjöö, **1996**

A general over-view of the change that occurred within Old Europe with the coming of the Kurgans is important if we are to have a whole picture of who we are. This transformation changed the way human beings lived, loved and died the world over. It is not a pretty picture because the dominator model is based on hierarchy, control, greed, and violence. Men are at the helm, women and children subject to their direction. It is a change that occurred in our not-so-distant past, the waves of which still lap at the shores of our consciousness. How this could have happened and why this happened will not be addressed here. I will focus on the fact that it did happen, and look at some of the consequences in order to facilitate an understanding about how we deal with death and how we might find peace in learning to trust the ancient wisdom of the matriarchal mind of our foremothers.

Marija Gimbutas has indicated in her exhaustive research into this subject that the ending of Old Europe came with three waves of Kurgan invasions — beginning in 4,400 BCE, with the middle wave occurring at c. 3,500 BCE and the final wave of destruction at c. 3,000 BCE. The Kurgans were a patriarchal, hierarchical pastoral people from areas surrounding the steppe regions of the Black Sea. Their cosmology was quite different from the Goddess cultures they invaded, as their deity was a male sky-god symbolized by the thunderbolt and solar connection. Beginning with these invasions, the two cultures collided over time, creating a drastic change in the consciousness of human beings. With the evidence Gimbutas has put forth in her work, it is clear that humans lived for millennia in harmonious, peaceful, egalitarian societies, the knowledge of which is encoded in our DNA.

The arrival of the Kurgans is a fairly recent event, even though we teach in our schools that history virtually began with the Bronze Age. In stark contrast to the gentle agriculturists of Old Europe, these semi-nomadic pastoralists, who had domesticated the horse, brandished an array of weapons — including daggers, spears, and bows and arrows. Up until the mid-fifth millennium BCE, weapons were not found in grave goods in Europe.

The Kurgan people also practiced different burial rituals than those of the peaceful peoples they conquered. Most notably, their graves were marked by attention paid to males and the warrior elite, unlike the more egalitarian agriculturalists, and they practiced suttee, or the hideous custom of sacrificing the consort or wife upon the death of the "esteemed" male. Animal sacrifice was also included in their funerary rituals. Their belief in the after-life differed significantly from the Old Europeans as well.

We have seen how the Goddess-based cultures maintained a strong belief in cyclical existence, with regeneration exemplified by the magnificent tomb as womb structures, accompanied by the profound birth-life-death and regeneration symbolism of eggs, cup marks, vulva-triangle, and anthropomorphic architecture, representing the body of the Goddess. Rebirth was represented by the communal burial of bones that was analogous to seeds being placed within the body of the Mother.

The Goddess was the giver, sustainer and taker of life, and all was returned to Her in Her never-ending cycle. The Kurgans, or Indo-Europeans, maintained a linear concept of death — the dying person assumed a new life in the world of the dead. Chieftains and "valiant" warriors were often buried with their entire household — wife/consort, children, animals, tools and weapons, to ensure a prosperous passage in the new world. Gimbutas gives us a disturbing picture of the afterlife views of the Kurgans:

"From comparative Indo-European mythologies and beliefs we know that the world of the dead was imagined as a cold, swampy, underground realm ruled by the sovereign male god. The journey to the gloomy underworld involved a road or a river, usually a three-day period of walking, riding, or travel in chariots. Souls drifted there in a pale and passive manner, and there was no belief in the possibility of rebirth." (Gimbutas, **Civilization of the Goddess,** p. 400)

It is my belief that herein lie the many seeds of the concepts of the patriarchal mind regarding life and death currently coming to fruition in the patriarchal culture in which we now live — our inheritance from our forefathers, not our foremothers.

The ideas of a frightening death, hell, sin, purgatory, the "evil" nature of the body and sex and the demonization of women find their roots in the Indo-European psyche. The many reflections of the father sky-god ideology we now see in current patriarchal religions grew over time, gathering momentum as swiftly as the older mythology of the Goddess could be replaced: the idea of Eve as the cause of original sin, the notions of brimstone and hellfire and eternal damnation, the caste system, the idea in Buddhism that one must have a male body to attain enlightenment, the Buddhist concept of the impure womb, the notion of the "grim reaper," the practice of suttee in India, as well as foot-binding in China and female genital mutilation in Africa and in the Middle East, the establishment of all-male hierarchical priesthoods, both in the West and the East, the veiling of women, the burning at the stake of wise women healers during the Inquisition, and basically, the general co-opting and stealing of the truth and wisdom of the Goddess, given over to a male "God" who lives outside the world, punishing wrong-doing and demanding the people live in fear of his anger. People believe, if they are "God-fearing," they have found peace. How does anyone find peace living in fear?

The ideology of these violent people slowly began to erode the worship and Goddess-based practices of the Old Europeans as well as transform the Goddess Herself. As the Goddess was demoted, so were Her priestesses, and women in general. The far-reaching effects of the ways of these patriarchal people were devastating, the details of which I will not attempt to go into here. The Goddess was eventually "dismembered" and split off, with the fragments of Herself named, over time, as different goddesses. At the same time, the male god took on the attributes of the Goddess, becoming the one who gives birth, as we see in the myths of Adam birthing Eve from his rib and Zeus birthing Athena from his forehead and co-opting the original trinity of Maiden, Mother and Crone as Father, Son, and Holy Ghost.

While the Goddess remains alive in different forms, She nonetheless becomes the goddess in patriarchy, with the patriarchal mind "allowing" Her presence, under the control of men who lived in fear of Her power. As long as the image of the Goddess is relegated to a pristine sexless virgin, like Mary, or to the image of the whore, like Mary Magdalene, men can feel in control of Her power. Or, as long as they can revere male Buddhas and Bodhisattvas who interestingly enough have acquired female attributes, such as Avalokiteshvara, they can honor the feminine if it is engendered in a male form. Their relationship to the Goddess becomes one of fear and domination — men's need to emulate Her power as their own, apart from Her actually causes a deep split in the psyche of all people who believe that their life lies in separation from the Mother Goddess — a fatal mistake. The distorted thinking from this split remains a grievous wound, reflected in the destruction of the rainforests and holes in the ozone, not to mention wanton raping, pillaging and plundering worldwide through war and men's notions of entitlement and privilege, supported by a male "God" who thrives on the bloodshed of conflict and the obscene suffering of his so-called son nailed to a cross, dripping with blood in agonizing pain.

Nothing appears to have changed much since the conquering Kurgans made their way into the abundant and verdant heart valley of the earth-Goddess so many centuries ago. Perhaps it is helpful to remember that 5,000 years of patriarchal rule is really not a long time in the story of humanity, and that, perhaps, this short-lived mistake will correct itself through our collective remembrance of the harmony, peace and egalitarianism of the Goddess, before we annihilate ourselves.

The Rise of Men's Fear of the Goddess

As patriarchy gained a foothold in the psyche of the people of Old Europe, and the clashing of the two cultures grew into a merging of one, much of the creativity and spirituality of the Goddess cultures was lost, and with that, the deep reverence for life and death that had previously reigned. Because of this shift in consciousness, the collective worldview was forced to undergo a drastic change in which "power-over" became the ruling paradigm. This kind of fear-based structure gave rise to dualistic thinking — good/evil, male/female, spirit/matter, and light/dark — where life and death were seen as oppositional. And since men rule in patriarchy, it was their fear that occupied psychic and physical space, giving rise to the notions of heroes, conquerors, and warrior-kings, always on the look-out for new territory to colonize, whether it was women's bodies and minds, the fruit of their wombs or the earth herself.

This fear of women's power grew so strong that men had to create myths for themselves where they became dragon-slayers (the dragon is an ancient symbol of women's power, earth wisdom and menstrual blood), be-headers of "demonic" goddesses in order to become immortal, and rapists in order to subdue the wild woman to become her possessor. Strange concepts developed cross-culturally, like the "vagina dentata," or "toothed vagina," believed to be the dark hole of the goddess whose teeth would clamp down on the male's valued sexual organ during intercourse, rendering it limp and useless. The idea of the "Terrible Mother" acting as devourer of her children is a dreadful concept that would scare anyone. This is a distortion of the Death-Wielding Goddess of Regeneration. When the distortion of the Goddess as the "Terrible Mother" found believers willing to project their fear onto women, women were then seen in the collective mind-set as this projection. Men's fear gave rise to misogyny, male superiority and an unspeakable terrible disregard for life.

As this fear grew, the church took an active role in its institution, when men became more and more convinced of their superiority as they saw themselves reflected in a male god, and a suffering male savior, even deciding in the sixth century that women did not possess a soul — as if it was their decision! Could the patriarchal male mind possibly be more arrogant than this? One would think not. And yet, this fear continued to find its disguise in numerous forms — including the very influential Cartesian hypotheses of the mechanistic nature of the world, having emerged from the unhealed grief of René Descartes over the loss of his mother when he was a little over a year old, in which men decided they had to extract — to take as if it was their right — the earth's gifts from her. (Sjöö and Mor, **The Great Cosmic Mother**, p. 324)

As these ideas took a stronghold, men continuously oppressed women and children. Women were considered often nothing more than "chattel," bought and sold as men's personal effects, which continues today in the world-wide sexual slave-trade market in such places as Sudan and Afghanistan, where women are openly regarded as men's possessions. An American fourth-grade schoolteacher and her students raised thousands of dollars to free some Sudanese women from this degradation. Can you imagine the impact of such a project on the gentle and tender minds and hearts of these children — that a school project becomes raising enough money not for the school soccer team, but to free women of color half-way around the world from blatant slavery? These women whose homeland was the birthplace of original Goddess worship? These women whose ancestors embodied the virtues of justice, compassion and equality?

Women and children became property — just as they had been in the early Kurgan societies. The institution of marriage changed the matrifocaled kinship structure to a patriarchal one, and bloodlines were lost. Do you know your mother's maiden name that wasn't her father's name? In order for women to find our names, we will have to make up new ones, and give them to our children.

Down through so-called history, we encounter a more recent notion of something we are asked to accept as sophisticated psychological theory emanating from the "brilliant" (deemed so by themselves, I might add) minds of our forefathers — something a man decided to call "penis envy." This apparently wise theory, considered to be so by many men at the time, became a foundation upon which men could decide about the sanity of women, and whole systems of thought emerged from this "discovery." As fast as men identified with heroism in this "truth," the insane asylums filled with women who were the "hysterical" objects of their newfound discoveries, placed there by fathers, husbands, uncles, grandfathers and brothers who found their sense of power in being the righteous judges of women's mental health.

The problem, however, is that this supposed truth is really an obvious projection of men's fear onto women. Freud was afraid to acknowledge that the women he was seeing were experiencing sexual abuse, so instead of telling the truth, some strange male theories were devised, placing the onus of the blame on women. This thinking has no place whatsoever in men's attempts to understand women. There is no way that any understanding can be reached when the viewing lens has cataracts of distortion and wrong thinking. Women's power of creation and capacity for sexual pleasure became a threat to men, (whose own power is really informed by the female Shakti, the snake power of creativity) to the point where the patriarchal mind devised many destructive ways of controlling and owning women's power to this day.

The controlling of women's reproductive rights by men is a most heinous crime committed against the Goddess, creating terrible karma. The insistence of male priesthoods that women are distractions, temptresses and hindrances to the male spiritual seeker is really a degradation of the very life — of their own mothers — that births them. In patriarchal consciousness, a spiritual seeker is usually considered to be male. With this fear growing exponentially over millennia, it is no wonder we find ourselves in the dire conditions we are in now. By the fifth century, the Church Council formally declared the cyclic reality of life — that which is related to the menstrual moon-mind of the female, including the teachings of reincarnation and regeneration — as heresy. This action gave permission for males to hate and persecute life itself through sanctioning hatred of the female.

With the social, economic and religious subjugation of women — daughters of the Goddess and heart and soul of all life — life itself is made to suffer. When all life suffers, humans become confused and bewildered, living in deep despair and ignorance. With this kind of experience, the grasping after life is increased in an attempt to avoid death. Desperate grasping, clinging and attachment to life while fearing death removes us from the wisdom of the earth, the cycles of life of the Great Round of the Goddess, the regenerative truth of our ancestors and the ability to listen with our hearts.

In patriarchy, the once sacred blood of women responsible for holding the clan and tribe together is feared and the belief in the defilement of women abounds. Again, I quote a sample of cross-cultural reflections from Barbara Walker on this grave and insane distortion:

> "The laws of Manu said if a man even approached a menstruating woman he would lose his wisdom, energy, sight, strength, and vitality. The Talmud said if a menstruating woman walked between two men, one of the men would surely die. Brahmans ruled that a man who lay with a menstruating woman must suffer punishment one-quarter as severe as the punishment for Brahmanicide, which was the worst crime a Brahman could imagine.
>
> "Vedic myths were designed to support the law, such as the myth that Vishnu dared copulate with the Goddess Earth while she was menstruating, which caused her to give birth to monsters that nearly destroyed the world. Persian patriarchs followed the Brahman lead in maintaining that menstruous women must be avoided like poison. They belonged to the devil; they were forbidden to look at the sun, to sit in water, to speak to a man, or to behold an altar fire. Zoroastrians held that any man who lay with a menstruating woman would beget a demon, and would be punished in hell by having filth poured into his mouth. Christians inherited all the ancient patriarchs' superstitious horrors. St. Jerome wrote: 'Nothing is so unclean as a woman in her periods; what she touches she causes to become unclean.' The superstition came down to the 20th century, when a Scottish medical text quoted an old rhyme to the effect that menstrual blood could destroy the entire world.
>
> "Christian women were commanded to despise the 'uncleanliness' of their own bodies, as in the Rule for Anchoresses: 'Art thou not formed of foul slime? Art thou not always full of uncleanness?'" (Walker, **Women's Encyclopedia of Myths and Secrets**, pp.641-643)

Walker's text cites numerous other examples of this terrible hatred and fear of the very blood from which all life is born, but I think the above examples sufficiently elucidate, beyond the shadow of a doubt, that men's fear of women's power became the governing force of their need to be in control — having dominion over all living things.

When men fear the Sacred Feminine, the Great Mother, and the Goddess in themselves and in the world, they become hopelessly lost. In our Western society, they are instructed by the patriarchal mind from an early age to "be a man" — and that if they are emotional and sensitive they are accused of "behaving like a girl," as if that is something to fear. The shame instilled in young boys about the feminine from which they come into this world sows the seeds within their psyche of misogynist acting out, and this, combined with high levels of testosterone which seem to climb in proportion to exposure to violence in puberty, is a near-death experience of their souls.

Their once innocent connection with their mothers becomes a twisted and distorted toxicity, over which they have no control. Disrespecting their mothers and women in general, who are survivors of a society that hates them, proves their "manliness." Their only relationship with the feminine becomes an accepted voyeuristic journey into pornographic sex, accompanied by the adrenaline rush of violence, where they are fueled by the unconscious rape mythology of their forefathers.

The antidote for fear is courage. It is my wish that the rampant fear of women's power that has created sexism and racism and all of the other "isms" we experience in patriarchy, not to mention the misogyny and self-hatred internalized by women and men alike, finds its transformation in the courage within each one of us. It is clear that humanity is indeed propelled in a downward spiral towards a kind of unknown destruction — the likes of which have not been seen before. This destruction is optional. We must begin to become vulnerable and open to express the courage to love.

And what does all of this have to do with death and dying? When you take a good look at the fear instilled in the hearts and minds of the people, which has caused a grievous amnesia of something once good and life-affirming, you can see that our beliefs about death are shaped by this grinding, gnawing fear. Our fear of death is so strong in Euro-Western society, that in order for most people to live their lives, they live in denial, and submerge themselves in delusional thinking that allows them to believe death will not happen to them — even while they are dying, they believe they are not.

Paradoxically, this fear and denial have created a death-wish fueled by an obsessive-compulsive preoccupation with violence, particularly violence against women. If the dying are fortunate, they will go through the steps of bargaining, anger, acceptance and surrender, but in the end, what are they surrendering to? If we had a sense about this while we actually live our lives, we wouldn't have to work so hard to avoid the truth of our mortality, since death would be our constant companion in our awareness while we live. Our awareness of death as part of life could serve, motivate and inspire us to live full, conscious, loving and good lives, developing the awareness that how we live will determine how we die.

We have seen enough of men's fear of the Goddess. It is not life affirming for anyone or anything. It is time now for all of us to open to the loving arms of the Mother and see Her in ourselves and in the eyes of each other, women and men alike.

Edges of Mystery

"Row row row your boat,
Gently down the stream.
Merrily, merrily, merrily,
Life is but a dream."

Death is not only letting go of the body. We have many opportunities in life to see death's many faces. If we are aware, we can learn from the experiences of our "little deaths" while alive, and become more prepared, given the time and space, to meet the "big one." Like the simple truthful song above, life is but a dream. How do we embrace our life in this manner? Can we really be merry? Can we really go gently downstream? Thus far in this book we have briefly explored the herstory of an older time in which our ancestors, regardless

Spirits of the Sky, Earth and Underworld, Monica Sjöö, 1996

of race and culture, lived in the knowledge of the sacredness of all life, held in the arms of a great Mother-Goddess. It is important not to romanticize these cultures, as they were not perfect utopias. But, they were peaceful, egalitarian and maintained a rich connection to the sacred in everyday living — all of which could certainly seem like utopias from our viewpoint at this time.

There is much to draw upon from them, as embracing the knowledge that humans have lived longer in peace than we have in war will help shift our collective consciousness away from fear towards a more loving, life-affirming way of being. We can use all the help we can get. I think it is important to look at some of the faces of death in an attempt to perhaps gain a deeper understanding of how to better live our lives.

The Dark and the Shadow

Because the Goddess was demonized and fragmented, Her domain, once considered whole and One, was split. Light and dark were no longer seen as parts of the whole, but were separated from each other. The Goddess' wheel of life became a straight line, with life at one end and death at the other, and the dark regenerative womb of the Goddess became a place of torture in patriarchy. That which was associated with goodness (God), the sun and light, was male; and that which was associated with evil (Eve), the earth and the dark was female. Everlasting life in the everlasting light has been a goal of patriarchal religions, while the fear of punishment, death and torture in hell (a derivative of the name of the Scandanavian Goddess, Hel, the Crone of regeneration whose name means "cave") in the burning fires in the underworld has caused a deep scarring/scaring in the human psyche.

Death became associated with the "frightening" dark and was split off from the process of life itself. Reclaiming the dark and "uncursing" the dark are essential to a healthy approach to death and dying. And in this reclaiming, I feel it is of utmost importance to remember the truth that all of humanity has emerged from the womb and belly of the Dark Mother of Africa — she is the Mother of us all, and reverence for her must be restored. In this context we must come into right understanding of the dark and embrace it for what it really is — the earth as daughter of the Great Dark Mother herself — the cosmos, the yoni-verse.

Meditation: Seed Self

(This section is to be read to you or recorded for listening to.)

Find a comfortable spot and lie down. Close your eyes and take several deep breaths. Allow yourself to fully relax and let go. Simply follow the gentle rhythm of your breath. Now imagine yourself as a seed buried in the sensuous dark soil of the earth. Within your seed-self lies all the potential of your being, given to you by the Great Cosmic Mother. You did not create the seed yourself. You simply are the seed of life, waiting for the right conditions to bring you into fruition. Imagine the generative qualities of the soil — her moisture, temperature and mineral rich content, all gathered to spark your growth.

As you lie in this soil you realize you are resting in the rich, nourishing dark womb of the Mother, who is gestating you. She is dreaming you into form. You begin to feel the stirrings of your roots in Her darkness. As your roots extend into the soil, you feel met and held by the gentle moist embrace of the earth Herself, Her soul-soil. She feeds you in Her sacred dark and you begin to grow. As you grow, feel the essence of the relationship you have with the dark soil, the Dark Mother.

113

Feel her love. Feel the embracing wisdom that holds you in the dark until you are ready to be in the light. You must be ready, for if you are exposed to the light too soon, you could die. Feel your rootedness in the dark. It is the Dark Mother who holds you and succors your tender growth. Without Her love, you would not realize your potential. Without Her love, you could lie forever on the top of the ground, in the light, and never grow. Now, after your roots are thoroughly embedded in the earth, you begin to feel your stem-self stretch upwards through the dark, rich soil. Soon, you feel your stem-self break through the surface and meet the warmth of the sun, ready to continue the journey of your unfolding and blossoming. The dark of the earth and the light of the sun are the arms of the Mother, who hold you with strong tenderness. You reclaim your connection to the Dark Mother, and let go of fear. You realize the potential of the sacred dark, and understand how it holds and supports you. You are happy that you have made this discovery. Now, when you are ready, gently open your eyes, and sit up slowly.

Take some time to write in your journal about your experience. What did you learn about the dark? What did you learn about the light? How did it feel to experience the dark as the regenerative womb? Did you encounter fear of the dark? If so, could you let it go? How did it feel to experience the sun and the soil as the loving arms of the Mother? Pay attention to how fear of the dark may be present in your life, and know that you have the power to transform it.

The ancients originally created their places of ritual in caves and in the dark recesses of the body of the earth — the dark was sought after because of its womb-like qualities. These places of worship were our first cathedrals. The dark played an important part in the ritual enactment of birth, death and regeneration — from the earliest times up until the time of the Greek Eleusinian Mysteries, practiced for about 2,000 years. Many myths tell of the descent of the initiate into the dark in order to experience rebirth, and transformation of consciousness. Cave sites in France reveal long passageways large enough for one person to crawl through, connecting with a cave-chamber deep within the earth where rituals were enacted. Descent myths relate to a kind of death and rebirth. One must learn to die to the old to make room for the new.

The pre-Hellenic myth of Demeter and Persephone tells of the descent of Persephone into the underworld of discovery, without rape and abduction by the male. It is a story of love and revelation — of transformation of the seasons and states of consciousness. The maiden Persephone hears the cries of the dead, and feels she must go to them in the underworld to help guide them, and must leave her beloved mother, Demeter. In her journey, she encounters her grandmother Hecate, queen of the underworld and holder of the secrets of life, death, sexuality and regeneration. Persephone journeys into the underworld to find herself and to learn the secrets of the mystery of the Goddess. She returns to Demeter, uniting with her mother in love, no longer a child, now a young woman. This story reveals a journey into the dark as a necessary entrance into the unknown in order to know oneself. When one takes the risk, the secrets are revealed. In patriarchy, the story was changed. Persephone was raped and abducted, tricked and held hostage.

This is not a story of discovery, but rather a story of domination and control. In this, the dark becomes a place of foreboding and fear — the female is disrespected and violated by the male, whose false sense of power is found through perpetration of injury on the female. This mythology considerably changed the face of the dark and the relationship of death to life. What lies in the dark is split off from the wholeness of the initiate and the split itself becomes part of the psyche. The journey for the initiate changes from exploring the nature of one's being and learning the secrets of the ancestors into having to navigate that which has been split off in order to find wholeness. With this change, the dark is no longer the domain of the Crone Goddess, but more the domain of the crying, despairing, abused self, living in loneliness and isolation. She must be recovered for healing to occur, but this journey is far more treacherous and difficult, for it is a journey to find the once-known, now-forgotten love of the female self, which the dominator mind does not want to see women retrieve, for it means empowerment and a shedding of ignorance, revealing the glistening truth of women's autonomy.

Meditation: Descent

(To be read to you or taped to listen to.)

Find a comfortable spot and lie down. Close your eyes and allow your body to relax. Follow the gentle rhythm of your breath to help you slow down. Feel yourself relaxing more and more until you sense a spaciousness and openness. Release an audible sigh: ahhhhhhhhh — on an outbreath. You may want to repeat this several times. Know there is nowhere to go and nothing to do. Just be. Now see yourself in an open field where the flowers are blooming, filling your senses with fragrance and color. The warmth of the sun lightly embraces you, and you feel a gentle breeze caressing your body. Just as you feel the love of the Mother surrounding you, She appears before you. Allow Her to be there for you however She chooses. She comes towards you, arms outstretched, and you see the love in Her eyes — a kind of eternal love flowing from an unending source in Her heart. You allow Her to enfold you in Her arms, and you feel one with Her. You walk together, dance lightly in the field, talk and share. You feel deeply contented with Her. As time passes, you find yourself hearing a distant calling — the voice of an ancient one from a far-off place. You leave your Mother's side to listen more closely. You discover that this voice is calling to you to come and find something lost to you. Before you, the earth opens, beckoning you to enter, and you know you must go. You tell your Mother that it is time for you to go, that you are being called. Her eyes well with tears of grief at the thought of your parting, but She knows She must let you go. You part in sweet embrace, and enter the earth.

You feel a sense of excitement as you enter the world of the unknown. You follow along a dark descending passageway. You smell the cool moist richness of the earth. The dark is somehow familiar, and you are not afraid. The passageway enters into a chamber in which there are two figures — one is timeless, with an ancient face of a mountain. The other is younger, sitting with the ancient one, crying. The grandmother speaks to you and tells you she is the Crone of the underworld, the one who can teach you of the lost magic of women. She says, however, that in order for you to remember the magic, you must reclaim the part of yourself you see before you. This part of your soul has been cast off for a very long time, as you have been an obedient girl, and behaved "well" in the world of the fathers. You have not gotten angry, except in secret at yourself, and you have done everything you were told. You have held your tongue, and have been an accepted daughter by the men. This part of you has not been allowed to live with you. She has been lost in the underworld, crying out, wailing in despair, unseen and unheard. She is your wild-self, the untameable part of your woman-soul that cannot live in the world of the fathers. She must live in the wild-zone of the Mothers, and she must be returned to you. The wise Crone instructs you to go to her just as your Mother came to you, with arms outstretched. And so you move towards her, opening your heart to her, retrieving the cast-off part of yourself, taking her deep inside to fill the emptiness in your heart. At once you feel a rush of warmth and love, filling your whole being. You hear a soft music, a kind of rejoicing echoing in the chamber of the earth. You feel alive in a way you have not known before. The Crone Grandmother moves towards you and gently kisses your cheek. Tears of joy stream from her eyes, as another daughter of the Goddess is re-united with Her-Self. She tells you that you will now remember the magic of the Goddess' love, which will be revealed to you in time. It is time now for you to leave the underworld to return to the waiting arms of your Mother. Grandmother Crone guides you to the passageway. You look at her with deep love and gratitude, and you know you will return to her again.

You begin your ascent. Finally, you arrive at the opening of the chasm where you are greeted by your Mother who gifts you with sweet smelling flowers. She has been awaiting your return. You embrace, and She nods with a knowingness that tells you of Her awareness of your reunion with your lost part. You both dance and dance in ecstasy, joyfully celebrating. You also know that in time, you will need to return to the domain of the Crone to assist others in finding their lost parts of themselves. Your Mother knows this is your work, and though it causes Her sadness to not be near you, She offers Her blessing. Now gently allow yourself to return to waking consciousness, slowly sitting up and opening your eyes when you feel ready.

Take some time to write in your journal. How did it feel to be unconditionally loved by the Mother? Did the dark frighten you? What did you feel when you retrieved your cast-off, wild part of your woman-soul? How did you experience the Grandmother Crone? Are you excited about remembering your woman-magic? Do you feel you can help empower other women to find their cast-off parts of their woman-souls?

Uncursing the Dark

Death and Rebirth Within the Cornish Quoit, Monica Sjöö, **1998**

I now refer to exploration of the cast-off parts of oneself as looking at the shadow and traveling in the shadowland. The dark for me now is a place of nurturing, and so if I make a reference to my "dark side," it is in a positive sense — that part of me that is connected to the untamed and chaotic menstrual moon-mind. Reference to the dark as "bad," opposing light as "good" implies negativity, particularly when referring to the earth, women and people of color.

My own journey of initiation into the shadowland began when I was nineteen with my first LSD experience, where I saw the treetops outside the window turn into the Four Horsemen of the Apocalypse. I wasn't wasting any time! The guidebook I used at the time was **The Psychedelic Experience** by Alpert, Leary and Metzner, based on the **Tibetan Book of the Dead.** I spent years traveling my shadowland, working with the sacred psychedelics LSD, psilocybin, mescaline, peyote and marijuana. The shadowland was a big place — and it contained not only my demons but also the cast-off parts of the collective unconscious, which were the same as my own, really. The darkness of the shadowland was terrifying and frightening at the time, since I later came to realize that the dark itself was cast-off by the patriarchal mind. I had no concept of the dark as nurturing and womb-like.

During this time, I constantly faced the fear of death — physical, emotional and psychic. My greatest fear was fear of complete dissolution into existential nothingness and loss of control. I encountered the many faces of schizophrenia, from hebrephrenic to catatonic. I was stalked by my fear of death and my fear of the dark everywhere I went. I could not go to the Fillmore and "trip out" on the Doors or Big Brother and the Holding Company as my friends could do. I was too immersed in trying to stay alive in the shadowland. I believe I am alive today because of the unseen guides and helpers who held me in Grace as I somehow made my way through the labyrinth of my being, which was threaded with voices of fear and distorted suffering faces, that found a lodging place within me, which I later learned were there to be embraced rather than resisted.

I later learned that descriptions of shamanic initiation include an experience of being suspended in sheer terror, without the sense of connection to anyone or anything — "it is a condition in which the man (sic) stands absolutely alone in space, and feels cut off from all life, even from that of the Logos; (*at this point I would add, Goddess*) and it is without doubt the most ghastly experience that it is possible for any human being to have. It is said to last only for a moment, but to those who have felt its supreme horror it seemed an eternity, for at that level time and space do not exist." (Leadbetter, **The Masters and the Path**, p. 220)

I had this experience, and had thought I was going crazy. Now as I look back on my life, I feel that many people experience this kind of shamanic-psychological-psychic terror in different ways. It would have indeed been very helpful had I had an experienced guide. I do not recommend delving into the shamanic realities without the assistance of trained guides. I also feel that our current guides such as therapists and psychologists need to learn of this shamanic initiation in order to validate a client's experience of the underworld and the shadowlands as part of the journey — and not something that necessarily needs to be fixed or drugged. I see the only way for this to occur is for the guides themselves to authentically visit their own unconscious rather than study from a book and then receive some type of stamp of approval. Nevertheless, I eventually came through to the other side of this immersion when I took an LSD trip alone, and sat in front of a mirror.

My intention was that I was not going to move until I could see myself clearly and wholly/holy — until I could completely love myself. I would not budge until I could embrace my wholeness, until I could accept myself exactly as I was. I could see in myself all of my inherited conditioning mostly from my parents' unhealed wounds. I also could see within myself their inherited wounding from their parents, and so on. I felt that I needed to end the legacy of self-loathing and fear — even though at the time I was not aware of the patriarchal mind as originator of this negativity in my ancestral line. I somehow knew that the only antidote for what I saw in the mirror was total and complete love and self-acceptance — that love had to come from within me. I knew I could not rely on an outside source to heal me — to love me. It had to come from within. This resonated with the Buddhist teaching "there is no refuge outside yourself." I was actually able to shed some of the unhealed energies I was carrying for others, and could give them back — another shamanic practice I later learned about — and I fell deeply in love with myself then and there, some thirty years ago, and have remained in love ever since. The radiance of my beauty beamed back at me from the mirror, and I became my own devoted lover.

I winked at myself, and felt a warm and gracious love and humor fill my body. I smiled at myself and felt healed. This is not narcissism. This is total self-love that becomes the path of selfless love in the world. I could see my own divine essence including my shadow, and so embracing my shadow as part of that divine essence became easier than fearing and resisting it. I cannot say that I am now "shadowless." That isn't really the point. What I can say is that I learned to integrate my shadow into the wholeness of my being so that I am much less terrified of the unknown, including death. For me to be able to say this as my truth is monumental, as fear of death and fear of the dark held me in a profoundly icy grip for several years during the time when I worked with my sacred hallucinogenic teachers.

This kind of descent into the shadowlands is also what is known in shamanism as "dismemberment," or a kind of death of the ego. In the Sumerian story of Innana, the hera goes to the underworld to meet her dark sister, Ereskigal. In her journey, Innana, Queen of Heaven, must pass through seven gates in which she surrenders something of her identity in order to go deeper. When she reaches the underworld, naked, she is hung on a meat hook to "rot" for three days. This is indeed a graphic depiction of the kind of required death experience of the seeker in order to know oneself. In other kinds of dismemberment journeys of shamans, the initiate goes into the underworld and is torn from limb to limb by animal spirits.

Having experienced this kind of journey, I can say that while it may sound violent, it really was not — it was more of an experience of having old outworn parts of my being stripped away by the benevolent spirits who were interested in my evolution and spiritual wholeness/holiness. When I was put back together, I was reborn — just like the butterfly emerging from the chrysalis. My new consciousness was fresh, wet and open. These experiences of journeying into the underworld, while dangerous at times, are also deeply ecstatic. This allows me to think that the letting go of the body in physical death, while perhaps frightening if one is not prepared, is also ecstatic. I feel that the Goddess finds a way for us to experience this kind of descent and dismemberment in order to come home to Her — and the path home is as varied as there are individuals. Some people descend through illness or addiction, while others may journey through complicated psychological states of despair and depression. Nevertheless, all paths lead home.

I also eventually experienced the dark womb as nurturing during a peyote trip when I did an overnight vision quest on a mountainside. I climbed into my sleeping bag, and almost immediately found myself inside the womb. I felt big and small simultaneously, and most of my consciousness was in my eyes. My eyes felt very large. I could see the veins of my mother's womb all around me, and I felt warm and peaceful. The womb was filled with light — a luminous reddish-orange light emanating from the dark. I was completely unafraid and was in total awe. There was no sense of engulfment — just pure safe protection and containment. I was the fetus growing inside my mother's belly. I don't know if I was in the womb of my biological mother, or in the womb of the Cosmic Mother — but in a sense, there was no difference. In that experience, I was remembering a sacredness about the beginning of my existence, which has stayed with me throughout my life's journey.

It was holy and beautiful. I consider this experience to be a return to the truth of womb-wisdom, which I was only able to find after plummeting the depths of my unconscious patriarchal conditioning. The dark in Goddess thealogy is a very different place indeed than the dark in patriarchal theology. I did not experience the slightest urge to escape from an impure place. The womb was not impure in any way. It was warm, luscious, nurturing and beautiful, and I was like a seed inside a plump, juicy pumpkin.

I have also found that sitting in the sweat lodge is a profoundly nurturing death and dark womb experience. As a facilitator of women's sweat lodge work, my approach, which is not traditional Native American Lakota, as I was not trained in that way, is to invite women into the dark, into the womb, in order to experience rebirth. The inside of the lodge is completely dark — so dark, that I have often seen light emanating from the covered bent willows criss-crossing overhead and around me. I have seen sparks of light moving around the inside of the lodge and have felt them to be connected to the spirits and ancestors we invoke. I have seen women, terrified of the dark, open and embrace the dark as Mother — as the womb from which we all emerge.

With this teaching, the association of dark with frightening death evaporates. Women have been able to feel how much fear is held in the body just from a lifetime condition of being afraid of the dark. We do not go for marathon heat — I feel women do not need that kind of purification. Rather, it is a gentle lodge, where we sit with the elements of earth, air, fire and water and we pray, sweat and cleanse together. We experience ourselves as One, ending the ceremony in a renewed sense of who we are as a community of women. The dark provides a place to let go into, to die to the old and to welcome the new.

When a snake sheds her skin, she goes blind for a period of time. Snakes have long symbolized the power of the kundalini shakti life force, and the ability of woman's body to transform. This temporary blinding is a good metaphor for the process of death in transformation — we become blind to what was, rest in the dark, and slowly open our eyes to the new. Death in this sense is essential for life to flow — all the changes we experience in our life as we grow are little deaths.

The truth of death and rebirth is the foundation for rites of passage ceremonies — desperately needed in our cold and linear patriarchal society. Our losses in relationship, within ourselves and with others, in jobs, and in changing consciousness are all experiences of dying to something outworn or outgrown, allowing space for something new to emerge. Embracing these changes as allies of death itself can help us to understand the necessity of letting go of egoic cravings and attachments. In understanding ego death, as shamanic and spiritual experiences demand, we can awaken to the true meaning of life.

Allies of Death

Trance states or altered states of consciousness, dreams, and oracular visioning are world-wide, often ecstatic experiences of shamans, witches, seers, visionaries and medicine people who travel into the unseen realms to access healing and knowledge. A practitioner entering such states learns to "die" to ordinary reality — just as we do when we sleep and dream. A shemama or shaman is one who moves back and forth between the worlds at will. This movement into altered states of consciousness teaches the practitioner about the nature of life and death, as one is exposed to realities beyond the physical. Necromancy — contact with the dead — is also part of this knowledge. In this section we will briefly visit these allies of death and see how gaining some understanding of these allies can help shape our attitude about our own death.

Fairie Queen, Monica Sjöö, **1980**

Trance

House of the Goddess, Monica Sjöö, **1994**

In some shamanic cultures, initiation into medicine ways occurs when one experiences "possession" by a dead shaman or healer. In my journey work and trance work with women, as I have mentioned previously, we contact the ancestral Grandmother spirits for guidance and wisdom. While we are not necessarily in contact with recently deceased relatives, though this does happen, we are able to access information from the collective ancestral wellspring of ancient women which helps us in many ways in our current lives. Practicing journey work and trance helps us to understand other realms of consciousness and serves to alleviate the fear of the dark and of death.

When we utilize ecstatic trance, we link up with our "ansisters" from the ancient woman-centered cultures who lived inside of an ecstatic reality on a daily basis. Their comprehension of life and death seems to be much more peaceful and much less fearful than ours. It is my wish that during my lifetime I will be able to truly comprehend and embody as much of this ancient knowing as possible, as I think that seeing the acceptance of death as an ecstatic experience as part of the great cosmic cycle is deeply and profoundly revolutionary. People in their dying process will often enter trance states. They may stare ahead without recognizing your presence and their heartbeat and breathing may be very slow. They may appear to not hear you. However, they are very much alive. They can emerge from such a state into "normal" consciousness, recognize their environment and resume communication.

When my mother entered a trance state in her dying process, I could feel that she was making connections somewhere else in time and space. Her look reminded me of the Tibetan teaching known as the Dzogchen (meaning "total completeness") gaze — the gazing into pure space allowing a dissolving of self into that vast limitless space. It was remarkable to witness her in this experience. The personality I knew as my mother was not present — she felt to me to be completely open, fearless and held in Mystery. In the Dzogchen teaching, it is said that we are already enlightened, already whole, and that we have to allow this reality to emerge in order to experience it. I felt my mother's presence in her trance state to be more of her true nature — her already pure, awake, unencumbered self. She came out of this state, her heartbeat and breathing became more normal, and she returned to a more identifiable form as "my mother." It was a profound teaching about the nature of impermanence and the fluidity of the nature of a human being.

Trance work can help us to open up to the world of magic and imagery — the imagination. The imagination or psychic world is a fluid world of color, sound, rhythm and pictures connected by life force or prana. This world is a vast web of information — which can be read and interpreted to inform our lives in the physical. When we experience trance work we learn that time and space are relative and that the past, present and future exist concurrently. Secrets about life and death are revealed in such states and the seriousness we interject into our identities and daily lives seems to fade as the "bigger picture" of the Great Mystery becomes more apparent.

When trance is used as a way to open up into one's inner life, the regular or ordinary world falls away, and the opportunity to connect with the deeper and more hidden aspects of life emerges. We have the opportunity to see ourselves as part of something greater and can learn to surrender to that greatness. Ecstatic trance dancing, drumming and singing were ways women used to access healing states of consciousness. What would a deathing be like attended by humming and drumming women who help the soul pass into a blissful state by bringing ecstasy to the experience of dying? Arnold Mindell, a therapist who has written extensively on shamanism and psychology, writes, "the shaman finds transformation and ecstasy — not tragedy or failure — in death." (Mindell, **The Shaman's Body**, p. 157) If we learn to live with the sacred as an everyday experience, our "shaman" or "shemama" selves will awaken and we will be able to develop the correct relationship to death while alive. Welcoming the Goddess into our lives will awaken this shamanic consciousness, and guide us to a more loving, less fearful experience of death.

Barbara's Story

My mother's passing was an extraordinary event in my life. Having tended to my father in his dying ten years prior, I had some idea of what to expect. But like birth, every death is different. Some things were familiar, and some were not. She was able to be at home with loved ones. My mother had been Director of Volunteer Services for the American Cancer Society in her county, and she was fully aware of what an individual and the family undergo when a loved one is seriously ill with cancer. When she was diagnosed with multiple myleoma, I felt she decided then and there that she was not going to stay around very long, as she didn't want to undergo extensive treatment.

My mother was like that. When she made up her mind, that was that. She was an amazing person — she had to be in order to marry my father, who didn't look like the rest of the guys, as he had a fused spine from birth, and was short, with a short, compacted torso, and long arms and legs. She was beautiful and very intelligent — entering UC Berkeley at the age of sixteen. She and my father moved to a country community outside of Berkeley when they were young to raise their family. In that community, she became well-known for her political views. She was an avid liberal democrat, and helped to found the Democratic Club in that town. This was quite an accomplishment for a woman in those days — the fifties. Most women were supposed to be Mrs. Cleaver. My mother breast-fed all of her babies — another unheard of thing at that time. So, I attribute much of my feistiness and love for justice to my mother.

She was also someone who had been very wounded in her childhood. People back then just went through life grinning and bearing their pain, but it took its toll on her. Being a mother in patriarchy, she did, of course, suffer from oppression, and did not have the conscious labeling to identify it. Because of that, I believe she suffered an ongoing depression that expressed itself in rageful fits. She was a rage-aholic. Her mother, Blanche, told her "it was a man's world" and committed suicide when my mother was in her twenties.

Author's mother, Barbara, photographer unknown

125

Even though my own wounding was a result of living with an alocholic father and a rage-aholic mother, to this day, I am in awe of what my mother accomplished in her life considering the pain she carried. How she managed to care for her five children, on welfare after divorcing my father, and then pursuing a job to support us in order to get off welfare, in a posh community, was amazing.

It was six months from the time of my mother's diagnosis to the time of her death. She tried chemotherapy, which almost killed her. She knew what she wanted, though she didn't consciously express it. She just never got out of bed again after her diagnosis. After her hospitalization, she was moved to a convalescent hospital, where I stayed with her as much as possible. She really didn't like it there, as she was very sensitive, and it felt unsafe to her. She was able to really connect with a couple of nurses who she felt truly cared about her when they were working. I had to find a way to move her closer to me, which meant changing her insurance in order for her to come to my county, which I was able to accomplish.

Still devoted to my commitment I made early on in my life to care for my aging parents, it was now very important for me to model this for my children, because they were of the age where they could see it. Prior to my mother's hospitalization, I had taken care of her in my home on several occasions, so my kids had been around her when she was sick, and had witnessed that this is what we do in our family. Because of my mother's rage, she was not easy to live with, but we worked on things, and were able to get things to a good enough place that I felt I could continue with her care in the future, whatever that would be, and have her around my kids.

When she moved to the nursing home close to me, I was with her as much as I could be, bringing her cat at times to comfort her. In all that time, she knew she was preparing to die. We had had a conversation about her dying when she was staying with me. She told me it was the one sure thing in life that we could count on. As she became weaker, I made plans to bring her home, so that she could die in peace. We ordered a hospital bed, connected with hospice and moved her into our living room. She remained conscious throughout her process. She had only a small dosage of medicine that kept her calmed down.

What was interesting was that she had been on much more medication in the hospital and in the nursing home, but when she came home to be with family, she didn't need much of anything, and had no morphine. At the time of moving her from the nursing home to the gurney to the waiting ambulance, she rested on the gurney in a somewhat upright position with her hands crossed over her chest. I looked at her — she was very inward — and she looked like an ancient spiritual being — a kind of deeply-practicing devotee. It was at that time that I began to get acquainted with her true nature in a way that I had never experienced before.

Even with all of her pain, anger and fear, a calmness and serenity began to exude from her. She stayed with us for three days, before passing. I had help so that I wasn't exhausted, and so that I could participate in her process in an appropriate way where I could show up, and give her all my presence. She went through various kinds of experiences, including deep trance states, with eyes wide open, and breathing about five breaths a minute. When she was in this stage, I climbed into bed with her, and held her hand, and talked with her, giving her permission to go, just loving her.

At other times, I stroked her, and told her how brave she was, and that she was doing a really good job. When I made this comment, she had been quietly resting on her belly. She smiled a faint wry smile, as if to say that she wasn't so sure she was doing such a great job — but she was. At another point in her process, she began to "root" like a newborn baby does when searching for the breast. This was extraordinary to witness. She was pursing her lips, as if to suck, while gently pushing into the pillows for the breast. It was unmistakable.

When it became clear that she was going to pass soon, I gathered my then partner and my daughters to her side and together we circled her with loving prayer. I was with my mother when she passed. It was at 5:45 in the morning, on tax day. Death and taxes — my mother's final political statement! I was holding her hand, and was whispering into her ear, guiding her to the light. She simply stopped breathing — the next breath just didn't come. There was no struggle, no pain, and no fear. There was a deep presence of her transformation.

At the moment of her death, the birds began welcoming the new day, and the sunlight was just breaking through the early morning mist. It was perfect. It was astonishingly beautiful — soft, golden, holy and peaceful. It felt just like a birth. What made my mother's passing so mysteriously beautiful was that she was able to shed her anger and fear in those three days she spent at home with us. I was witness to her process, and as she went deeper into it, her true being emerged. This is not something that I can easily put into words, as I felt I was dwelling in the realm of the unspeakable with her, completely privileged to be with such a being.

It is said somewhere that our true essence is 10,000 times brighter than the sun. I really had a glimpse of this truth while sharing with my mother in her deathing. I do not know what she felt, or if she had a sense of her own mystery. But I can say that she was extraordinarily peaceful, which was not a common state for my mother. It was this experience I shared with her that inspired me to write this book. I felt I learned first hand that death is beautiful. I had a sense of this with my father, but since I was not with him right when he passed, I did not have the same knowledge that I gained from being with my mother.

A day or so later after my mother's passing, I saw a good friend, and she asked me how I was doing. I replied "I am drowning in grief and swimming in joy." Midwifing my mother in her dying gave me many precious gifts. One of them was a new understanding of the grief process. I felt an instant grief when she passed because things changed for me and I knew I would never be the same.

It wasn't a grief about her having died — it was about me. I didn't feel anything to grieve about her experience — she had been in complete peace and surrender when she died. The grief I felt was about who I was without my mother. The feeling of knowing that the woman who brought me into this world, who suckled me at her breast, who changed my diapers, who worried about me when I was growing up, who loved me in the best way she knew how, who called me to wish me happy birthday, was no longer in body for me to connect with, was what I grieved.

Simultaneously, alongside this grief was a tremendous joy. Her passing had been so full of Grace that it filled my heart. I felt like celebrating. The experience of feeling the birth energy when she passed was rich with love. There is such an energy at a natural birthing that is absolutely delectable. To have experienced this with my mother in her death was a teaching about the mystery of life. How can we understand the Goddess if we don't experience Her in Her very process of creation and dissolution? How can we know about dying if we don't allow ourselves to be with it?

Another gift I received was the knowledge that I am next in line — I am now the elder. With this realization came the wisdom that I have time to prepare for what I want and to educate my children about death and dying. I have time to create my own ritual, and pass on a wisdom to my children that has been lost. I realized we can be empowered in our death. My parents were lucky in that they had me — someone who was willing to be with them all the way through. This should not be lucky — it should be the normal thing to do. Again, as with my father, my siblings were not present for my mother, and I know that it was because they were not able to be for their own reasons. One of my brothers did come and spend a short time with her before she died. But he didn't stay.

We kept my mother's body at home for three days. During this time, I sat with her, prayed, played music, kept candles lit and talked to her. She looked very young. No wrinkles or lines remained in her face. There was never any odor. I felt I had complete closure with her. The only thing I would have changed if I had it to do again was that I would have called in my women friends to help me bathe and anoint her body. I now feel that this is a sacred act that women have done for millennia. I would have chosen for us to sing and pray together for her while bathing her. My sister talked me out of doing this at the time, and I now realize it was because she couldn't do it. But with my women friends, we could have. I was fortunate enough to experience doing this for the mother of a close friend who died not long after my mother. So, in a sense, I had some kind of completion with what I would have chosen to do for my own mother.

The particular act of bathing and anointing the body of my friend's mother with wonderful smelling oils while we sang was truly sacred. I felt that we were ancient priestesses together, caretaking the life that comes through us, and blessing it on its journey. The most profound teaching I received from midwifing my mother in her death was that we need the teachings that will help those of us left behind to practice dying in order to learn how to live. The teachings we need are the Goddess earth-based ones that teach us about love, compassion, forgiveness, gentleness, beauty, celebration and love of the body, that can mother us into our death. If we truly understand what jumping into the lap of the Mother is while we are alive, then in our death, we will be able to find the lap of the Great Mother on the other shore.

Dreams

Maltese Goddess of Upper and Underworld, Monica Sjöö, **1998**

Dreams are a way that we can connect our unconscious with our conscious in order to truly "wake up." Some dreams are a continued processing of the day's activities, and others are more connected with deeper transformation, while still others are premonitions. Many cultures, such as the Malaysian Senoi, value dreams as an integral part of the fabric of the well-being of the community. Important dreams are listened to and acted upon. In very early times, women who bled together would no doubt dream together, accessing wisdom and knowledge for their communities. The Dreaming Goddess of Malta, mentioned earlier, sleeps in the dream position now seen practiced in Tibetan dream yoga, lying on the right side with the right arm placed under the head. She speaks to dream incubation — where a person might enter the temple bringing a question of importance to ask the Goddess for a healing dream. Similar reclining images have been found carved into the rock entranceway of the Paleolithic cave of La Magdeleine in France.

The Tibetan "delog" (pronounced DAY-loak) tradition is a truly incredible practice in which the practitioner's body actually dies for about five days. The body has no appearance of life as it lays cold and breathless, without a heartbeat. This practice is perhaps beyond dreaming, dream incubation and trance. However, it reveals the ability of consciousness to separate from the living body to journey into other realms and lands of being. It is a true account of the experience of the practitioner in what happens after death who returns to tell the story. It is neither a near-death experience nor a visionary experience. It is a true death experience. A noted delog, Dawa Drolma, who

130

passed away in 1941, received instructions from the Goddess White Tara in her youth in visions and dreams to prepare for such a journey.

At sixteen, against the advice of all her lamas and teachers, she entered into the death state and began her journey of consciousness through "the pure and impure displays of mind," often accompanied by Tara from land to land. (Drolma, **Delog**, p .ix) Upon her return, she was able to vividly remember everything she saw and heard. In her own words, "I let my mind settle. In a spacious and extremely blissful frame of mind, I experienced a state of sheer lucidity . . . .I was fully aware of the fundamental condition of my mind in all its ordinariness. Because that awareness was unimpeded, it was as though I could hear all sounds and voices in all lands, not just those in my immediate environment." (ibid. p. ix,x) She received information from relatives and teachers in the land beyond death of people that she knew in her life, and gave them important messages upon her return to the land of the living.

As an ally of death, dreams reflect a microcosmic aspect of the macrocosmic creative cycle of the universe. We sleep and dream, and awaken again. In the dreamstate, if we are lucky and have learned to pay attention, at least some of the time, we can continue to learn about our own mysterious being. If we cultivate a relationship with our dreams, we can actually learn to "practice" dying — that is, we can acknowledge our surrender to the numinous dark before we fall asleep, affirm our trust and faith in the greater whole, and let go into the experience, perhaps with an intention. We can enter into the reality of the dreamstate and acknowledge its importance as much as our waking reality — that which we often refer to as the only reality. In this way, we expand our consciousness and open ourselves to getting messages that can change our lives.

I had a premonition dream of the 1989 Loma Prieta earthquake in San Francisco the morning of its occurrence. I listened to the dream — though not as thoroughly as I needed to — but was able to take care of some details about my house prior to the earthquake — like making sure I knew where a wrench was in the event I needed to turn off the gas. I woke up from that dream asking my then partner to leave a wrench out before he left in the morning. In my dream, I found myself in a building in which I often worked holding classes and private sessions. When the earthquake occurred, I was in that building, in private session. Following that dream, I had another premonition dream of an earthquake in the Bay Area where my mother lived, and was able to call her ahead of time to warn her. The tremor was not as severe as the one before it, but my mother was glad to have had some notice. I have had dreams in which I have encountered my deceased parents, and upon waking have had the distinct feeling that they are simply in another form. I have also had dreams at the time of death of two friends — one woke me up when I heard my name being called by her, and the other woke me up when I experienced an intense display of light pouring from a fountain. I felt I was being directly contacted by both of these women as they were dying. My limited experience with dreamwork has taught me to have less fear of death.

A woman in one of my journey circles revealed to the circle of women some of her dream experience relating to death. Her experience shows how dreams can be a doorway into another realm beyond what we identify as "life," calling us to expand our definition of what we refer to as "death." Kim's friend, Glenna, was diagnosed with Hodgkin's disease when she was in her twenties. She was the first close person in Kim's life to die and Glenna's death had a profound impact on her. Kim had a series of dreams about her friend, and the ones I include here are the ones dealing with messages and teachings from Glenna.

Kim's dreams:

I see Glenna dancing and so happy that it makes me happy too. She turns, looks at me and says "You the living should not be sad about us. We are in a much better place." I stepped towards her to tell her how much I miss her and she disappeared before my eyes.

The next dream occurred during a time when Kim practiced a technique prior to falling asleep that produced dreams of a psychic nature. She would place her hands on the area of her ovaries and breathe into them. As she fell asleep she would ask a question. On the night of the following dream, her question before falling asleep was "Where is Glenna?"

Glenna and I were having a conversation just like we had done so many times. I asked her what it is like to die. She said that is like the best acid trip that you've ever had, only much much better. She went on to say that at first the light is painfully blinding. It was as if you see the energetic light being emitted from everything in the universe (Mother Luminosity?) She said that you then become aware of your "essence." I asked her to show me and she suddenly became a substance that looked similar to mercury except that it was made up of pure light. It was incredibly silver, shimmering, and anything within sight of it was reflected both inside it and on its surface at the same time. It seemed both solid yet fluid and transparent. It was so beautiful that I began to cry and I told her that I love her and that I miss her. She said, "I know" and then she was gone. When I awoke I was crying but I finally felt a sense of peace and acceptance regarding the loss of my friend. I have not dreamed about her again.

Kim felt these dreams to be actual communications between herself and Glenna regarding death. Kim has related to me that these dreams have helped her in lessening her own fear about dying.

Two years following my mother's death, my sister had a dream in which she was talking to my mother on the telephone. My mother said to my sister in this dream, "It's a mistake. I didn't die." Jamie and I discussed what the meaning of this dream might be and came to the conclusion that perhaps my mother was trying to communicate that it is a mistake for us to think that we die when our bodies die. She said my mother appeared fine, and was talking with her in a very "normal" way. It was such a strong dream for Jamie that it woke her up from a sound sleep.

Because sleeping and dreaming are akin to dying and entering another world, like traveling between the worlds as the shemama/shaman does, perhaps we can learn to place less emphasis on our identity as the body, and learn to embrace our wholeness as beings who are not bound by the limiting beliefs of the mind that thrives on the need to control. If we can learn to surrender this identity and need, we can open to a less linear and more circular way of experiencing life and ourselves.

Dreams help us to see that we are more than the body. They help us to encounter other realms where it is possible to access information and healing. This access of course requires attention — lucid dreaming and Tibetan dream yoga are two examples of this kind of attention to dreams that enables the practitioner to gain knowledge and insight. There are a number of hidden Tibetan spiritual teachings called *termas*, meaning "mother treasures," that have come through dreams to certain practitioners down through time. These extensive and detailed termas were often hidden by predecessors in remote geographical places with predictions made about when they would be discovered in future times. Writer Vicki Noble told me that she felt her Motherpeace Tarot was a terma, as much of the information and imagery she incorporated into her work was revealed to her in her dreams.

The patriarchal mind set (what I call PMS) does not really understand dying. It tries to avoid it. If we can learn to really embrace death as a time of great transformation, we can learn to be more present in our lives. Many myths tell us of events taking place in the spirit world or dreamtime before they actualize in the physical world. This means that the spirit world gives birth to the physical — what manifests physically has a reality first in the world of spirit. Where were you before you were born?

Holger Kalweit quotes a Netsilik Eskimo in **Dreamtime and Inner Space**: "The world is not only that which we can see. It is enormous and also has room for people when they die and no more walk about down here on earth. Mankind (sic) does not end its existence because sickness or some other accident kills its animal spirit down here on earth. We live on, and there are those who say that it is what we call the soul that prevents us from dying. This is not simply what the shamans tell us, those who understand the hidden things; ordinary people who know how to dream have many times seen that the dead appeared to them, just as they were in life. Therefore we believe that life does not end here on earth." (Kalweit, **Dreamtime and Inner Space**, p. 8) For these Eskimos, dreams of ordinary people in addition to those of shamans contain information about the true nature of death allowing people to accept that the death of the body or "animal spirit" is not the end of life.

Oracles

Perhaps a lesser-known ally of death is the oracle. According to Dianne Skafte, an oracle "is the instrumentality or medium by which a deity makes known its will. Communications inspired by divine inspiration are also known as oracles." (Skafte, **Listening to the Oracle**, p.3) Because oracular divination reaches out to us from the numinous mysterious space beyond ordinary reality, it would seem that the world beyond death intersects this same reality from which oracles emerge — as in dreams and trance. During the time of the proliferation of the Goddess cultures, women gathered together in a collective, practicing their divinatory rituals rooted in menstrual wisdom, would serve as the channel for the oracle. Across time, these practices took new forms as in the oracle of Delphi in early Greece. Delphi means "womb" and in this oracle, the great Earth Mother was worshipped as Delphyne, Womb of Creation.

It has been said that the priestess would enter a trance state after breathing in vapors emitted from cracks in the earth and from chewing laurel leaves. She would then serve as wise counsel to those who came to her. Whether or not the breathing in of the vapors of the earth was actually true (some writers have noted that there are no geothermal sites at Delphi and so question the source of these vapors) the metaphor of connecting to the earth in order to receive wisdom reveals that the earth herself is the living deity — the primal Ge, or Gaia. The priestess breathing in the vapor-breath of the living earth to mingle with her own, whether it was a psychic or physical phenomena or both, would undoubtedly undergo a transformation in consciousness. The priestess was referred to as the pythoness or pythia, a remembrance of the early Neolithic Snake Goddess who was symbolic of divine female power and connection to the primal creative shakti. From the depths of the earth, the pythia would draw upon the realms associated with "dreams, healing, communication with the dead, artistic inspiration, prophecy, and second sight."(ibid., p.69)

The oracle at Delphi was overtaken in patriarchal times and became known as Apollos's oracle after he murdered Delphyne. However, this is just another story of the co-option of the Goddess and Her powers as men's distorted desire to be as powerful as the Goddess grew. And of course, because of greed, domination and fear, the oracle was eventually destroyed, as are all things in the end when consumed by this malignancy. The Christian emperor, Theodosius, closed the oracle and Arcadius finished the takeover by having the temple completely destroyed. Nevertheless, in this consumption, there is always rebirth, and with the emergence of Goddess spirituality today, we are seeing the return of oracular wisdom, based on woman's way of knowing the world — through the womb, the heart, the mother-mind and the earth.

Many other oracular sites existed in the Mediterranean area, as in

Greece and Malta. The rock-cut city of the dead on Malta, the Hal Saflieni Hypogeum, mentioned earlier in the discussion of megalithic tombs, has a chamber within it now noted as the Oracle Room. The recess within this room provides extraordinary acoustics, probably accentuating the oracular communications from those who spoke with the dead. I had the wonderful experience of sitting in the Hypogeum with several women chanting to the Goddess. Our voices became one, and filled the space with a kind of numinous quality; other women in the group who heard us were very moved by the sound. Other temples of Malta — Mnajdra, Hagar Qim and Tarxien — also include similar architecture in which acoustical reverberation allows for a voice to be heard throughout the vaults — probably a stunning and mind-altering experience. It does not seem any accident that these oracular chambers were placed within the womb-tomb-temples, where the living and the dead were joined together in spiritual union.

Even though we hear about priestesses and priests serving the Goddess as channels for the oracle, I believe that we are all channels for Her wisdom, and that we don't necessarily need a medium to connect to the guidance emanating from the earth and the realms of mystery. I believe there is a deep longing in the individual and collective human psyche crying to be in connection with these realms and that oracular wisdom is actually all around us. Dreams, divination tools such as the Tarot and Runes, a message from the radio at the right time or an appearance of an animal offering a telepathic communication are all examples of oracular presence, if we pay attention.

We can learn to feel in harmony with our uni-verse (or yoni-verse, as "uni" is a cognate of "yoni," meaning "source") in a multi-leveled way whereby we feel simultaneously connected to the earth and to the numinous world as an everyday experience. With a connection such as this, our fear of death and dying would be greatly diminished because we would know that we are more than just our bodies, and that our consciousness is interconnected in a vast sacred web of life. We would know and feel in our bodies a sense of being held by something greater than ourselves and by experiencing direct communication with that Greatness/Goddess, we would learn to trust our coming and going as a part of the dance of the Mystery. A flower and a tree do not have any intermediaries informing them of how to find connection to the earth. They do it themselves. By experiencing this connectedness on a daily basis, we would be in tune with our environment and be skilled in hearing and reading the messages from our surroundings.

When we live in harmony rather than in isolation created by belief in separation, telepathy increases. I believe telepathy to be a major component of oracular wisdom. Telepathy is based on the interconnectedness of all beings — as the Vietnamese Buddhist monk, Thich Nhat Hanh, calls "interbeing." We find this telepathy when we acknowledge the fluidity of our true nature. When I lived in the spiritual community mentioned earlier, we referred to ourselves as a "mental nudist colony" — another way of saying that we recognized telepathy. We were even able to mirror to each other when we were out of "sync" — when we were not paying attention to the telepathy, and we would remind each other of our telepathic communion and our responsibility to it. I raised my children to honor telepathy, and have said things to them like "you were very telepathic when you did that." They have grown up with a strong sense of what telepathy is and they are smarter, more attentive human beings because of this wisdom. Oracles serve to remind us of this connection and help us to feel the Mystery of the unseen numinous realms, connecting us to the unknown and showing us doorways between the worlds.

A very particular oracular practice in some cultures is the practice of necromancy, receiving oracles from the dead. Since all that lives is born from the body of Earth, all that dies returns to her. Earth, then, is the home of the dead — a reality our ancestors deeply revered. "Spirits who joined with all-knowing Earth became wise. They acquired power to see the future, reveal secrets, and provide beneficial guidance. If a living person contacted them, he or she could gain knowledge of many hidden things." (ibid., p. 214) If we truly believed our ancestors to be there for us beyond the veil, how would this inform our lives? How could we experience more joy and ecstasy in our daily life experience by connecting to the wisdom of our beloved dead? What would they tell us?

Necromancy was not only a practice of the ancient world. Even though it appears that consulting with the dead was a well-developed practice among the Egyptians, Assyro-Babylonians and Etruscans, there is also an indication that people practiced this art during the classical period. Odysseus was said to have consulted with the oracle at Epiris about his journey homeward, a site associated with Persephone, goddess of the underworld and land of the dead. In the medieval and Renaissance periods of Europe, wise healers would summon the dead to ask for assistance in healing and possible curing of illnesses. (ibid., p. 216)

In modern-day Greece, in the province of Inner Mani, elder women, said to be knowledgeable in the secrets of the grave, exhume and read the bones of loved ones. They come face-to-face with the Goddess' process of decay as they unearth the remains and literally put their hands into the decaying corpse. They wash and scrape the bones and lay them in the sun to dry. Coming face-to-face with the actual decay process is no doubt a sobering and deeply authentic experience of what happens to the body in death. It would be very difficult to maintain a denial of death under these circumstances. Author and therapist Dianne Skafte writes, "I believe that we can strengthen our connection to oracles by devoting mindful thoughts to images of bodily decay. Only after studying ancient practices for a long time did I finally recognize the intimate connection between oracles and the buried dead. I began to understand that in the earliest times people looked downward into the earthy dark for guidance and comfort. The caves, the snug womb-like shelters, the moist hollows in rocks and trees — these were our first temples. The earth pressed oracles upon us, body to body. And where the body is, death will naturally follow." (ibid., p. 220) I, like Skafte, believe that apprehension of oracular wisdom is blocked if our consciousness is locked into a fear of death — a fear of dissolution of the "me."

When we open to understanding the cycle of life we begin to know that dissolution is a part of the whole. In this understanding, we can learn to let go of our fear and to embrace the dance of life itself. We can learn to connect directly with the earth herself to find healing, solace, love and nurturing, like a tree or plant. Life is not static — on the contrary, it is ecstatic. In letting go of fear about death, I believe only then are we able to open into the experience of life as it was truly meant to be lived. In this openness, we can feel the warm breath of the magical and unspoken realms melt away the cold beliefs in lonely endings.

Ralph's Story

Author's father, Ralph, photographer unknown

My first profound experience with death and dying was with my father, Ralph, who passed over seventeen years ago. He was an unusual human being. I am convinced that he would have been a shaman had be been born into a shamanic culture. Ralph was born with a fused spine — he had no discs between his vertebrae. This made his life experience very different than that of most people. He had to endure ridicule and the stigma of looking and being different. His own very "Christian" family emotionally rejected him, causing a deep wound of abandonment. He was told he would never find a woman who would want to marry him and have children with him, and to not hope for it. He was also told it would be very difficult for him to be "successful" in the work place. He eventually defied all of these negative messages, married my mother and together they had five children.

He was very successful in business, but he was not really of that world, and so could not maintain the necessary façade to live in it. He was an alcoholic — that eventually caused much suffering for our family. My parents divorced when I was fourteen. In a posh community, my mother and her five children went on welfare, and my father left the family, moving to Mexico to find a way to establish a business. He had been in love with Mexico and the Mexican people for a long time. For a while, due to his alcoholism, he struggled, living in his car for a time, and would have died had it not been for the loving kindness of a family that cared for him. After that experience, something changed in him, and he was able to eventually stop drinking — no AA, no twelve-step — he just stopped.

My father was, perhaps, an early beatnik. He loved simplicity, nature and authentic people. He was artistic, sensitive and kind-hearted, and, deeply wounded. When he became sick in his sixties, I was living in the spiritual community I mentioned earlier in this book, which had a sister satellite community in California. He came to live with us there after being hospitalized so that I could care for him. He needed to sleep in an iron lung at night, so we parked his lung in our living room and the people living with my then partner and myself shared his nighttime care with us. When I learned I was pregnant, there came a point where I needed to go back to the "mother community" in Tennessee to have my baby. Other community members continued to live with him and care for him as long as the city community existed. When it was time to move on, they moved my father back to his home where my mother continued care for him.

Even though my parents had divorced years before, they lived together after my father stopped his drinking. All this time, he slept at night in the iron lung. His experience with the iron lung lasted about ten years. In the late summer of 1986, my father became ill and was hospitalized, never to return home. He had expressed at the beginning of that year that he knew it was probably the year in which he would die.

We left the Farm community in 1984 and moved back to California. I was able to be around for my parents. When my father became ill in 1986, I tended to him in the hospital as best I could, and then moved him to a nearby convalescent hospital, where I spent as much time with him as possible. My children were very little, and so I had to juggle my life in order to make things work. In my psychedelic days, I had promised myself that I would take care of my elders, my aging parents in their later years. It felt like the only right thing to do.

It was by no means a picnic. I had to speak my mind and come from the heart in caring for him. And I had to learn very quickly about the best way to help him pass on, since I felt neither the rest of my siblings, my mother, nor my father's siblings knew how to be emotionally present. I am not sure that my father's mother, sisters and brother even wanted to be. My father was seventy, and I did let his family know that if they wanted to see him, they had better come. His ninety-three-year-old mother came and visited him; she tried to "mother" him, but I could see it was too late for that — he had too much anger and unhealed wounding to allow that.

My father was not one to have "processed" his wounding the way so many people do today. But, he had a kind of acceptance and surrender that seemed to come naturally from within him. The night before he died, he told me he was going to die. It felt as though he was actually consciously choosing to go. This was after we had spent some time together in preceding days when he was asking me about people he could see walking around — all of whom were dead. He told me of a "fog" he could see, and he spoke to me of "restitution" and of a "divine presence." It was as if he had lost all fear, and was in some kind of preparatory stage, waiting to go on a journey.

The most amazing thing about my father's passing was that he often suffered from high carbon-dioxide counts, called carbon dioxide poisoning, which frequently gave him a grayish hue. The night before he died, he was glowing pink, like a newborn baby. His aura was sparkling and he was surrounded by light. I felt very privileged to be in his presence, sharing his process. The privilege I felt came from experiencing the greatness of his true being, not from being with his personality. His essence was more present, more luminous, as he was making his way to the other shore. I told him that it was okay for him to die, and that from what I had heard, it was supposed to be a most amazing experience. That permission helped him to go. He had asked me to take him off of all drugs, which I was able to get permission to do.

So, Ralph passed on in a conscious state, after making his own choice. I was not with him when he actually left the body. I don't think I was prepared well enough to have kept my grief quiet in order to let him have the space to do what he needed. And I think he knew this, as he didn't ask me to stay the night with him. He passed alone. The nurses had come in to feed him, giving him some of his favorite food, mandarin oranges, and left the room for about fifteen minutes, and came back to check on him and found him gone. He had waited until he was alone. His roommate, whom my father told he was "leaving," had gone home for the weekend. I had gone home for the night. The nurses had left the room. I knew from the night before when I saw how he looked that he was entering a state of grace, and was passing into the Mystery.

He was more than my father; he was a most amazing being whose light was a blessing for anyone able to feel and see it. My father had a life of difficulty, and so, could be quite difficult. But the true nature of his being was pure, and in his death, I felt he was released from the ignorance suffered by the personality. I arrived shortly after he passed, and read from the **Tibetan Book of the Dead** to help guide him in the bardos. The feeling in his room was holy. It was not scary or weird. I could feel that his spirit had expanded to fill the room. Comparing this to what I have witnessed in the **Tibetan Book of the Dead** videos leaves me feeling that something is missing in those teachings.

Because I have spent much time with natural childbirth, both as birthing mother and assistant midwife, and have now spent some time with death, I can say that the energy feels the same. I was not well versed in death at all at the time of my father's passing, but I know what I felt in that room, and it felt just like a birth. I really don't know how the concept of failure, as is warned against in the Tibetan teachings, enters into such an experience.

To have closure with my father's passing meant to me that only loved ones who really knew him could authentically facilitate his memorial. I chose to eulogize my father and share with others the experiences I had with him in his dying process. I felt that it was important not only for people to see and feel the real way to have a meaningful memorial service, but also to know that death doesn't have to be hidden from view, that we can share it with one another, and that it is a privilege to do so. The authenticity of the memorial touched everyone's heart, in a very real way. I could sense a deep and profound closure, one that helped to make the meaning of life more visible.

Because I chose to facilitate his service, I had a realization about how the patriarchal way of "doing" funerals protects most people from experiencing true feeling and how difficult it is for people to feel safe enough to truly express themselves, wholly/holy in the body. What is missed in celebrating a loved one's life in their passage of death is cause enough for grief, let alone the passing of the being. My father's service was very simple. I also realized that people engage in elaborate distractions and attending to detail to avoid the real feelings of loss, sadness and grief. If a funeral is perfectly planned and "performed" then people won't have to be real together. Our denial about death and our dissociated funerary rituals are a perfect match.

To have taken care of him in his sickness, helped him through his death and facilitated his memorial, felt as natural as anything I could have done. It felt right. Being with him through the experiences of caretaker and death-rebirth midwife allowed for much healing. Because my father had been an alcoholic during my growing-up years, needless to say, I suffered in a dysfunctional household. But, being with him, his pain and his suffering in his later years — just being with him — created room for compassion and forgiveness. I do not know if I could have done this with him had he sexually abused me, or more deeply emotionally and/or physically abused me, without any prior healing of that.

I am not saying that all people should caretake their elders if they have had deep psychological and or physical wounding inflicted by them. I do know the power of forgiveness and compassion, but I do not know that in the accomplishment of this healing, one is then ready to be in intimate contact with the abuser. I could forgive my father's abusiveness while at the same time create boundaries with him regarding how I needed to be treated by him if I was to caretake him. And I did have to say that I couldn't continue if he could not treat me respectfully. I do not mean to say that as a child I was not hurt by his behavior — I was. But, I was able to do my own healing work, and come to terms with my own pain in my adult life, and develop compassion for his suffering.

In some teachings about death, as in **The Tibetan Book of Living and Dying,** we are instructed to observe that sometimes dying people will release a lot of anger and fear, and say and do things reflecting this. When this happens, the book instructs us to not react, just to let the person do what they need to do. I feel that when reactive anger and fear behaviors are no longer personal, and one is not the target of a person's anger, then it is acceptable to let it go. I had to be in a relationship with my father where it was simply not okay for him to act out his pain on me. I could be compassionate with it, but not take it. I also had to create this boundary with my mother when I took care of her in her last days.

There was no other way for me to do what I had to do. It was good for them to have been given that boundary because it allowed each of them to have more peace. When a person is not busy spewing out controlling, demanding, angry directives, but instead, is gratefully and respectfully asking for help, the energy around them has a very strong healing quality, because love and respect create spaciousness. Both of my parents were able to learn about this — not perfectly, but they could hear it, and work with it.

In the time I spent with my father through his dying process, I became the mother — not inappropriately or co-dependently, but authentically. It makes perfect sense to me that in the times in history, when women were loved and respected, we were not only the bringers and nurturers of life, but were also the lovers who said good-bye, bidding the sweet fruit of our wombs farewell, bestowing blessings and guidance on the journey life takes back to the Great Womb of the Great Mother.

I believe that women's funerary practices and rituals are very different than what has been given to us by male dominated religions founded by men who have suffered from the very painful and life-denying separation from the Goddess. Because women bleed, grow life inside our wombs, nurture, teach, create, and selflessly love, our rituals of birth and death are born from a place that most men do not know, though their passage into this world is through it. No woman in her wisdom-state would succumb to the idea that her womb is impure. That would mean that we would have to say that all life is impure and defective. No mother, in her natural wisdom-state looks into the wide-open gaze of her newborn child and thinks her child to be an impure fruit of her womb, plagued with aggression and poisonous passion. The only thing passed between mother and child in that moment is an indescribably delicious, succulent love.

When I felt like a mother to my father in his dying, who looked like a newborn, I felt a tremendous love for his being — it was different than what I felt for my babies, and yet, at the same time, it was a very familiar feeling. This is the gift I think people who are prepared to midwife a loved-one in a loving way in their dying receive — a sense of the Sacred, and a glimpse of what lies ahead for oneself. This experience of love opens the heart where transformation can occur.

This transformation in dying is something that can benefit all who are able to fully show up and be present — the dying person as well as those who attend. My father's deathing changed my life, and opened doors for me into my spiritual path in ways that could not have been planned. Nor could I have learned it in school or from books. I learned it by becoming an apprentice to life itself — the way women used to pass on their teachings. I was opened up, my heart was pierced, and Goddess entered me. I have been walking that path ever since, uncovering hidden truths and claiming my Sacred Feminine Authority.

Death and Sacred Sexuality

Yin and Yang Within the Goddess, Monica Sjöö, **1980**

Certainly in our Euro-Western, patriarchal puritanical so-called culture we find it very difficult, nearly unthinkable, to find a holistic, healthy association between death and sexuality. The only currently "acceptable" connection is through misogyny, domination, violence towards women and sado-masochism. Since patriarchal religions are founded on a split between mind and body — with body, earth, dark, blood, and female being "bad" and "wrong" and the intellect, light, mind and male being "good" and "right" — there is no view within this framework that allows for the sacredness of the body.

Liberation is pursued away from the body. The body is seen as defiled. How can we expect any kind of spiritual salvation for humanity when the collective mind of the world's major religions regards the body (read "female") as unclean and impure? The degradation of the earth and our cold, isolating fear of death are directly related to this ignorant and confused ideology. If we do not accept that we return to the body of the Mother, the earth, in our death, how can we find peace in dying? And, of course, with denial of the sacredness of the body, earth and female, comes the anti-pleasure judgment of sexuality as sinful.

What was it that the ancients knew and revered about death and sexuality? As I have stated earlier, I do not believe our ancestors were ignorant about the nature of sexuality and procreation. We have also seen how our ancestors believed in death and regeneration as part of life. It would seem, then, that they embodied knowledge of life and death that understood the role of sexuality — not just as a function of procreation, but also as a celebration of life. Not that they understood the scientific data as we do today, but nevertheless embraced wisdom about life, sex, death and regeneration. In **Sacred Pleasure**, author Riane Eisler states, " Specifically, what I am suggesting is that our ancestors celebrated sex not only in relation to birth and procreation, but as the mysterious — and in that sense, magical — source of both pleasure and life." (Eisler, **Sacred Pleasure**, p. 58) This indeed, is not the usual interpretation among the mostly male scholars who have studied the Paleolithic and Neolithic.

Many images from the Paleolithic in cave art show representations of female and male animals in pairs relating to new life in spring as well as of female and male sexual organs together. (ibid., p. 61) The discovery of a stone engraving from Isturitz in the French Pyrenees dated to be some 20,000 years old depicting a phallus inside a vagina, indicates, according to Eisler, "not only a religious association with the act of coitus but also an understanding of the role of sexual intercourse in the birth (or in their terms, rebirth) of life. "(ibid.) It is important to remember that our early ancestors did not live in a split world. They did not separate themselves from nature, nature from the spiritual, or the spiritual from day-to-day living. Sexuality, by definition, was sacred.

Because of androcentric biases in archeological scholarship, the importance of women and the significance of women's reality have been criminally overlooked. It has become quite obvious with current feminist scholarship that early people deeply respected and were awe-struck by the creative sexual power incarnated in the body of woman — so much so, that most of the images we see from the Paleolithic and Neolithic are female.

Many, such as the Acheulian Goddess from the Israeli-Syrian border area, thought to be dated somewhere between 232,000-800,000 BCE, the Goddess of Willendorf from Austria dated 25,000-30,000 BCE and and the Goddess of Laussel from France, dated 25,000 BCE are wide-hipped, large-bellied, perhaps pregnant, and large-breasted, depicting the mysterious, creative revitalizing powers of the uni(yoni)verse embodied by woman. It appears to me that because our ancestors lived in close communion with the earth and cosmos they were able to experience their natural, organic shameless birthright — love, pleasure and ecstasy. Because death and rebirth were united, sacred sexual rituals were enacted as part of funerary practices. (ibid., p. 64)

Why would sacred sexual rituals be included in funerary practices of the ancients? Since it seems that the ancients experienced a comprehension of the relationship of sexuality and birth, it would make sense that they also saw a connection between sexuality and rebirth. It would seem that sexuality was considered the basis of the revitalizing principle of life itself, hence the evolution of later pagan celebrations such as Beltane, known to many as the time of the Maypole dance.

This ritual was originally a celebration of sacred sexuality in which people made love in the fields to ensure the fertility and abundance of the crops and to ensure the nurturing of the new life of spring. Many of the womb-tombs previously discussed had narrow openings facing east which would receive the rays of the sun. Eisler gives us a reason to ponder as to why this was important in her discussion of Aegean tombs: "So the additional puzzle that the small opening of many round Aegean tombs faced east to the rising sun is solved if, as Goodison proposes, the vitalizing sun was in prehistoric belief systems associated with woman's life-giving powers.

"Moreover, the association of sex, woman, and the sun would further explain why, as Goodison documents, solar and feminine symbols are so often found in prehistoric Aegean tombs — for they would both be symbolic of regeneration or rebirth." (ibid., p. 65) The sun was considered female by numerous early cultures long before its association with the male appeared. In what Eisler presents, we are shown that the penetrating rays of the sun into the tombs were symbolic of the Goddess' creative powers, stirring life anew inside the tomb, much like the life force stirs with the first "quickening" within the womb.

The so-called "Minoan" culture of Crete evidenced an unabashed respect for the place of sexuality in the peaceful, creative culture that flourished there from 3,000 — 1,500 BCE. The Cretans enjoyed a vital faith in the Goddess and the feminine principle, reinforced by a woman-centered society. Their dedication to the Goddess "involved a glorification of the meaning of sex. Fertility and abundance were the purpose and the desire, sex was the instrument, and for this reason its symbols were everywhere." (Gadon, **Once and Future Goddess**, p. 87)

A woman's body is equipped with the only organ in existence designed entirely for the experience of ecstasy. The orgasmic capability of the clitoris in sacred sexuality is much more significant than just a simple release of tension as a result of genital stimulation. The female orgasm is a pathway to experiencing the bliss and sacredness of surrender to the Goddess in an egoless opening to the vastness of her mystery and magic — a way to contact the unveiled presence of her love through sacred trance. When women experience this, they are transformed into priestesses, channeling the wisdom and love of the Goddess for the good of all. This is not to say, however, that just having orgasms is the key to this ministry. A spiritual intention in sacred lovemaking creates the openness for ecstatic union with the Goddess.

Understanding the nature of sacred sexuality is, however a powerful key, and seeing its relationship to death and rebirth is extremely important. The good news is that we don't have to fear death and we don't have to live in denial of the cyclical nature of the cosmos. Women can know this from being in tune with our fertility and menstrual cycles, the rhythms of the moon as well as with the tantric nature of our sexuality. For men, the post-coital state is sometimes referred to as "le petit mort" — the little death. He is spent. For women, this is not the case. A woman's sexual capacity is multi-orgasmic and as a result, she can reach heightened spiritual states. Researchers have noted that within women there are actual neurological connections between female sexuality and trance experience.

> "In women's brains there are unique neural links between the fore-brain and the cerebellum, which allow sensations of physical pleasure to be directly integrated into the neocortex, or high brain center.
> This explains why some women experience orgasm so intense they enter religious trance, or altered states of consciousness. And this ecstatic female orgasmic experience, in which the physical and the spiritual are fused and realized as one, is at the core of all mystical experience. This is why, in the original religion of the Great Mother, body and mind and spirit are always integrated." (Sjöö and Mor, **The Great Cosmic Mother**, p.53)

In sacred sexuality the experience of egolessness in union is truly ecstatic. Since egolessness is a kind of death and can be associated with ecstasy, what are the implications for humanity if we approach our own death of the body in this light?

Sacred sexuality is a journey through death and rebirth, as one surrenders to the greater whole and comes alive again in joyous, pristine awakening. In some spiritual teachings it is said that when death is received in joy it is itself the greatest total cosmic orgasm — it is making love with the Divine. I have experienced in sacred orgasm — that is, orgasm of the spirit as well as of the body — an expansive merging with a pure, warm and luscious white light, causing within my body an unspeakable experience expressed in the flowing of tears of joy. Is this the Mother Luminosity following death in Tibetan Buddhism? I think so. I have experienced this state with and without a partner.

There is a reason why patriarchal religions haven't wanted women to know our sexual capacities. There is a reason why the heinous crime of clitorectomy has been performed for centuries and continues to be — women's sexual anatomy/autonomy is a threat to the patriarchal mind.

I include here a reprinting of a Gnostic mythology, origins unknown to me, given to me by a dear friend, emphasizing women's creative psycho-spiritual sexual potential:

"The title of this talk, 'And the Fifth Element Was Her Laughter,' comes from a Gnostic creation myth in which Sophia, the embodiment of wisdom, begins the creation of the universe by masturbating. Her orgasm releases a flow of vital ethers which coalesce into a new being, Sophia Achamoth. In her turn, the second Sophia also masturbates, and her orgasmic flow fills all of space, creating the first matter of the cosmos. Her passions become the four elements, and her laughter is the fifth, which was called the luminous substance of the universe."

The Gnostic doctrine goes on to say that creation is not a one-time event, but a continuous process. Every time a woman has an orgasm, she releases an energy similar to that of the original Sophia's, a subtle etheric substance which eventually coalesces into matter. What's worth noticing here is that the goddess' organ of generation is not the womb, but the clitoris. The paradigm of creativity is not birthgiving, but self-stimulated orgasm."

It is very interesting to note that science is now devising theories about what existed prior to the big bang — what I term the big, "shebang." One such theory is called the "Mother Universe, a timeless dimension that has always existed and always will, bearing daughter universes down an endless corridor of time." (**US News & World Report**, *Mysteries of Outer Space*, p. 14) Princeton astrophysicist, J. Richard Gott, says of this theory, "This first universe created itself and was its own mother making the first matter in some way we will never be able to know." (**ibid.**, p. 23) It seems perhaps that the original Sophia might be able to help Dr. Gott answer what he sees as unanswerable.

Not only does this myth reveal the power of woman's creative potential, it emphasizes her ability to experience this awesome state alone. She is whole unto herself — continuously creating form out of her own sacred sexual pleasuring.

Again, I mention here the significance of the translation of "Om Mane Padme Hum" — the well-known Buddhist chant, meaning "hail to the deity of the clitoris vagina" which is certainly different from the more commonly accepted "hail to the jewel in the lotus." We can now agree that we know what the jewel and the lotus are. What do we feel in the body when we recognize that creativity is sexual at its core? What are the implications of this that relate to death and dying? To one feminist writer, Susun Weed, it seems that dying laughing with our eyes wide open would be a good way to pass from this world. Why not?

If the passions of the Goddess created the elements, our returning to those elements, her passions, while being embraced by her laughter seems to me to be a lot more fun than what I have been taught — to fear the sharp sickle of the grim reaper, to only land in burning fires if I have not been saved by the angry sky god's son, or to fight at the entrance of a womb for a space which I detest but must choose in order to purify my aggression and loathing towards my parents and my paltry human existence.

I find it deeply disturbing that in our own culture we are separated from the sacredness of the place of sexuality in death and from the truth of our ancestors regarding rebirth. The notions that impregnation occurs without sex for Mary and that birth for Athena is from the forehead of her father are very strange and peculiar ideas — only made possible by a need to see sexuality as sinful and dirty and by a fear of woman's creative power. A culture that emphasizes the power to punish and kill rather than the power to give life is grievously wounded. A culture that suffers from a blatant absence of the female magical life-giving images of pregnancy and birth in its religious-spiritual teachings, art and history is crippled by a rupture, a tear, in the very fabric of that which has given birth to it. This tear can only be mended by the restoration of the wisdom-view of the Goddess herself, coming alive in the hearts, minds and souls of Her children.

As the Hindu story of the great goddess Durga, The Chundi, reminds us — the gods themselves could not subdue the out-of-control demons destroying the land. This demonic force has been referred to as the "out of control male ego" in this mythology. The gods had to summon Durga, the Great Mother, to come and restore the harmony needed for life to flourish. Durga's promise is to always return to restore this harmony. We are in this time now where calling once again on the vast restorative powers of the Great Mother is what is needed to bring peace, unity and a remembrance of the sacred. Life and death are one. Sexuality in its sacred, honored place in the dance of life and death, as necessary as the warp thread is in the weaving of fabric, holds the delicate threads of life in the creation of an exquisite tapestry. This is a non-dualistic, non-objectified sexuality. It is a life-affirming, respectful enactment of the cyclical regenerative powers of the cosmos. Why is it that our ancestors lived in this reality and we have forgotten? What has happened to us that we have de-sacralized the very essence of life itself and replaced this truth with a twisted, distorted confusion and self-inflicted painful ignorance, steeped in violence, domination and hatred of women? We are far from the wisdom of revering our ancestors and what they knew and practiced.

In early human experience, the Goddess was seen as parthenogenic — she who gives birth to herself — the "Virgin Goddess." In this model, there is no separation. She is the All. All comes from Her womb, born through the gate of Her sacred yoni, and all returns to Her in death. She was the self-seeding Goddess. What does this mean? Because we are so accustomed to dualistic thinking, it might be difficult to imagine such a notion. For the ancients, this truth seems to have been a direct experience. The self-seeding Goddess loves Herself, and through this love she brings life into form. Science is coming to a realization of the parthenogenic mother.

The phallus belongs to the Goddess. It is Hers. It is not a separate appendage floating around in the sky to be used by the sky-gods to rape and

148

plunder — though this is what it has become in the current ruling paradigm. This condition is born of separation — the illusion fostered by patriarchy that men are separate from the Mother. Since nothing can be truly separate from Her, the desperation men feel at this loss is reflected in rape, violent sex and pornography — all, in my opinion, a frantic attempt, in its shadowy form, to reconnect with the feminine, with the Goddess.

Men without the Goddess get crazy. All one has to do is look at the Washington monument and realize the statement this structure makes as a metaphor of our times. However, in truth, the phallus emerges from the yoni. This is the true union. It is not the other way around. In sexual embrace between woman and man, the Goddess is loving Herself. There is Oneness experiencing Her own Oneness. Heterosexual union within the Goddess is Her sacred self-expression of regeneration. Other forms of sexual expression, i.e., lesbian, gay and autoerotic are also Her rituals of love and pleasure, all celebrating the magic and mystery of Her form.

Many forms of the phallic-headed Goddess were found in Neolithic graves, suggesting Her regenerative function. In a Cucuteni gravesite in northern Moldavia, thirty-two female figurines with snake or phallic shaped heads were excavated. One of these figures holds what appears to be an erect phallus. (Reis, **Through the Goddess**, p. 42) Gimbutas suggests that they were not necessarily male symbols, but perhaps, more accurately, portrayals of the spontaneous and life-promoting power of the Goddess. Patricia Reis contends that even though snakes and phalli were found conjoined in a single image of the female deity, revealing the bisexual nature of the Goddess, she *remained definitively female* (italics mine). "These are profound images of a religious nature which demonstrates an ancient concept of female wholeness. These phallic Goddesses provide a visual experience of unity and wholeness, a kind of coherence.

"They contain within one image the *complete* (italics mine) powers of self-conceiving regeneration." (ibid., p.45) These holistic images of the Goddess in her power of creation and regeneration emphasize unity rather than duality. Nothing is separated out into "a little man inside a woman" and a "little woman inside a man," or two halves of a whole that need to rely on the other half in order to feel complete. The Goddess is complete unto herself, giving birth to both forms. Monica Sjöö has expressed this idea of wholeness of the Goddess in her painting, "Yin/Yang Within the Goddess." (see page 95) This experience of wholeness within the One allows death to be a necessary part of the completion of the life cycle, meeting sexuality as the channel for regeneration.

Pitifully, what has been handed down to us in modern times as a recollection of this virginal Goddess is the Virgin Mary — a rather powerless, sexless image whose power is defined by her adoration of her son and who is impregnated by some guy in the sky who we can't be sure even asked for her consent. However, even with this co-opted image of the Goddess, many Catholics are now returning to the worship of Mary as the Black Madonna. It is as if the people are experiencing a kind of collective memory of the underlying power of the Goddess and see it and feel it reflected in the Black Madonna, much to the consternation of the male hierarchy within the church. Mary was not supposed to be worshipped, only respected as the Mother of Jesus, and in this, was considered less than her son.

Several evolutions of the Neolithic fish/toad goddess come to us as the Greek Baubo, also called Iambe, and as Heket, the Egyptian frog goddess known as the primordial mother of all existence. Baubo is the crone who lifts her skirts displaying her vulva to bring humor to Demeter as she mourns for Persephone in the underworld. Demeter's anger melts into laughter bringing a Spring thaw, and new life returns to the once frozen landscape. The sexuality of the crone is an important aspect of Baubo, as it is in the Celtic Sheela-na-gigs, another form of the fish/toad goddess. Both goddess forms are symbolic of the fertility and fecundity of She who is divine birthgiver and regeneratrix.

Shamanic practitioner Penny Barham states ,"The healing power of sexual humor was recognized and it was older women who had the maturity and confidence to deal with it." (Barham, **Goddessing**, p. 19) The crone, as the third face of the Goddess, reminds us of impermanence and transformation; her sexuality is vibrant, mature, and she uses it in sacred humor, not in a seductive or male-pleasing manner, but to remind us of where we come from, and where we go in our death. It has been said that the skirt-lifting and other Baubo-related behaviors were performed by women for women, restoring harmony and fruitfulness to the natural world as well as to the community.

There is no doubt that sexuality is what brings us the opportunity to experience physical form. However, sex alone is not enough. The body of our biological mother is the safe warm place of our gestation. Without this containment, we have no place to flourish. She nourishes us and brings us to wholeness, birthing us from her sacred yoni into form and continues to sustain us as we grow. And the whole entire cycle of life, birth, death, sexuality and rebirth is contained within the sacred body of our Great Mother. She is the Holiest of Holies. Reclaiming the sacredness of sex and shedding the fear of death will restore for humanity the ability to experience the sacred dance of coming and going in our daily lives, as the ancients were able to experience for millennia.

Remembering Vera

I just returned from the hospital tonight. Vera died about three hours ago. I didn't know Vera until I met her on her deathbed. She was in her eighties. Two nights ago, Teresa, a woman who attends my teaching circles, shared in circle about her experiences as caretaker for an elderly woman who was in the hospital. Teresa shared about how privileged she felt to be in the company of this woman and her daughter who looked to her

Vera, photo by Pam Sellars

as someone who could really be of help to them. I asked Teresa the woman's name and she said Vera. Teresa asked me to pray for her and I said I would.

Secretly, I wanted to tell Teresa she could call me if she needed to, but for some reason, I didn't say this to her. Today, I received a call from Kim, another woman who attends a different teaching circle. Kim said she was at the hospital with her friend and her friend's mother, Vera, and that Vera was dying. The family wanted me to come and be with them and help Vera pass over. Kim said Teresa was there too. I thought how amazing the Goddess is — how She holds within Her overlapping circles within circles. The synchronicity was beautiful. I didn't know Kim and Teresa knew one another, nor did they know they were both in relationship with me.

When I went to see Vera in the afternoon, she was conscious. I could see she was struggling with her breathing, but she was fully awake. The doctor had told her early in the day that she was probably not going to make it through the afternoon. I talked to her about dying, and she said she wasn't afraid. I told her it was fine for her to die, and that dying was part of the journey of life, and that we were all there to share with her. We held hands around her and formed a prayer circle. Her daughter, Pam, gave her permission to go whenever she needed to. She seemed to relax and move into a deeper surrender. Before I left, I told Vera that it was a privilege to meet her. She looked at me with clear eyes and said "thank you." I came back later in the evening, and she had been given some morphine shortly before I got there.

There was definitely a difference in her consciousness — she was not as present. She hadn't complained of any pain at all, and then seemed to have some pain of some kind and wanted morphine. I was sad that she was given the morphine, because I think it removed her somewhat from the experience she was having. I think sometimes that because we are not trained in the art

151

of dying, we don't understand the agitation and psychic pain that sometimes arise, and we think we have to deaden it, or make it go away.

If we had the teachings that there is nothing to fear, I don't think we would suffer from as much confusion during this time, when the elements of our being, as we know it, dissolve. We would be trained in what to expect, and could learn to go with the flow — to be present with the experience without having to change it. But still, she did remarkably well. We formed another prayer circle around her, and spoke lovingly to her and gave her as much permission as she needed to surrender.

During this circle, Vera died. Her breathing slowed down, and she simply took one last breath. We removed the flowers from the vases in the room and spread them out over her body. Music was playing. Even though this was a hospital setting, we were able to make it pretty and made it feel like a holy place. I hadn't been there but about forty minutes before she passed. The timing was exquisite.

The whole experience with Vera flowed from a place of Mystery that included me along the way. I was blessed to be part of it. To witness yet another being die in peace, surrounded by love, showed me even more the deep need to create empowering death-bed rituals. The ritual with Vera continued afterwards, as her body was honored with gentle washing and annointing with oil. She was in the tender hands of the Goddess — the women who loved her and cared for her.

How could it be any better? Loving women tending the dying, creating safe and sacred space for the loved one to pass from this world. It feels so natural and right, and at the same time I feel sadness at what we are offered instead. It is a total blessing to have the privilege to be with someone who is dying — they are the teachers of what we all eventually face. To have the opportunity to be in connection with someone in this transition allows us to shed our fear about the unknown and to be engaged in the living process of dying.

Death and the Sacred Body of the Goddess

Triple Cerridwen at Pentre Ifan Gromlech, Monica Sjöö, **1990**

To the ancients the body of the Goddess was sacred. From cave sites to large megalithic tombs, the legacy of the Goddess left to us by our ancestors is astounding, beautiful and magical. It is unbelievable that it has taken so long for us to see and hear what they have been saying to us. I suppose not too surprising since it is really recent feminist scholarship that has literally unearthed the Goddess for us to comprehend without male fear and bias.

It is not to say that the prospect of death did not frighten the ancients. I am sure that they experienced fear in their own way about death, as well as grieved their losses, but I think they embraced death in a much healthier way than that to which we are accustomed. Because much of the iconography from the Paleolithic and Neolithic is mostly female with accentuation on body parts affirming the generative and nourishing powers of the Goddess, how could meditating on these images help us in approaching a peaceful death?

The breasts of the Goddess were as important a symbol of nourishment to the dead as to the living. Gimbutas states, "As the most important attributes of the Goddess, they symbolize her presence and her regenerative potential in the grave. From the breasts on the walls of funerary monuments as well as from their association with vultures and owls it can be perceived that the breast symbolism is more complex than it appears. The breasts are not nourishing the living alone; more importantly, they are regenerating the dead." (Gimbutas, **Language of the Goddess**, p. 40-41) To consider being nourished at the breast in life and death might help us face our death with a kind of awe and wonder rather than fear and loathing.

This would of course require a shift in the consciousness of the current mind-set we experience, as in this mind-set, the body of the Goddess is not revered, but rather scorned and objectified. People do not want to embrace that which they scorn. It makes no sense. Men scorn the Goddess' body as they create the pornography that allows them to feel superior to that which has birthed them. Women scorn our own bodies by internalizing the messages from the patriarchal mind, learning to hate our own life-giving powerful creativity, seeking approval from the men who hate us. None of this makes any sense. And inside of this reality, the Goddess is not seen for who She is, as we slowly deprive ourselves of the beauty, grace and wisdom that we were meant to experience in life and in death.

In returning to a deep reverence of the cosmic mother in our daily lives — She whose milk has given name to the "Milky Way" and to "galaxy" (from the Greek "laktos," meaning "milk") — what would awaken in our consciousness that could help us understand the cyclical nature of life where we would not be so frightened of death that we would have to deny it, as we do now?

As has been previously revealed, a very sacred part of the body of the Goddess was the vulva — the gateway of life and death. The Indo-European word "cunt" is derived from the Goddess Kunda or Cunti, symbolized by the Goddess Kali who personified the sacred yoni. Such words as "cunning," "ken," "kin" and "country" are cognates of "cunt." How quite amazing that this word is used today as a pejorative and a profanity to cast insult. Why and how do you suppose this has come to be? What are the implications of this condition?

For the ancients, however, the vulva was the gateway of life and death — the place of sacred emergence and return. Aurignacian rock engravings dated at 30,000 years BCE show schematic drawings of the vulva symbolizing womb and vulva. Upper Paleolithic vulva symbolism includes different categories of vulva-consciousness: aquatic symbolism of the womb of the Goddess and her life-giving waters, seed and sprout as the sprouting of life, and oval swollen vulvas as the giving of birth. It is the seed/vulva symbolism that is of particular interest here in relationship to death. Vulva imagery was also depicted as seeds characterized by a dot in the center of a type of enclosure.

Sometimes a branch or budding tree was shown as a substitute for the vulva. As a symbol of the source of all life and cosmic womb, the vulva is analogous to the blossoming bud, unfolding its precious new life and coming into wholeness. It is well known that reference to flowers such as the lotus in more recent religions, like Hinduism, is really a reference to the vulva. Many spiritual teachers (mostly males we hear about) from Eastern traditions are considered to be "lotus born." What does it really mean to be "lotus born"? In Lepenski Vir, a Neolithic settlement of the late seventh and early sixth mil-

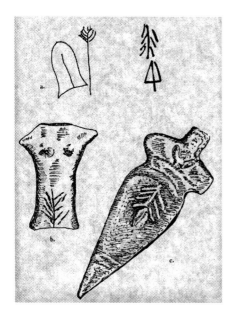

lennium BCE in northern Yugoslavia in the Danube River Basin, the large fish goddess figurines found there, carved on egg-shaped stones, show a female figure with incised vulva as well as labrynthine patterns symbolic of regeneration.

The floor plans of the temples themselves were in the shape of the female pubic triangle. The fish is a worldwide Goddess symbol; womb and fish, "delphos," are synonymous in Greek. Sheela-na-gigs, Irish carved symbols of squatting women revealing their vulvas, found on many churches prior to the sixteenth century, closely resemble the yonic statues of the Hindu Kali. Like the Kali statues, Sheela-na-gigs were representations of the Irish Caillech (pronounced like "Kali") or "Old Woman" Creatrix and death goddess; they protected doorways and were perhaps touched by the spiritual aspirant upon entrance, signifying a womb/vulva blessing, perhaps of protection, as one entered the womb-building.

Many church doors and windows are yonic in shape and seem symbolic of the womb, as does the vesica pisces, the aura surrounding Mary, in many herstorical images of her. There are even images of buddhas surrounded by a similar motif. The shape of the apse of a church is no doubt a remnant of the deep-seated imprint in the collective unconscious of the primal yonic-womb source. Though the Sheela-Na-Gigs are thought by some to be a precursor of the classic symbol of the vulva, the horseshoe, this symbol is actually quite old, dating back to the Paleolithic Horse Goddess. When a horse hoof is turned over, the image revealed is that of a yoni, and this symbol is found on Paleolithic cave walls and repeated much later in Etruscan pottery. In contemporary art, e.g., Georgia O'Keefe, the likeness of flowers to vulva is undeniable. On Cycladic platters found in tombs from the Aegean Bronze Age, vulvas and plants are seen together along with representations of the Goddess of Death and Regeneration.

From other finds in Old Europe, Gimbutas theorizes that pots decorated with dotted lozenges or filled with seeds could have symbolized the Mother's womb, and the seeds inside were perhaps the souls of the dead. She states, "In ancient Greece, pots with corn seeds kept near the household hearth

Above: a. *vulvas paired with branches, Upper Paleolithic caves, El Castillo, N. Spain and La Mouthe, S. France; b. early Vinca terracotta figure with branches at vulva, Jela, N. Yugoslavia, c. 5,200 BCE; c. bone plate, Neolithic figurine with branches and vulva, Gaban cave, N. Italy,* drawn by Melissa Meltzer

symbolized the dead who rest in the womb (pot) and are resurrected in the spring. The dead were called 'Demetrioi,' those who belong to Demeter, the Grain Mother, and who rest, like the corn, in the womb of that Goddess." (ibid., p. 145) In reference to the Hypogeum of Malta, Sybille von Cles-Reden says, "The Hypogeum consists entirely of curved lines, concave surfaces and rounded vaults. In the flickering light . . . these caverns must have suggested the protective darkness of the maternal womb in which the dead were laid out like seeds to be regenerated and made fertile again." (von Cles-Reden, **Realm of the Great Goddess**, p. 94) Here the dead are the seeds themselves. Cristina Biaggi also describes a tree with large round fruits, perhaps pomegranates, painted in red ochre on the ceiling of the Oracle room in the Hypogeum and suggests this to be a theme of death and rebirth. Perhaps the red pomegranates symbolize the womb, filled with the promise of seeds of fertility and eternal rebirth.

With the metaphor of interchangeable seed, vulva and plant lasting for millennia, rebirth was as much a part of death as dying itself. Returning to the sacred vulva of the Goddess in death was itself the promise of new life. If you seriously contemplate this truth of our ancestors, what do you feel about your own death?

From another perspective on the sacred body of the Goddess, feminist cultural anthropologist and art historian, Veronica Veen, discusses in her booklet **The Goddess of Malta,** the importance of recognizing symbolism, mostly in pottery decoration, as a revelation of the religious and world view of the early Maltese, as well as other Neolithic people. Symbols have been the language of cultures based on oral tradition. "Symbolic thinking" uses imagery in creative endeavors, such as pot-making, in which the object itself is symbolic of an important aspect of life and represents a connection to the greater whole.

For example, Veen notes the significance of pot, house, temple and tomb as interwoven manifestations of the Goddess Herself. Not only does the earth herself provide her body for people to mold her into shapes and forms, but she also remains a divine presence into which the dead are placed for rebirth. It is well known that many worldly myths speak of the first people being molded out of clay. Women were the first potters, taking the very substance of the Goddess in their hands and creating sacred womb-like vessels used for the purpose of containment. The house and temple of Neolithic construction were made from earth and stone as well as vegetable matter including straw and twigs — all materials of the body of the Goddess.

Water as a component of clay could be seen as the same amniotic waters necessary in creating life in the womb. Just like potters, mothers as life-givers and hearth tenders in their houses, enact the sacred creative act of shaping and molding children. Veen writes, " . . . an oven sanctuary of the Danube Culture displays a ritual of the transformation of corn into bread. Here the oven, like the pot (also made of earth), is the container where a

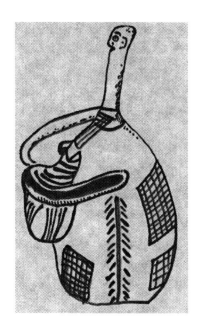

(raw) product of nature is transformed into a product of culture. The same can be seen in relation to the womb and house, the creation and education containers of human life, respectively." (Veen, **The Goddess of Malta**, p. 17) A marvelous ceramic pot from Myrtos, Crete, circa 2,800 BCE, shows the unmistakable connection with pot and Goddess as the mother pot encircles her baby pot with her arm as the baby pot rests on her hip.

In Africa, the ancient gravesite of the Akan was called an "asensie" meaning "place of pots." (Van Sertima, **Black Women in Antiquity**, p. 105) Many pots were inscribed with snakes (python, symbolic of female power), snails, lizards, frogs and crocodiles who were said to greet the deceased as they entered mother earth, the domain of Odiarouno, the regenerating goddess, after they left the world of Atoapoma, she who gives life. Many pot lids were formed in the likeness of family members and placed in the ground. The creatrix Atoapoma, considered to be self-begotton and self-born, eternal and infinite, gave birth to the entire firmament of stars, moon and sun without the help of a male partner. Again and again cross cultural references refer to a parthenogenic Mother/Goddess.

From gravesites in ancient Nubia, 3,500 BCE, and Badarian graves in predynastaic Egypt (Nakada I period), small clay female figurines were found buried with the dead. Some of them were women holding a child, upon which a message was written for the deceased. It has been speculated by Rosalind Jeffries that these figurines were "letters to the dead" — bearing messages from the living for the dead as they went on their long journey into the afterlife. Both women and men were buried with these female figures indicating that both were children of the Great Mother. It is interesting to consider the image of mother and child as a symbol used in death. (ibid., p. 101) It seems to me to be a loving image in which the return of the child to her/his mother is honored.

Temples were places where spiritual transformation took place — another form of shaping and molding. As we have seen, our early ancestors ceaselessly honored the temple tomb as womb. The great trilithon stone structures at the entrance of the temples of Malta and Gozo represent the yoni/gate of the Goddess. As I entered and exited these thresholds of passage myself, I

Above: Anthropomorphic mother-pot with baby, Early Minoan II, Myrtos, S. Crete, 2,900-2,600 BCE, drawn by by Melissa Meltzer

157

felt a deep spiritual stirring that helped awaken me to a profound respect for the wisdom of the ancient ones who built and celebrated life within those hallowed stone structures.

At the temple of Mnajdra in Malta overlooking the glistening blue-green Mediterranean, I had a vision of the people who lived there. I could see brown-skinned people, living simply, moving in unhurried gait, laughing and singing. I could feel their connection to the earth and their spirit of celebration — a kind of celebration that characterized daily life. An overwhelming feeling of peace filled me with a serenity and an abundant calm for which I think most of us spend a lifetime of longing. I thought how amazing it would be to live in community with such spirit — in simple reverence for life and for each other, truly enjoying the ordinary as sacred. Even though I was not due to bleed, I began to menstruate, as did another woman I was with. I felt deeply touched by the living truth of the simplicity and ancient wisdom of these ancestors, the temple itself and the beauty of the sacred land.

The body of the Goddess is the very substance of life itself. I feel that I started to bleed in the temple of Mnajdra as a reminder of this truth. My flowing blood was connecting me to the flowing blood of all the women who perhaps even bled directly onto the land in that sacred place, or who perhaps gave birth there some thousands of years earlier. In life, the Goddess emerges from Herself, and in death She returns to Herself. Understanding the sacredness of death in the context of the cycle of life is essential to re-forming our collective beliefs about our own mortality.

To comprehend the body of the original Mother as place of sacred emergence and renewal is to restore an ancient truth and reverse the concepts of original sin and the impure womb, which are themselves patriarchal reversals of the original truth. Restoring sexuality to a place of honor in spiritual experience is a welcome relief for our psyches from bearing the burden of the life-negating, dominating puritanical/patriarchal cloak of disrespect and fear coloring current spiritual traditions that are not coincidentally male-dominated. Freedom awaits us in life and in death when we finally shed the outworn conditions of our self-inflicted suffering of the last 5,000 years and embrace the truth of our ancestors known for much longer.

When Mary is allowed to remove her robes and reveal her vulva as the gateway of life, and when she is seen as the Black Madonna, she can restore us to the earth that is our home and to the dark matter (read "mater" or "mother") of space, and when Queen Maya (Buddha's mother) is allowed to be revered as the living Goddess, not one who dies from illness after giving birth, then I think a true spiritual revolution — a turning of the wheel for spiritual awakening — will be birthed.

The Labyrinth

Ishtar/Inanna, Queen of Heaven and the Underworld, Monica Sjöö, 1991

The labyrinth is an age-old symbol of death, regeneration and rebirth, found cross-culturally, from the Hopi to Crete to India. "Labyrinth" comes from "labrys," the double-axe, which comes from "labia." The double-axe in Crete is symbolic of the double powers of the Goddess — death and regeneration. And of course, the labium, the outer and inner lips of the vulva, bring to mind the place of emergence and return of all that is born from the body of woman.

This place of primacy is the entrance into the labyrinth whose path spirals into the very center of the womb of the mother — the place of conception, and so, the place of transformation. The labyrinth is not a maze — there are no tricks or sudden dead ends. The path brings one into the center and then out again, born anew. What does the labyrinth have to do with death and dying? As a metaphor, it reminds us that life is a process of transformation, continuously held by the one changeless constant in the yoni-verse — change. The warm, moist, dark, cave-like space of our mother's womb not only provides us with containment, but also itself grows a special and unique organ, the placenta, to nourish and feed us as we grow deep within the core of her being.

Our very being is formed in the center of the labyrinth of our mother's body. Spiritually, I feel that if we do not have a conscious connection to this womb-wisdom after emerging from this place — this holiest of holy — we cannot fully blossom from potential to full flowering. We can struggle along, even appear to be doing quite well, in fact. But, the lack of connection to the mother's womb-wisdom eventually surfaces in painful reminders of our separation from our true nature, our primordial ground of being. We often continue to create pain through our own bewilderment, denial and fearful confusion about who we really are. To enter the labyrinth is to courageously enter the path of life as it takes us deeper and deeper into intimacy with ourselves and with the realms of spirit, where we learn to let go of all that does not serve us in our journey to freedom.

Embracing the deep dark core of our inner self, the very heart of our being, we follow the path out into the world, more aware of life's mysteries. Death can be seen as part of the labyrinth experience of life, rather than something ominous, with jaws agape, waiting in the shadows to devour us. The opportunities to practice letting go consciously walking the labyrinth of life prepares us for the supreme letting go at death. Monica Sjöö and Barbara Mor tell us that the labyrinth was a symbol of the complexity of life. They write, "the initiate had to find the way through the underworld — the womb of the Mother — going through symbolic death to be reborn again through her on a larger psychic level . . . .The ecstatic center of the labyrinth was the no-mind center of orgasm experienced as death, creative madness, and the loss of conditioned 'self.'" (Sjöö and Mor, **The Great Cosmic Mother**, p. 75)

According to feminist herstorian and writer, Heide Göttner-Abendroth, the labyrinth evolved from the sacred dancing grounds of moon priestesses. The basic spiral pattern was patterned after the movements of the dancers. A double spiral pattern was symbolic of the moon Goddess in which counter-clockwise dancing from the outside to the center reflected the waxing moon, reaching fullness at the center, and clockwise dancing from the center to the outside reflected the waning moon and emergence, the new moon. Gottner-Abendroth states: " . . . the mystical spiral was the image of the Moon goddess herself and her dual power: of passing from darkness to light, from death to life; and from light to darkness, from life to death." (Gottner-Abendroth, **The Dancing Goddess**, p. 39) Göttner-Abendroth relates that the dancing grounds served as calendars that were later frozen in time in the many stone circles like the ones found in Europe.

She sees the labyrinth of our ancestors as an initiation into moon-magic in which the initiate dances into the center to either experience the ecstatic center of light, "the divine climax" or seeks the mysteries of the underworld in death. In her view, the spiral-labyrinth is the womb and uterus. The experience of the ecstatic light or death was determined by the time of year the ritual took place as well as the kind of ritual being celebrated. Either way, the emergence from the labyrinth was a rebirth — rebirth through ecstasy and/or rebirth through a kind of death — depending on the course of the moon at the time.

The Hypogeum at Hal Saflieni in Malta, mentioned earlier, is an astounding labyrinth structure that housed the dead for about one thousand years. When I visited the Hypogeum, I felt a sense that the journey of life for our ancestors included death, where rebirth was celebrated in beauty and with a deep reverence for the cyclical process of the cosmos. As we sat and chanted in one of the carved-out limestone chamber-rooms, the sound of our combined voices filled the whole inside of the sanctuary with a sacred breathtaking resonance. It was as if we were the voice of the Goddess singing to the living and to the dead — to the ancestors and to ourselves, all present together in a timeless sharing. I thought how beautiful it would be to honor the dead in this manner as a natural part of our lives. I felt held by a sacredness beyond all words. In an extremely unusual turn of events during that time, one of my traveling companions began to weep in the Hypogeum, feeling a profound sense of grief.

Later, as we chanted together, that same grief swept over her, and she found herself in an altered state. When we returned to our hotel there was a message for her saying that her mother had been gravely injured in a car accident in Oregon and was on life-support. What Jamie wasn't told was that her mother had actually died at the scene, which she learned later when she left our pilgrimage to be with her mother. In our time in the Hypogeum, we had thought that maybe Jamie was in empathetic grief with our ancestors, and maybe she was. We also realized, however, that she was feeling her own grief at the passing of her mother. Without consciously knowing it, we were together in this sacred place, singing and chanting with the ancestors and with the newly dead, Jamie's mother.

Animal Spirits

Epona, White Mare Goddess, Monica Sjöö, **1989**

The Goddess is all-inclusive. In Goddess spirituality as well as in shamanic traditions, animals are not considered "less than." In shamanic tradition, animals are considered our closet relatives, as they were here before we were. The Goddess' domain is the all and all Her creatures exist in equality without hierarchy — worlds within worlds within worlds. I learned this on my first LSD trip. She is the birth-giver and protectress of all life. As protectress of animals She was the Lady of the Beasts. In earlier times, animals were the Goddess Herself — archetypes and symbols of fertility and death, standing by the Great Mother "in what can only be described as an epiphany."(Buffie Johnson, **Lady of the Beasts**, p. 3) In later times, she became known as the nurturer of humans and animals, exemplified by the many-breasted Roman black Diana of Ephesus, whose images can be seen today in the Capitoline Museum in Rome, as well as by images of the Mayan Goddess, Ixchel, arm and arm with her rabbit companion.

The community in which I lived for many years (though a patriarchal hierarchy — I did not know enough about Goddess spirituality then to have that awareness) followed a teaching set forth by the father-figure guru who claimed that pets were an extension of peoples' egos. Perhaps in some situations they are — but certainly not all, and it is not the animal deciding that. Sometimes animals are the only sentient beings that are kind to humans. In this community, my home for a long time was a birthing center open to women to come and give birth.

One time, a dog came to my door, and I realized she was pregnant. She did not live in our community — she belonged to a neighbor. Our community was 1,750 acres, so she definitely had to do some walking to find my home. She came to give birth. She knew what she wanted, and stayed with us until she had her puppies. This dog was very intuitive. Recently, when my daughter was sad and crying, a friend's dog, Rose, an English bulldog, jumped up on the couch next to her, placed her head on her shoulder in the crook of my daughter's neck and placed her paw around her shoulder. It was awesome. The empathy Rose had for my daughter was undeniable. I think it is important to regard the animals in our families as feeling beings who love us and enjoy being connected to us. We can honor their deaths in ways that mirror our respect of their lives. The following stories are about some special pets.

Cleo

Cleo was our cat that had been given to us. I had decided that I didn't want a cat or a dog but a friend came over with Cleo, a beautiful Abyssinian, and said that a family he knew had moved out of state and left her behind. He thought that maybe we would want her. I looked at her and had an unusual feeling that somehow she and I were being reunited — that she was a familiar. We thought about it, and agreed to try having her in our home. Well, of course, when you do that, you bond, and then saying "no" becomes very difficult.

Cleo became a part of our family, and shared life with us for a few short years. She really felt like my familiar, and joined me in my work. Sometimes she would come into the room and lie on a person right where they might be experiencing pain. Or she would just hang out in my healing room, adding her healing energy. People really liked her, and felt her energy to be special. I felt happy to have her assistance. She taught me about the loving bond and telepathy between humans and animals.

I didn't know much about Abyssinians, and later learned that many of them suffer from kidney problems. She became sick after being treated for fleas, and I was surprised at how rapidly she was declining. We took her to the vet, who administered an I.V. of fluids and then we took her home. She continued to decline. We took her to the animal emergency hospital, and were told she was in renal failure, and that putting her to sleep was our only option. I decided to bring her home and be with her rather than take her to a back room for an injection.

I placed Cleo on a heating pad in front of my altar in the healing room. I talked with her, telling her how happy I was that she came back to me, stroked her and held her paw until she passed. During her process, I looked at her and felt a strong presence of the mystery of death, and I felt that the least amount of interference and intervention was the most compassionate way to be with her. In that moment I felt this to be true about humans too. It is such holy work to die.

Unnecessary interference with a being's process in their dying is really disrespectful. Once, a client revealed to me that a hospice worker told her at the time of her mother's dying, that she wasn't supposed to say anything, but that with just a little more morphine, her mother would die sooner. After all, the doctor said she would die in a day or so, so what would be the difference? I reeled upon hearing this. Who are these people to feel they could control someone's process like that? The family was vulnerable and not well prepared for her death; they didn't know how to handle the intensity of what was before them.

The suggestion to administer more morphine seemed like a relief for them, thinking it would be a relief for their mother. But who is to say? The mother didn't ask for more morphine. This is not the way to handle a death. Don't do anyone any favors by hastening their process for your sake, thinking it's for theirs, if they didn't ask. The family is not to blame — they just didn't know.

I brought in my daughters to create a prayer circle for Cleo. We all shared through our tears our love for her and told stories about her. The room was filled with peace, loss, grief and love. We lit candles for her and we let her stay in the room in front of the altar. I was so grateful that we were present as a family being real with death, and not hiding it somewhere. My daughters loved Cleo, and felt their hearts pierced when she died. She was a full family member. For them to grieve all together with family allowed them to not feel ashamed of such a powerful emotion. Later we buried her in a simple ceremony placing her in the ground under the altar of the sweat lodge in the back yard, invoking the Goddess to be with her. I felt Cleo would grace us in our ceremonies and continue to be my familiar in a different way. And indeed she has.

Bun-bun

Bun-bun was a cherished bunny we had in our family who gave much joy to my children when they were younger. He was a sweet, gentle, soft and cuddly animal that truly loved being with humans. Bun-bun developed a growth on his jaw that puzzled the veterinarian. After a biopsy, without any conclusive results, on the advice of the vet, we decided to keep him at home and just watch him for a while. He didn't seem impeded by the growth — he was frisky and maintained a good appetite. However, I did not have a good feeling about the situation. In my heart I knew that Bun-bun would not be with us long, and really didn't want to put him through surgery without knowing what we were dealing with. We didn't even know if surgery would help him or if he would even survive it. So, I felt that nature taking her course was the best remedy, though it would mean he would die.

One day, just kind of suddenly, Bun-bun ran out of energy. It was very quick. I had gone out to see him in the morning, and he was lying on his side. He was alive, but he didn't get up to greet me as usual. I knew he was dying. I asked him to please wait until I took my kids to school, that I wanted to be with him, and that I would come back for him. I did not tell my girls, as I knew that it would be too disruptive for them to have to go to school on that note. They of course knew that he was dealing with something unknown, and knew that he might die from it. I quickly got them ready for school and after driving them, immediately came home and went to Bun-bun. He was still in the same position, and I knew he had waited for me.

There is just a certain kind of telepathy one develops with the animals in one's family where you just "know." I gently picked him up and brought him into the house and held him on my lap. I talked with him, stroked him, and soothed him. He was calm — so sweet and gentle. I was amazed at how much emotion I felt. Through my tears I was still able to be there for him, and I could feel a deep surrender within him. This is what amazed me the most about the whole experience of being with this animal in his passing. The kind of surrender was a very powerful teaching for me. He was not fighting, resisting or angry. He was simply dying. It was death — calm, quiet and loving. He passed knowing he was safe and that it was okay to go. He knew he was being loved, and I felt he showed me that it is possible for any sentient being to pass peacefully when one feels supported by loving arms. I will always be grateful to him for this teaching.

Ephende, Yassir and August

All living beings share the same reality of life and death — simply, those that live, die. Today, I spent the morning with my friend Keni sharing with her the euthanising of her three horses. Two were mother and daughter, and the third was a horse that had been with the other two for a very long time. The daughter, Ephende, had been Keni's companion since Keni was seven. She is now thirty-six. Ephende was twenty-nine. The circumstances under which these loving beings "had" to be put "to sleep" were difficult and disturbing. Due to difficulties within the family, some family members simply did not want to care for them any more, nor did they give Keni a choice about what to do. She was informed that it had been decided that the horses were to be euthanized. Keni's shock and grief were more than any one person without support could bear. These animals had been her family — they had been there for her when her own flesh and blood had not. It was her family that was being "put to sleep" this morning. While it was true that they were old and had some health problems, it was a decision that was made by other family members without much thought.

I had never participated in anything quite like this. I arrived an hour before the scheduled time. We spent time with them, talking to them and stroking them. Keni had spent some time the previous day telling them of what was coming. Several days prior, Keni had to put down a sick dog, and Yassir, the male horse, came to the side of the house (her horses roamed free) where he could look in the window and see her. He watched everything, looking Keni in the eyes. She felt from him that he knew that he would die soon. And she felt that he communicated to her that if he had to go, it was okay with him if she would hold him just like she was holding her dog. She promised him she would.

As the time approached, we decided to cut some of their tail hair. We did that, and created an altar. The hair was placed on the altar, along with some apples, sage and the skull from a pony that Keni used to have. We brought the horses out, as the vet arrived. A man and his grandson were there to take the bodies away. A few other family members were present. No one but Keni and I had an understanding that these were sacred beings, and that what was about to take place had to happen in a sacred way. We asked for silence. I lit the sage and made a prayer, thanking the horses and asked for a safe passage for their spirits. It is beyond words what I felt as I saw the large needle of sedating drug go into the neck of the first horse. As soon as the drug started to take effect, the vet injected her with a large dose of phenobarbital, which is the drug that stops the heart. Her legs began to give way and her great body fell to the ground. She died as she had lived, unafraid. Ephende, the daughter, had a wild kind of spirit. Yassir soon followed, and then Ephende's mother, August. Amidst tears, we stroked them and whispered in their ears comforting and loving words. The onlookers were choked with their own feelings, unfortunately, taking care not to express them. I wondered how all this was for the grandson. He was a young boy of about ten or eleven. At that age children still have innocence. I am sure that his grandfather had never seen a ritual given to horses that were being euthanized. We showered their bodies with flower petals, lit more sage, and said more prayers. It was an extraordinary event. It was very difficult for me to be with the fact that these beings were killed that morning. There is no way I can say that it was anything different. Needles were placed in their necks, as they stood there, waiting. We think they knew what was going on. We think they surrendered to it. There was a sense of peace, except for August, the mother. She resisted at first. One moment we were standing with them in the pasture, stroking them and looking into their sweet eyes, and the next moment, their strength was removed from them, and they lay listless on the ground, the flies quickly gathering. I don't know about right and wrong in this. What I do know is that it seemed that it had to happen because of the decision of some humans, and so I was there to make it as sacred as possible. It was very difficult. Both Keni and I had attended a slide presentation by Vicki Noble several days earlier in which she spoke about the Amazon priestesses who were buried with their horses. Had Keni been able to have her way, that is what she would have wanted.

We did not witness them being put into the truck. We were told it would be better not to. After they were taken away, we stood on the ground where they had died, and spoke of them. I closed my eyes and I saw them as young horses and could feel their spirits circling us. As we were quietly sharing about what has just transpired, Keni pointed up to the sky and we watched a circling vulture overhead. I felt the presence of the Black Dakini — the vulture goddess. And then shortly after, there were three more. It seemed as though they were there blessing the passage of the three horses, and helping their spirits cross over from this world to the next.

Another of the family horses, Rebo, was taken away from the others and placed in a strange place without his friends. No one had informed Keni of this. She simply never saw him again. A year after this separation, the horse died as a result of refusing to drink water. I feel he died of a broken heart.

A Shamanic Journey to the Ancestors

As I was writing this book, I asked my friend, Joan, if she wanted to enter into dialogue with me on the subject of death, dying and the Goddess. Joan was an early editor of Maria Gimbutas' book, **Language of the Goddess**. She was also involved in intense Zen koan practice, and is now a roshi — a teacher of Zen. We spent several hours together discussing, from a spiritual feminist perspective, death and dying. One of the experiences we shared together was a shamanic journey to the ancestors, facilitated by a constant drumbeat. We lay down, and listened to the beating drum, on tape. A shamanic journey is an entering into a state of non-ordinary reality, in trance. We journeyed together at the same time, with the same intention, which was to explore the ancient wisdom of our ancestors about death and what they wanted to share with us at the time. What follows is a description of both of our experiences in our journeys.

Meeting Our Ancestors at Avebury, Monica Sjöö, **1993**

Leslene: What did you learn?

Joan: There were two parts. And one was sort of experiencing the dying process myself and the other was a bit of image from the old times. So the part about experiencing dying — it felt like there were a couple of different passages in it. One was of great peace, where it felt so peaceful and wonderful to just experience kind of being in this very big spacious consciousness. There was one passage where I felt like I was tumbling away from life, and there was some discomfort and fear attached to that, a sense of free-fall away from life. So that was interesting, because I could understand where fear would come up. But I also felt it was a time of getting a different equilibrium — part of the threshold moment from one state of consciousness to another that didn't feel like the thing, it just felt like a moment in the thing where one is regaining one's balance in a new way.

Leslene: Was that a tumbling away from life as you know it? Away from consciousness all together?

Joan: The main thing that I felt was that being alive and being dead are on a continuum, more of one kind of consciousness in one and more of another kind in the other. So when I could feel myself as alive, I was also really aware of the presence of the death consciousness in me also. I have an ear ache right now and I was really aware of the processes of destruction and transformation going on, you know, in my ear, because I have an infection, and that was an example of the way our living consciousness always carries our death consciousness as well, which aren't really different. They are part of the same continuum, but they have different kinds of qualities, and so the process of dying felt like a moving from one end of that spectrum of consciousness into another — from where life predominates to where death predominates. So when I talk about that tumbling as a falling away from life, I mean away from living consciousness into this other consciousness, which is just different.

Leslene: So you are saying there can be fear there because it's the un-known, or it's just different . . . .

Joan: It's different. And so it's like there's a moment where you lose your equilibrium and then you have to find your equilibrium in your new conscious-ness. In that also, next to that, not simultaneous — it was like there were all these different passages — there was a grief. I thought, "Oh, I'll never open my eyes again" and there was grief — there was a sense of loss in that, about the world, about the beauty of the world. A strong sense of the difference between being afraid of dying and just knowing it's not your time yet, that you're connected still to the earth, that there's more to do. And I felt that very strong. The feeling was, "this is fine and this is good, just not now."

The overwhelming feeling was this kind of peace and then a sense that there was a tremendous amount of energy devoted to maintaining life con-sciousness and that there's something very relaxing and peaceful about letting that go — so that was interesting. There's will to be alive, and how lovely it is to just let that go, and just float.

Leslene: Yes, I really get that. I really understand.

Joan: Do you? So that was the personal part, and then I did have this one really strong series of images about deathing in the old way. It happened outside, which is surprising to me. Did you get the same thing?

Leslene: Yes.

Joan: And the person who was dying in the first image was lying flat on her/his back (I couldn't tell who it was) and there was a group of women, and that was really important that you were received back by a group of women. And they made a semi-circle around the upper part of the dying person's body and they would just stroke her, and give her a little bit of water, and just be present with her, and as her dying proceeded, what happened was she contracted from the prone position into the fetal position, and there was this clear return, and as she retracted into the fetal position, what had been the semi-circle of women surrounding her when she was prone — she pulled into them and so she was completely taken back into the circle of women. And somehow that was exactly the reverse of the birth process, and like there was part of her sticking out of the birth canal that came back in.

Leslene: (joking) . . . so, I'm just musing, is there Cesarean, is there breech?

Joan: Oh that's great, a breech death! Maybe that's what assisted suicide is, a kind of Cesarean death . . .

Leslene: Oh, that's interesting . . . that's a whole other area to look at . . . wow, this is lovely.

Joan: And the one sense I had of the women is a kind of anonymity to them. They had an archetypal flavor, but they were really strong. I was trying to notice are they old, are they young, what are they? And much more what came out was this feeling of tremendous strength, whatever their age was, and they were deep, and able to hold what was happening, no words — just stroking, and touching.

Leslene: Well, thank you for sharing this.

Joan: Thank you for asking.

After Joan shared her experience, I shared mine with her.

Leslene: Well, so, there are a lot of similarities. We're doing this together, in the same time and the same place, and I love that.

Joan: Great! Tell me!

Leslene: So, when I went, I was just sort of pulled into this tunnel, and sort of just released, into the Lower World (a shamanic non-ordinary reality). It felt birthing-like, so I just went with that, and it was really fast. I wasn't used to that, but it was okay. I was just in a scene of a circle of women and there was a fire. I could tell right away they were celebrating somebody's passing. Somebody was passing — it felt like a woman to me. Like you, I couldn't really distinguish between young and old. It was definitely an archetypal presence of women. I was connected with/by a grandmother person who was my guide, my ancestor, my ansister.

Joan: Ansister, I like that.

Leslene: In the circle was a woman who was dancing. She was doing some really ecstatic dancing. They told me she was doing the snake dance for the woman who was dying. It was a dance celebrating and honoring transformation and letting go. What the grandmother was telling me was that it's really important to have a celebration of the actual processes that life goes through while someone is dying. So there was this dancing going on, and there were also people around — I couldn't see them, but I could feel them — making love. They were celebrating sexual relating — celebrating that. She said that was an offering for the passage of this person that aided her passage.

Joan: That's really interesting. I'm just remembering when you say that there was part of the passage in my own death. I was passing through all of that kind of life stuff — people making love, eating and dancing . . . .all of that . . .

Leslene: Oh . . . that's interesting . . .so maybe it was your death I was attending . . .

Joan: (laughter . . .)

Leslene: (laugher) You know, you were doing the dying and there was all this celebrating . . . I don't know, but we're doing this journey thing . . . .and time and space changes . . . so that's not scary, right?

Joan: Oh, no, no . . .

Leslene: To me, oh wow, it was really beautiful, and they were accentuating celebration, and said it was really important — celebration is really important. And so after that, she took me outside and laid me down under a tree and had me go through the death process.

Joan: It was under a tree for me too, outside.

Leslene: I love the synchronicity! She brushed my hair and did all this stuff with me, and then asked me to lie down, and then asked me to "just dissolve".

Joan: laugher, oh, just dissolve, okay! That's great.

Leslene: And so, I did. I just dissolved and went into the earth and I became the roots and I went up the roots into the tree and went into the branches and became this tree and became an apple, and then dropped into the hands of someone who ate the apple. And it was all the same thing — all the same. It was just energy expressing itself. Hard to talk about it. It was like being a human being wasn't more important than being an apple. There was a strong sense of sharing when the apple I had become was consumed. I could see that human consciousness, while wonderful and unique, is not better than any other consciousness.

So somehow I came back to my body. She took me into this very simple and beautiful temple. There were a lot of, like you, you said, images from those times. There were bucranium (bulls' heads) and she was showing me egg-shaped graves cut into rock and there were people in the fetal position put in there. So that's really interesting about your fetal position, and they were all in the fetal position in these places. She was saying over and over how important it is to honor the mystery of rebirth — that that's really important, that you can't really grasp it, but it really needs to be honored. And she was talking to me a lot about what's missing now and what's needed to bring back. And she just said that over and over — the mystery of rebirth. And there was talk about the womb and the importance of really coming back to that wisdom.

The image of the Goddess of Laussel pointing at her sacred triangle came in. She was instructing me. And then she took me somewhere, I think we were still in the temple. And she started handing me all these bones. She wanted me to feel them, touch them, hold them and kiss them. She said they were the bones of my ancestors and that I needed to learn to kiss the bones of my ancestors and not be afraid. So that was quite an amazing experience, holding those bones, and feeling my fear, and all my stuff around "this is weird, etc.," and what's really in the way of kissing the bones of one's ancestors, and what does it really mean to kiss the bones of the ancestors.

I was able to kiss the bones, and I don't really know if I can put into words what I felt. I don't think I can really describe what that was — a deep kind of connection. Finally she said, like you were talking about the stroking, it was really important to emphasize the passage from one shore to the next with deep love — to help the loved one feel deeply held and to really teach and absorb and embody the understanding it's really okay to die. It's really really okay. And that deep love is what's missing, and the presence of that is the medicine of what's needed. She said it does reside within the hands of women to bring that — it's something innate to women. Not that men can't do it, but it was like, oh yes, that's what women do — in the sense of the circle of life that women bring through, to see it from beginning to end. It's really women's place to do that. So, that's what I got.

Joan: That's wonderful.

Leslene: So now, to bring that through. There was a sense that just surrounding a person with presence and profound loving — it was really like that kind of loving of mother and child in its most whole natural state. That anybody would feel safe with that and anybody would have a safe passage with that.

Joan: That's beautiful.

Leslene: Thanks! I feel really blessed to be able to access some of this. The snake dance was really interesting. She somehow kept producing layers of skin and letting them go and you could see she was there in another form, and then another, and it was like she was showing that death really serves life — really serves the continuation.

Joan: One thing that kind of floated through was something my mother has been saying a lot lately is that she just feels like her time is passed, and that it's not her time anymore. And she's a person who really loves life who really lives it quite to the full, but she just doesn't feel like it's her world in some ways anymore — that she's kind of falling further and further away from it and I'm really interested in that because she is a person who loves life and who has a very good life, she feels. But just that sense of how death serves life by allowing the continuation of life and watching her prepare.

Leslene: That's really interesting, she's talking about it.

Joan: Yes, she's talking about it. And she's sixty-seven and she's not that old, and her health is good and it's not like it's really an imminent event for her, but it's some kind of shift in her consciousness. It's interesting to me because it doesn't feel like depression or illness or anything like that in her because she does have a life she really loves — it just really does feel like something that happens, maybe, as you get older where you begin to feel like the wheel is turning and it's my time to step off.

Leslene: I'm wondering, and we'll see what happens with her, how that can inform her dying, and the fear level. When you were talking about falling away from life, do you feel the fear of that was something you experienced while still being in the life consciousness as you approached the death — it wasn't something that happened after you were out of the body?

Joan: No, it was like the transition. And the feeling that was uncomfortable was a tumbling, kind of through space, and I thought "oh, I hope this isn't it . . ." and then that stopped. And it was like I said, a kind of disequilibrium — moving from one form of consciousness to another . . .

Leslene: I wonder if there is something like that when one is born . . . you know Stan Grof has this whole theory about birth being so terribly and horribly traumatic and awful, because you're pushed and that whole thing, which I have a really hard time with . . .

Joan: That sounds sort of woman-hating to me, too.

Leslene: Yes. He's written a book about death, too, and I think it's all kind of around the same thing, and I just, well I just don't really like that. There's a whole thing in Tibetan Buddhism too where pregnancy is described as profoundly hard for the baby in the womb, and that rebirth is a fight for finding a womb to enter — like flies on a piece of meat. It's horrible. I'm wondering if a baby being born, in patriarchal decor, if you come into a hospital setting, like most of us have — bright lights and people taking you away, and hitting your bottom — seems to me to be a really sort of frightening tumble into life. But if it's not that way, but you come into the hands, into the circle of women, then there may still be sense of transition . . . but far more gentle . . .

Joan: There's got to be. I mean you're in an oceanic float, in the womb. I mean it's got to be a transition.

Leslene: Yes, and they do call it transition . . . and it really is, or can be, the most intense time. It's kind of like where the mother, if you're going to lose it, they say that's the point where you might really lose is at that point. So, the child is so one with the mother, if the mother is losing it, the child will have that sense. If the mother isn't losing it the child will have that sense of not . . . because of that oneness. Just thinking of that tumbling thing you were talking about . . . .do you see how it's related (laugher) . . .

Joan: (laughing) Yes, I do.

Leslene: (laughing) Oh, good. Sort of tumbling into life and tumbling out of life and tumbling into death . . . So what can we do to take care of that? I know more about what to do about it in birth, because I know what to say to a woman and it's been said to me, so I've experienced that. What do you think we can say to someone who is leaving who may encounter what you experienced?

Joan: It seems to me some form of it is going to happen, that it's just part of the threshold, so knowing that it is going to happen is the key. I had been in this very peaceful kind of blissful place, and it was kind of a shock. But if I had known this is part of it and it will end, then it would have been all right.

Leslene: So what can we say to somebody we are assisting? We have to create our own instructions.

Joan: Well, I guess we can say that. I don't know if my experience is *the* experience . . .

Leslene: Well, it's your experience, and you count, and it's something that came up around this as a possibility and we are exploring this . . . so maybe we could address possibilities. It's always tricky around addressing possibilities without suggestions . . .

Joan: Exactly.

Leslene: How do you prepare somebody for possibilities say in mountain climbing? They are prepared for situations that may not arise.

Joan: I think you just lay it out, in a simple straightforward way, like this may happen and that may happen, but underneath it all you're held.

Leslene: Yes, you're held. I think that's really the bottom line. That's what the ansister said. It's important for people to feel they are deeply held. And she said it's not really happening right now. I felt grief too around that — it's not really happening right now. She said we're not being held and we don't know how to hold each other. That's essential for safe passage. It seems to me if you are out in fear you can get lost in that fear until it subsides, or . . .

Joan: I would think, because it seems to be part of life consciousness, so it would be part of death consciousness, but how sad to have your last moments of life consciousness be spent in fear . . .

Leslene: Yeah . . . I don't think that's a good idea . . . (laughter)

Joan: (laughter) Yeah, probably not . . .

Leslene: So for right now, in these times, there is so much fear. We all embody some of that — it's in us, until we come face to face with it however we can in whatever ways we do so we don't carry that with us. I think that's really the challenge right now is in dissipating or transforming or finding a way to be released or transformed, I guess would be the best thing. Releasing it into the cosmos — seems like we can do better than that, because we don't need psychic debris. That's what the snake dance was about — was really transformation. They were saying it was really important to have someone enacting that — doing that — for the dying person.

Joan: So something that's occurring to me as you're talking is if you're doing a deathing where you know enough ahead of time to really have a chance to do this, that at some point earlier on, not at those last hours or days, but sometime earlier on, it's really important to go into that fear, and do that work, which is probably really intense, difficult and painful work, but to go through that and come out the other side.

Leslene: I totally agree. I really think we need to practice, and to do this and find out what it is we even need to practice. Anything we can do to bring more love into this world, quickly.

Joan: (laughing) Yes, quickly. Well, I have to go put theory into practice.

Leslene: Oh, yes. Thank you.

Ancestor Worship

Are there Great Female Beings out there waiting for us to be free... , Monica Sjöö, **1996**

The practice of ancestor worship seems to be long-forgotten in Western culture. What does it mean to worship one's ancestors? I am sure that you have gained an understanding of my respect for the ancestors as I have revealed it in this book. Simply put, without our ancestors, we wouldn't be here. In ancestor worship we are acknowledging the threads of life energy that create a vast web of life with no beginning and no end across time, holding us all together. The long lineage of ancestors does indeed trace back to one common ancestor we all share — the first African mother. Stretching out like many branches from one tree, all people everywhere are connected by this one common ancestor. So ancestor worship involves paying homage to those ancestors in our immediate lineage (if possible) as well as honoring what "The People" (Native Americans) refer to as "all our relations" — all forms of life. For instance, rocks, plants and animals have been here longer than we have.

Our ancestors are not all necessarily human. Sometimes I tap into the vast energy of a mountain, which is much older than I and so is an ancestor that lives in the present. Sometimes I feel the sacredness of a grandmother tree that reaches out to me from the timeless unspoken realms to guide me. Sometimes I feel the presence of an ancestral animal spirit that comes to me to give a special offering. Some cultures feel that their children are reincarnated ancestors.

In my home I have several altars that have my parents' ashes on them, along with photographs. The ashes are placed in containers I consider sacred.

Because we live in an abusive and violent society, it might be difficult to put pictures of family members on an altar if one was not close to or was hurt by them. This is understandable. When I invoke the ancestors in ceremony, I am usually calling in those wise women, "the grandmothers," who were not abused or violated. They in fact seem to have no knowledge of such behavior, though they understand that we do.

My immediate ancestors were all people who suffered in one way or another, and I want them to find healing too. Invoking the "grandmothers" summons a healing energy from across time — a time in which women were loved and respected — that I call upon to be available to all who have suffered in my lineage. Their energy is strong, loving and kind. It is fathomless and fills me with joy and love. When I am with other women who summon the "grandmothers," they also feel the same warm presence. As I have mentioned previously, I work with women in circle in which we invoke and journey in non-ordinary reality with the grandmothers. They give us guidance and opportunity to see ourselves in ways that call us to go deeper into our healing.

Because I feel that much has been denied to us (humankind in general) regarding our spiritual heritage, I have found it vitally important to especially remember the ancestors of pre-Bronze age antiquity. This includes going all the way back to the first African mother. For me, remembering these very early roots of my being, the memory of which resides in my cells, I feel I can tap into a source of profound strength and healing wisdom. This is something that I don't think can really be taught — it is more of a transmission. It is as if I call upon the spirit of Gaia herself — She who has given us form and sustenance. And Gaia herself has her ancestors — stretching all the way back to what I call the "Big She-Bang." Connection to this ancestral wisdom is itself, a state of grace.

In his Mother Universe theory, Astrophysicist J. Richard Gott claims, "If a time traveller could follow the chain of genesis backward, he (sic) would eventually find the Mother Universe. But from that point he (sic) would have nowhere else to go." (J. Richard Gott, **US News & World Report**, *Mysteries of Outer Space*, p. 23)

The original Halloween, referred to earlier, is a time when the veils between worlds are thought to be very thin. This means that it is an optimal time to enter sacred space and invoke the ancestors. I feel if this was a collective practice in our society, we would see much less preoccupation with the shadow aspects of death — i.e., violent acting out and the numbness that goes with it. In the practice of invoking the ancestors, we invite them to be with us, dance with us, and offer messages, and we show them we remember them and that they are not forgotten, for what is remembered lives. Also included in ancestor worship is the recognition of those "not yet born." These are the ancestors of the future. It is for them that some of the indigenous peoples of the Americas live their lives by the teaching of being mindful of the decisions one makes in the moment and the impact they have on the next seven generations.

If the arrogant men who carelessly play with nuclear power had this in mind, we wouldn't be faced with where to dump nuclear waste from nuclear power plants that does not break down for 250,000 years as well as renders the environment in which it is housed radioactive through uncontrollable leakage. This is a prime example of the danger created when one loses contact with and respect for ancestral wisdom.

Heide Göttner-Abendroth tells us the role of the Moon goddess in matrifocaled cultures relates to death and to the ancestors. She maintains that all religions involved with ancestor worship have their origins in ancient matriarchal conceptions of the Moon goddess. "During their absence, the souls of the ancestors abided in the arms of the Moon goddess or in the wings of the Goddess of the Night (Egypt), where they awaited rebirth." (Göttner-Abendroth, **Dancing Goddess,** p.34)

Because women are daughters of the Moon goddess and reflect the moon's cycle of continuous change, ancient women were one with the Goddess — really were the Goddess Herself — and their death practices ensured that every person's death was followed by a series of rebirths. Göttner-Abendroth relates that the origins of the legends of the fountain of youth arise from early thoughts about women, like the moon, not dying at all, but just undergoing change. She says that like the moon shedding her black veil or the serpent her shriveled skin, women were thought to retreat into solitude and shed their skin.

Göttner-Abendroth writes, "Since the people aided the Moon goddess in her resurrection, they were convinced she would aid them in their return from death. They considered human existence to be nothing more than a chain of decline and advance, of death and resurrection that transcended the death of the individual. Existence was a cycle of phases as eternal as those of the goddess, who was expressly named 'the eternal one' by many peoples. The conception of death as the irrevocable cessation of life — that sad notion of patriarchal peoples — did not exist for matriarchal societies. Everything in nature, including human existence, followed the example of the Moon goddess." (ibid.)

Feminist artist, Judy Chicago, created her magnificent piece "The Dinner Party" as a huge triangular table set with thirty-nine places honoring female ancestors. Though I have only seen pictures of this majestic artistic endeavor, the feeling of connection I have experienced in looking at the pictures of those who have gone before me — my foremothers — has felt very strong. The place settings are reminiscent of "ancient matriarchal death rites in which places were set at the table for the dead, who were invited to bless the living with their presence. That, of course, was Chicago's intention, since women's most urgent need in their process of self-discovery is the knowledge and reassuring spiritual presence of their great predecessors who have been suppressed by patriarchal historians." (ibid., p. 106)

Considering that patriarchal culture is founded on the notion of the individual and the subsequent development of the "ego," I believe the fear-inducing beliefs of the cessation of life at death and the judgment of an angry father-god in life as well as in death are tools of manipulation, domination and control. People cannot access ecstasy in a state of fear. If people are fear-ridden, then their experience of the sensuous and erotic nature of life is thwarted. How can we expect ourselves to embrace death if our lives are governed by an unnamed ever-present fear that has become "normal"? Göttner-Abendroth's research shows that women used dancing, originating with women in Africa, as a way of calling the waning moon Goddess to life. It was their religious practice.

This constant dancing that went on for days resulted in trance and ecstatic experience. What would it be like for you to consider a religious practice based on dance, trance and ecstasy? How do you think it would change your thoughts about death and dying? Can you envision how trance dancing could connect you to the essence of the life force? Perhaps you would need to try it first to know!

Perhaps you might be inspired to create an ancestor altar in your home where you can place photos of loved ones who have gone before you. This altar can be a reminder for you of your origins, and if you have had difficulty with family, then you can use sacred objects that connect you to an ancestral heritage you can respect. Because hurtful people are suffering in ignorance, they, too, need healing. You can bring that intention to your ancestor altar. You might be surprised how any anger you may have been holding on to can dissolve when you ask for healing from those you trust in the unseen worlds for those who have hurt you.

Connecting to the ancestral world also expands your consciousness and your sense of "self." One can experience a profound sense of tribe — something our linear, hierarchical, patriarchal society has basically destroyed. Most of us suffer, whether we know it or not, from a deep kind of loneliness. I feel this is the spiritual longing for our tribe and our loneliness we experience is a kind of collective soul loss of the absence of our tribe.

My own connection with the ancestors has helped me tremendously with this condition. I do not feel so alone and separate (though I understand it is an illusion to think one is separate, I witness it to be a pervasive experience in this society, and with the presence of tribe, I don't think it would be such a strong illusion). Including my chosen ancestors as part of my family and everyday experience, I am able to feel more grounded in living my life. Spending special time with them in ceremony strengthens my connections and brings much needed joy and reverence to my life.

A Simple Practice For Calling Upon the Ancestors

Cave of Yew Trees, Monica Sjöö, 1994.

Meditation
To be read or taped.

Find a comfortable place to sit for about a half-hour where you will not be disturbed. You may want to play a tape or CD of some gentle flute music or rhythmic drumming. Perhaps you might want to light some incense or burn some sage. Allow yourself to relax with your breathing, close your eyes and let yourself simply open. Soften your belly and quiet your mind. When you feel deeply relaxed, allow yourself to open to a loved one who you would like to connect with who has gone before you. See and/or feel them in front of you gently reaching out to take your hand. If you do not have any loved ones who have gone before, then allow yourself to be open to an ancient grandmother spirit who wishes to be there for you. She also will reach out to you. Allow yourself to extend your hand in a gesture of greeting. Feel your ancestor take your hand, holding it with warmth and tenderness. Notice how you feel. Spend your time with your ancestor in openness and love. See what emerges and arises in the experience and just go with the flow. Perhaps there will be a message for you, and perhaps you might have a question or two. When you feel complete with this meeting, bring yourself back to present time and open your eyes. Remember that you can call on this ancestor whenever you wish and that you can place a photo or piece of sacred art on your altar to remind you of your connection.

Midwifing Children — Ellie's Story

The following story is my friend Donna's account of her midwifing her daughter in her death. Her daughter, Ellie, lived to be twenty — surpassing the prognosis that she could only survive Infantile Polycystic Kidney Disease for two years. I think Donna's story is important because not only does she share about Ellie's last days, she also emphasizes how she stayed in her power in the hospital with the doctors to ensure that Ellie's choices were respected. Donna was an amazon-mother with Ellie. And Ellie was an amazon-daughter. You will no doubt feel Ellie's great courage and wisdom in reading about her in this story. I had the honor of observing Donna's devotion to her daughter's health care for many years. She was immovable in her love and flexibility  in caring for Ellie. I do not know of any greater love. Even now, in writing this, the tears are welling up from deep in my heart as I remember Ellie and her great beauty and love of life.

What a teacher she was — in life and in death!

It was a warm evening in June and the sunset had turned the mountain bright pink and orange. Ellie was sitting on the couch and asked me to sit next to her. She said she wanted to talk. This was a rare occurrence. Ellie had been pulling away from me and the rest of the family for months now. A few weeks earlier, on her twentieth birthday she had stayed with friends out in the desert and wouldn't come home even for a party. I figured she was "cutting the apron strings," so I wasn't worried. After all, we had been very close for all her life and it was time for her to develop some independence. So when she said she wanted to talk I considered myself incredibly lucky and I cuddled up to her on the old blue couch.

Ellie told me we had something important to discuss. She told me she was going to die soon and I was going to need to know. "Whoa, babe! Did you have a bad day or what?" I wanted to know. "No." she insisted calmly, " I had a good day and I've had a good life. But I've completed my soul's purpose for this lifetime. I'm going to go soon and you will need to know. Please pay attention because you will need to know how to handle this. I don't want to be kept alive. No heroic measures to keep me going. I'm done and I'm happy with what I've done." I told her that I understood and I would do as she requested. This was her choice and I respected her decision.

Above: *Ellie*, photo by R&R Photographers

We talked a long time that evening as the sunset blazed across the mountain and then slowly faded into dark. We talked about her life and the things she had done. She was very proud of her accomplishments, and so was I. She had always loved to travel and in the last couple of years she had been to Hawaii, and Mexico, and out to visit her beloved grandparents and the ocean in California. She said that traveling had been wonderful but that she no longer wanted to travel. She had completed her goals of learning to drive, having her own car, graduating from high school, having a job that she loved, and being part of a wonderful group of friends. Most importantly, she had fallen in love.

All this had been wonderful and she loved it all, but now she was done. We cuddled in silence for a while watching the stars and then I kissed her on the cheek and went into the kitchen to make dinner. I knew that Ellie was serious and sincere. Her intentions had been the focus of our efforts for many years. Ellie had a strong intention to live when she was born with Infantile Polycystic Kidney Disease.

The doctors said she would never live past the age of two. We did not accept this prognosis and we did everything we could to keep her immune system strong. We were a group effort. Ellie's brother and two sisters, myself, my then husband, my parents and our extended family worked hard to fulfill her dreams of life. We stretched in every direction to build her strength and joy and eventually she thrived.

As she grew old enough to understand her challenge, she took charge of her own healing process. We faced many choices that were life threatening. Many times we had been at the critical edge of a health crisis with only our combined intuitive efforts to pull her through. Her intention had always been to live well with soul's purpose. We always respected her intentions and her intuition. Bright stars were turning into a desert sunrise of purple and peach the next morning as I was driving to work at St. Mary's hospital.

I had become a respiratory therapist the year before and was now working in critical care with the ventilators. This was not my favorite job, but I knew intuitively that I needed professional experience in this field to have any power over our choices if Ellie was ever hospitalized again. I got a call from home telling me that Ellie had been watching TV when she suddenly screamed in pain and asked for an ambulance.

She was on her way to another hospital and the family met me there. My supervisor gave me leave and took over my patients as I drove to the hospital, still in my respiratory uniform. When I got to the emergency room Ellie was in a coma and she was breathing with the help of a manual squeeze bag. No one knew what was wrong yet, and they wanted to put her on a ventilator and do some tests. She already had the tube down her trachea, and she could not feel anything while comatose, so I agreed.

Tests proved that Ellie had two broken blood vessels in her head. This condition was not critical—it was terminal. It was only a matter of time before she would die. The choice now was how to let her die gracefully.

182

We sat in the waiting room while Ellie was taken to intensive care. Ellie's regular doctor had stopped by earlier to tell us he had retired from practice that morning because he was taking his wife home from the hospital with terminal brain cancer. It was time for the specialist to take over because this had gotten very complicated. We thanked him for his help. He had been very compassionate through all our changes with him, but now he was gone.

The new doctor had not asked our opinion of the situation. He didn't know us and he didn't know Ellie. He only knew that she was a beautiful young woman and he did not want her to die on his shift. We were all in agreement about that. The specialist said that the broken veins were in her brain stem and behind her eyes. He pointed out that she was alive and stable on the ventilator and on dialysis. He planned to keep her on the machines for a few weeks and then try to repair the veins with radical surgery that would require draining all the blood from her body and inserting pins to hold the veins together. If she survived all that, he explained, she could start rehabilitation. Then he admitted that the chances of recovery were slim because of her disease process.

We had a family meeting in the waiting room. We were in unanimous agreement. We agreed to never let her be alone in the hospital. We had never let her be alone in the hospital and we would take shifts sleeping so we could maintain our standard. Also, we agreed that we could not let her suffer on the ventilator in a state of medicated limbo that is standard procedure in this type of situation. We told the doctor that we wanted to get her off the ventilator and take her home to die. He said, "NO! I don't want her to die in my care!"

Can't say that I blamed him. We took turns sitting and singing softly to Ellie all night. In the morning, with everyone fresh and rested, I tried again. I explained to the doctor that she had told us her wishes two days ago. I told him she did not want heroic measures. We could not let her suffer because of our fear of death.

I explained that because I was a respiratory therapist I could get her off the ventilator if he gave me weaning parameters. Then we could take her home and she would not die in his care. He said, "NO! I will not be responsible for her death!" I told him I understood his position and I did not want to pressure him. I knew I needed to find another way to get what I needed with my daughter. I called Ellie's old doctor at home. "Just sign one more order for me. Please!" I begged. I explained our situation and that all I needed was weaning parameters.

He said that he knew us and he knew Ellie and that she was always the one in charge of her life. "She has survived her whole life on instincts. I believe we must respect her wishes here as well. I'll make sure you get the support you need," he said. I had a very small window of opportunity. Ellie had just been dialyzed to reduce the swelling caused by the intravenous fluids.

She was not quite comatose and I could just barely get her attention. The nurse and respiratory therapist on her case were with me and we got the two easiest measurements of breathing that we needed to get her off the machine. All we needed now was the large double breath. "Eloise!" I hollered, "If you want off this machine you have to breathe deep! NOW!" I shook her by the shoulders and she gave a large gasp. The therapist whipped the meter into place and we got the measurement we needed to get her off.

"Oh my God! Now we have to take her off the ventilator," groaned the doctor at the foot of the bed. "I never thought you could really do it." "It's okay." I told him, "She will be fine. We will take her home. She will not die until we take her home."

The next day, with her condition stable and the doctors satisfied that we knew what we were doing, Ellie came home. Ellie was with us for another week and a half. She had to spend time with her friends and let them know she was ready to pass. Only her sweetheart had known of her condition when she was in the hospital, so the whole group came over to see her many times throughout the next week. She would come out of coma when they came in the door and tease them with dry humor.

"Who are these troublemakers?" she teased. They laughed and joked about the gifts they brought her. They grieved together over the sudden accidental death that same week of Ellie's best friend, Pam, who died in a car accident. We made a safe place for them to express their grief. She would fall back into coma again as soon as they left. When her brother asked her where she went when she was not with us, she explained that she was floating above us, watching us. She threatened to throw bright red and yellow bricks from up above at her father, who she knew needed to take more responsibility in the family for many things. She had no tolerance for being sentimental. Once, when I told her how much we loved her, she said, "What's this, a guilt trip?" We all laughed. She talked about her body of light and that she was ready for it now. She had no complaints and she had no pain. We never left her side. Her peace was contagious.

On a scarlet sunrise morning at 6:12 a.m. she took her last breath. This seemed like perfect synchronicity because she was born on 6/12/72. Another reassurance of perfection. Our vigil was done. Her soul's purpose was completed in grace as she intended. We were and are very blessed to be a part of this miracle. I share it in hope of giving strength to the power of following personal intuitive guidance. It was not easy. Sometimes the grief and struggle of it all is still overwhelming. Still, I am very grateful to have the peace of knowing we did our best.

Dying as a Living Practice

Lammas Mother of the Harvest, Monica Sjöö, **1994**

To really die peacefully we must not wait our whole lives to admit that we do die, after all, only to find ourselves on our deathbeds, desperately trying to figure out how to get out of it. All of our distractions worked before when we encountered something we didn't like. Why not when we are dying? Well, it just appears that the final act comes for everyone — saint and sinner alike. So, the only way is through. It is said that in order for us to truly meet our death we must practice dying while living. I take this to mean that loving ourselves and understanding the fundamentals of kindness and compassion are requirements to this practice — not just in word, but more importantly, in deed. I feel it also means to come to an understanding embodied by the ancients — that life is, in and of itself, whole, sacred and purposeful in its very existence. Included in this understanding is the comprehension that death is not an enemy or something to be overcome or conquered — it is part of life experiencing itself moving through many passages, shedding the skin of the past in the present, making way for the new in the future.

As a shemama, a shamanic practitioner, I feel I have had to learn about the oneness of life and death in order to be effective in what I do. In my early spiritual practice, the teaching of making friends with death became a mantra for me — especially as I spent many hours immersed in psychedelic states where "ego death" was a prerequisite for me to make it through the psychic terrain of my mind and psyche without becoming permanently psychotic. Not that I knew what that meant when I signed up to explore consciousness in the 1960's through the use of psychedelics!

The same was true for me in giving birth — I was taken to the edge of life and death without knowing if I would come back. Although the fear of going crazy was not an issue during childbirth, I encountered other kinds of challenges that taught me that I had to really let go in order to push my baby out. There was a direct connection to any resistance I embodied and the closing down of my cervix, as well as a direct relationship between how open I could be and how open my cervix was. There was no way "out" — I simply had to learn to surrender. I feel women intuitively know a great deal about this magic through our menstrual mysteries. You can't fake your way in giving birth. That just makes things much more difficult.

So, learning to die while living means learning to give up control — not power, control. The ego is very busy grasping for what makes it feel good — and this can become very tricky, because the ego can feel really good when people do truly good things. But if the ego takes a "hit" for itself, then one is in trouble. Identifying with one's deeds or the fruits of one's labor as the "doer" is a mistake, and will make it hard to let go at the time of death if one hasn't figured out that one is not the doer of great deeds. Fame and fortune can do nothing for the dying person. Letting go of the need to be right, to be in charge, to be seen, to know, to have, to be adored, to having agendas, whatever . . . is all about dying while living. It is in this letting go that one can truly be alive and be fully present in the moment. Allowing oneself to live in the "I don't know" reality creates spaciousness and makes room for possibility and spontaneity. If one already "knows," then there is no space for not knowing.

Learning the art of the "giveaway" is extremely important in becoming conscious about death while alive. The giveaway, well known in traditions of The People (Native Americans), is about learning to give without expectation and attachment. In fact, the giveaway teaches one how to be non-attached. This kind of non-attachment is not about indifference. It is about true authentic compassion without the need to fix, control or possess. The ancestors are the masters of the art of giveaway. They give their knowledge as food and sustenance to feed the new life that comes from the womb of creation.

Knowledge, wisdom and love are not commodities to be bought and sold. They are given when the time is right, when the receiver is open and ready to humbly accept the responsibility of authentic living. Mothers, when allowed to be in our power, give this depth of attention naturally to our children. In the macrocosm, the Great Mother gives this love and attention to all

186

Her children — but those who do not heed Her, cannot know Her in their hearts. Without this knowledge, Her children live in fear, and many have become believers in an angry father-god figure who keeps tabs on his servants through intimidation.

It is very hard indeed to find a way to accept death when one fears the great cosmic being as a punishing parent. Consequently, many people die in distorted states of anguish, despair, regret, fear, anger, and resentment — much in the same way they have lived their lives. This is totally optional.

Learning to live with death, as an ally, is part of our healing from living in a male-dominated, god-fearing culture. This teaching was brought home to me through my experience with my friend Deb, a wonderful goddess-witch-drummer-musician, who was diagnosed with tongue cancer during the writing of this book. At the time the only option offered to her if she was to survive was to have surgery, which required the removal of most of her tongue. She was told that even with reconstruction, her speech would be inaudible and that she would not be able to use her tongue in talking. At the time of this diagnosis, Deb was only thirty-eight years old. I met with her before she left for the east coast to be at home with her parents to be cared for following the surgery.

We sat together in front of her altar sipping hot tea and conversed about her life. I offered Deb a "death meditation" practice in which we rattled softly together and I began to speak as she listened. Since this wasn't planned, I asked the Goddess to provide the words in harmony with her needs. The words came effortlessly as I asked her to feel the truth of the upcoming event of the shamanic death of the Deb that she and friends and family now knew and the rebirth of the Deb she and they would be getting to know.

I asked her to feel what it felt like for her to invite "the unknown" into her sacred circle, giving it a place to be next to her, allowing that presence to be okay. She said she could feel more comfort and ease with the unknown being with her rather than having it be outside of her circle. I asked her to listen to the words that came from a well-known song "gently down the stream, merrily, merrily, merrily, life is but a dream." We both knew that even though we were addressing her shamanic death, the possibility of her physical death had become much more of a reality with the diagnosis of this particular cancer.

So, in addressing her shamanic death and the unknown, she was able to connect with this possibility and not recoil in fear. She said she could feel the presence of fear but along side it was also the presence of strength. I suggested that prior to her return in six months, her women friends could gather and prepare her home to receive the newly rebirthed Deb and celebrate the initiation and emergence of her new life. She felt deeply embraced by this love and it made her feel not so alone in her journey.

We talked about how it would be a rebirth for all those who love and care for her as others would need to find authentic ways to relate and communicate with her while learning to deal with their own issues that her changes might bring up for them. Many people, in the face of life/death issues of others become uncomfortable and feel at a loss as to what "to do." There is nothing to do. There is only being. However, knowing how to be in this kind of life situation requires great skill.

Many feel their own need to fill the space with what they want to give, do, and say — their own agendas develop in order for them to feel better as their own nervousness, anxiety and fear about their own death comes to the surface. Deb and I discussed this at length, and she said very directly that she knew this was one of the lessons for her at this time — to be able to say what she needed and to not take care of others around what they need. This skill can certainly come from living with death as an ally.

Sometimes just being together in the silence to witness together what wants to emerge is the greatest gift we can give another. Deb is a courageous and wise woman who will be forever changed and transformed by the teacher of illness. This teacher is providing her the opportunity to connect with the Goddess within and without in a most profound way where she will learn about the secrets of life and death. In this kind of stripping away, all distraction is quickly shed as the Goddess calls to Deb from the depths of Mystery to look into Her luminous/numinous mirror.

As it turned out, Deb did not lose her tongue, as the chemotherapy she endured worked. But, of course, she did not know this outcome when she first went for treatment, and had to prepare to step into the unknown, which she did with grace and courage. She is currently cancer-free.

Once, on my return trip home from a women's Buddhist workshop on "fierce compassion," I stopped by the roadside to visit a shrine placed in the honor of a bicyclist who was fatally injured there by a drunk driver. The woman, Ceci, had been killed only two weeks before. This shrine, placed on a roadside bluff overlooking a beautiful verdant California valley, was a painful and wonderful place to visit. I read something there that I found interesting. In the newspaper article reporting on her accident, placed there among many other momentos, her friends were quoted as saying that when she was hit, they went to her and they all felt like little children — that there was nothing they could do.

Well, yes, being there for someone in the face of death and dying that shows itself completely unexpectedly can be completely shocking. I reflected that it is not about doing — save for the obvious first-aid and CPR one could offer — but I am talking about something different. It is about being so present in the moment that one knows how to be with that person and the unknown in complete compassion. It is possible to be like a loving tender mother in the face of something as shocking as Ceci's accident — to really be there for her, offering loving comfort, and refuge in safety, acknowledging the circumstances, helping her to understand what happened, and helping her to come to peace.

It must be terribly shocking for a person to be feeling one's passion in her bicycling, enjoying nature in one moment and in the next moment be pinned up against a rock embankment by a mass of heavy, hot, twisted metal, feeling her life force ebbing from her body. Knowing how to help someone to make such a transition comes from a deep inner knowing about letting go, allowing one to be present and ready in the moment. It allows one to *be* peace rather than think about it.

My friend, Kendra, had just that experience of being called to the moment when she was witness to a fatal motorcycle accident. The young man was bleeding profusely under his helmet and Kendra went to him, when others gathered nearby would not (she had thought maybe they were afraid of AIDS). She had to ask others to call 911. She was the only one who went to his side. She could feel him dying. She talked soothingly to him, and touched him and felt that she could help him find peace in that moment of his dying by embodying it herself. Her compassion emerged from a deep loving kindness as she surrendered to its presence rather than allowing aversion and fear to dominate. Kendra is a passionate lover of the Goddess, nature and Mother Earth. She is grounded in the healing energy of women's wisdom. Because Kendra is open to and trusts the wisdom and truth of the Goddess, I believe it was this intelligence that guided her in that moment.

She hasn't done many years of spiritual practice of this meditation or that, nor has she spent long studious hours poring over spiritual texts (though these activities in and of themselves can be very helpful). She is simply a serious student of the living Goddess and learns from the earth herself about being alive. Even though Kendra is a young woman of twenty-four, she was the elder on the scene of that accident. She felt blessed and honored to be there, helping this young man go from this world into the next. But she could only do that by being present to the surprise of the moment, accepting and trusting it. I had no doubt that the young man felt he was in the hands of a beautiful angel, which he most certainly was.

In some indigenous cultures of the Americas there is the practice of finding one's death song while alive. This song becomes the ally of the person throughout their lives, so that they become very acquainted with what the song means during their lifetime.

Death then, is a companion of life, and is never forgotten. In the hour of death, these people would, if they were able to, sing their death song — exiting this world with song on their lips and no doubt feeling the power their ally-song had gathered by being with them in their life. I can see that a death song would provide a connection between the person and the cycles of life, guiding the dying person into the next world and helping to allay fear. It seems to me that such a song would also bring the mystery of death into one's life, making it a spiritual presence calling for acceptance — rather than having it be something hidden away to be forgotten and denied.

Because we come into and exit this world alone, a song one has found in one's life to be used at one's death would seem to me to be comforting as well as empowering. With a sense of sovereignty and dignity, one could open to the unknown in death, accompanied by the familiar presence of one's song of death. And if one was unable to sing it for oneself, it could be taught to others who could sing it.

Meditation

The Womb/Tomb Temple of theVala (Swedish Kivik Grave), Monica Sjöö, **1997**

To be read, or taped and listened to. Find a comfortable spot and lie down.
Be sure you are not going to be disturbed. Perhaps you can have a friend beat
a light heartbeat rhythm on a drum.

*Now take some deep breaths, and allow yourself to release any tension in your
body. Just take slow relaxing, cleansing breaths, from your belly. Feel your belly
soften. Allow your consciousness to deepen and soften into a different place than
ordinary consciousness. Feel the spaciousness. Perhaps it is darker here. It is qui-
eter and more still than everyday consciousness. Allow yourself to be completely
relaxed. Now allow your attention to focus on "I." See who this "I" is and see if
you can locate where in the body "I" is. Notice how you identify with this "I" in
your daily life. "I" said this, "I" am angry, "I" want this, "I" don't like that, etc.
Really go into this "I."*

*Now, see yourself approaching your death. See yourself in bed, weak and
tired. What happens to this "I"? Do any of the possessions, accomplishments and
thoughts of this "I" matter now? What is it that you need the most at this time? If
you could create your own death ritual, what would you want? Are you afraid?
What are you afraid of? Can you surrender? Can you let go of "I"? What happens
when you let go of "I"? Can you sense the presence of a loving Mother-Goddess
who gave birth to you who is waiting for you in your death? What does She feel
and look like? How does if feel to let go into Her arms, to be held at Her breast?
Can you sense the timeless antiquity of Her being — known for millennia by your
ancestors? Allow all fear to dissolve into the warm golden love of a mother who has
never stopped loving you — even if you have forgotten and denied Her. A vessel*

191

appears for you — a magnificent boat, shaped like a vulva, etched with drawings of snakes, spirals and animals, with priestesses in feathered robes coming to attend you. The boat sets sail to cross the great uterine waters of the Mother's womb, carrying you to visit others who have gone before you — carrying you to the land of regeneration and other generations. You hear a gentle humming sound — the chanting of the priestesses to help soothe you as you journey. You have an opportunity to look at the life you just left. You realize how hard you tried to hold onto that life, how afraid you were to die, thinking you were your body and that you would be nothing when you died. You see how you could have prepared for your death while you were alive so that you could have had less fear. You notice that now there is nothing to fear, and realize that you are experiencing death as a doorway into another life. There is a profound sense of peace and you notice the presence of a sweet aroma. It is the scent of love itself. You realize that the Mother's love is what gives you life and that in death She simply breathes you back into Herself. Her rhythmic breathing and beating of Her heart are creation and dissolution. In and out, in and out — ebb and flow, ebb and flow . . . a never ending circle of the dance of the cosmos, of which you are a part. In between the ebb and flow is a great nurturing silence — a pause of restfulness between creation, dissolution and creation again.

The vessel reaches a shore of soft sand. You feel the boat come to a stop, nestling into the gentle grasp of the wet earth, the water making delicate lapping sounds on the sides of the boat. The priestesses take your hands and escort you ashore. There is soft music and an air of celebration. The air is filled with a sweet-smelling aroma of fruit. You look ahead of you and see someone coming towards you. It is a loved one who has gone before you to greet you — hands outstretched — with a look of joy. You take the loved one's hands and s/he takes you ashore, guiding you towards a beautiful apple orchard. Together you walk through the orchard, breathing in the succulent aroma, sharing, laughing, crying and loving. You feel so safe and loved. You are surrounded in magnificence. You now know that you are joining those in this world, and that here you will heal and learn about love. This is the land between birth and death, the resting place, the pause, and you know you will be here for as long as you need to be. You understand that life goes on, and that you are now an ancestor. It is your wish that the ones you left behind, so to speak, will hear you in their dreams, and come to know that death is a return to the heart of the Mother.

When you feel ready, begin to bring yourself back from the journey into present time, fully into your body. Feel all of your attention returning. Begin to move fingers and toes, and sit up when you feel ready. Take some deep breaths, and slowly orient yourself to the present.

Spend some time journaling. What ideas did you have about death and dying that may have changed as a result of this journey? What do you feel about "I"? How did it feel to connect with a loving, female Mother presence? What kind of difference do you feel it makes for you to surrender to the Mother Goddess of our ancestors in death rather than to the patriarchal intimidating father sky-god of recent times?

Charles' Story

Missing You, Monica Sjöö, **1995**

Several nights ago my friend, Ann, called me and asked if I could come to the bedside of her dying father, who she was caring for in her home. Charles had been suffering from an aggressive form of brain cancer, and had become bedridden. He was a sixty-nine year-old retired military man who had never really thought much about spiritual things. However, he was open to my coming and being with him. In the unseasonably cool "El Niño" mist, I drove across town late at night to be with a dying man I had never met whose background was vastly different from mine. Ann thought he was taking a turn for the worse.

He had been restless all day. I entered his room and found a pink-faced rather cherubic man lying in his bed. Whatever notions I had about a "military man" vanished then and there. He was soft to the touch, and was happy to let me hold his hand. I introduced myself, and sat in a chair next to his bed. I held his hand for a while, and gently began to talk with him. Though I did not feel that he was going anywhere soon, one never knows. I tried to feel out the most compassionate way to be with him, and decided to talk to him about dying. He seemed open and willing to discuss the topic. I began with asking him some questions, and learning about him and his views on his predicament. I could feel that he had come to some acceptance — not resignation, but acceptance.

It is important to understand the difference. I told him that I was aware of some instructions about dying that I found helpful in working with other people. I told him about the Tibetan view of dissolution of the body elements, and that once this had taken place, he would be the child luminosity looking to merge with the Mother luminosity after he left his body. He listened intently and openly, which really amazed me. I felt that it was a privilege to be with this man who didn't know me but who could let me into his very personal process of his dying and want to know what I had to say. He did not die that night.

The second time I visited Charles, we had a discussion about his life and I asked him what he thought the point of life was. He became very quiet, and said that he didn't think he was, like most men he experienced, a very deep thinker. I was taken by surprise by his comment, as I thought being a military man, he would have had a great deal invested in the importance of men's thinking. He said men were too busy cutting each other up to think about important things. I am still stunned by his comment. However, we continued on, and I said to him that I thought he certainly had something important to offer, and that when he was ready, I would like to hear what he had to say.

After a long silence, he said he did think he was philosophical about his predicament. I asked him what he meant, and he said that so far he was able to take what had come to him and was able to smile. I remarked to him that I thought he was very courageous, and that he was teaching those around him how to be graceful in the face of death. He smiled and lit up, as if he didn't know that.

He then asked if Ann could come into the room. She came and sat with us, and then Charles spoke to his deep concern about not wanting to be a "vegetable" or a burden. We continued the discussion for a short while, and I felt that Charles was really attempting to find a way to let go gracefully, but that he was burdened himself by a pervading concern for the welfare of his daughter and his granddaughter. I felt that he would not leave his body until he was able to come to a resolution with this issue.

Ann had to move Charles to a near-by nursing home because she just couldn't care for him at home any longer. She also had her hands full with her lovely teenage daughter who had special needs and who was about to start high school. Charles lived for several months, surprising everyone. He often came to an edge of what looked like transition, and would bounce back with smiles and talk of eating ice cream. Two days prior to his death, looking pale and swollen from his medications, he rested listlessly in his bed, responding only with an occasional opening of his eyes. He even reached a place in which there was no response to voice or to touch.

One day before his death, he rallied and responded with attempts to talk and communicate and of course, with smiles. The day of his death, he then went into a state of labored breathing with no visual or somatic response. Once again, we thought this was it. And it was. Charles died about one and a half days ago at 4:30 in the morning. Though I was not with him at the moment of death, I was called to his side at 11:00 PM and was able to stay with him for most of his process. Though Ann did not feel like she wanted to be present for his passing, he was in the company of two wonderful women, Pam and Renny, who had been caring for him at different times. They could stay for the duration. There were also nurses in the facility who were administering care.

There are several important points to share about Charles' passing. When it became clear that he was not going to bounce back from where he was, we had the oxygen tube and the catheter removed from his body. I suggested removing the subcutaneous morphine drip tube, but I think that was too frightening of a thought for others to consider. One nurse had a very difficult time with the thought of removing any tubes at all, and her control issues about so-called patient care became self-evident. However, the removing of these tubes gave Charles back to himself to complete his work. The truth of this was clearly reflected by the energy in the room as Renny, an off-duty nurse, remarked how freeing she felt that to be — something she had not experienced before.

When Charles' breathing became more rattled and he began to make groaning sounds with his breath, I went to his side and began to talk quietly into his ear. I felt he was entering the final phase of letting go. I reminded him of the dissolution of the body and that he was now leaving his body and that it was okay to let go. I continuously talked to him and his breathing relaxed as he heard what was said to him. I talked to him about surrender and letting go of attachments and letting go of fear. I did this for several hours by his side.

I am convinced that this kind of connected loving communication is as effective as morphine — more effective, in fact because it doesn't cause a person to disengage from what is happening to them. I am not saying that morphine should not be used, but I think it should be used correctly. It definitely should not be used for the sake of allaying the fears of people who can't handle what they are seeing. Charles' rattling breathing would probably frighten anyone, and the tendency in Western medicine is to fix it. However, in witnessing his breath, we could see he was not distressed. One of the other nurses came in and confirmed this as well. She did not have an agenda about what should be done, and was not invested in medicating her own fear. She was very respectful of how we wanted to handle things, and was willing to serve in the best way we thought she could. What a relief it was to have a medical authority be as kind as she was. His breathing was labored and wet, but he was okay.

However, not everyone would see this unless one was paying really good attention without projecting one's own fears and agendas onto the situation.

And, he was telepathically responding to the auditory coaching he was receiving. I also breathed with him, sighing "Ahhhhhhhh" on the exhale. He was comforted by this and could relax into letting go every time he heard me breathe with him. The experience was much like assisting a woman in conscious labor, only Charles was laboring to birth himself. He also telepathed to me that it was hard at times and that he was afraid, and I would telepath back to him that yes, I understood and that I knew he could do it. He would relax even more with this kind of communication. He felt to me like a butterfly working hard to emerge from the chrysalis. Because circumstances would not allow me to stay through the night, I asked Pam, who had been closely watching me work with Charles if she would take over for me. She was an experienced hospice worker and was happy to continue talking into his ear and guiding him. I asked Pam if she wanted to guide him after his transition and she was happy to help with that part of the midwifing, even though she had not done it before. I suggested that she guide him towards the blue light and tell him that he is loved and that loving arms await him as he leaves his body. I shared with Pam to guide him by telling him not to be afraid of what he encounters, and not to react in aversion or grasping. I also suggested that she practice the prayer/visualization of heart-merging described in the next section.

It was a gift for her to be able to participate in this manner, as she had quit hospice due to the "fix it" attitude that she could no longer endure. I trusted her and knew Charles was in really good hands. I felt okay about having to leave, and felt that he would continue right on through without any problems, which is what happened. I felt I gave him what he needed to make his transition, and that it really didn't matter who guided him. I felt that guidance was the important issue — not that I had to be the one who gave it. It actually felt really good to me to be able to share with another sister in such an organic way (because I did not know her before) who could continue the work without any conflicts or suspicions. She was there, I had to leave, she wanted to take over and Charles got what he needed. It was perfect. It gave me a wonderful boost of faith in how effortlessly and gracefully women can work together, especially in life/death circumstances.

Charles died peacefully about one and a half hours after I left. He simply took one large breath as his last. Renny, the other sitter, remarked that on a scale of deaths she had witnessed, most of which were not good, Charles' was a ten on a scale of one to ten. His rattling breath continued until his last, and there was no need to fix anything. I feel allowing him to breathe through whatever he had to empowered him in his dying.

Practices

Shamanka on Glastonbury Tor,
Monica Sjöö, **1993**

What are our practices at the bedside of the dying and for preparation for our own death and what rituals do we have to truly honor the passage of loved ones? What do we do? I have said that it really isn't about doing, but more about who we are in the moment. We can be present with who we are which includes the offering of helpful practices that can facilitate a peaceful death. Being centered and grounded at the bedside of the dying can inspire them. I feel the most important practice at the bedside is that of compassionate attention — simply being there and being present to what is. I have already indicated what a helpful motherly state of mind might look like. I will share several practices I have found to be quite beneficial at the bedside as well as in preparing for one's own death.

The following is a prayer practice that can be offered whenever you are sitting with the dying, even if you cannot be physically close to them. This can be taught to the dying for them to do for themselves as well. This practice is an adaptation of the Tibetan phowa practice. Visualize in the space in front of them an embodiment of the divine. I use an image of the Goddess that comes to me in the moment — a Great Mother figure who is strong and compassionate. Notice her beauty and her radiant light emanating from her heart. See Her light connecting to the heart of the dying person. Now see the dying person's light emanating from her/his heart. See these two lights merging and meeting as one. See all the karma of the dying person purifying and dissolving into the light of the Goddess. Then visualize the person merging with the image of the divine. In truth, there is no separation from the divine, so in this practice, we are reminding ourselves of this oneness. I believe this practice can bring peace to the bedside of the dying, as well as to one's life. This practice can be done even when you are not with the dying person. You can do it when you think of them. You can do it as you sit with them, either on your own, or with them. It is said that this visualization helps the dying to let go and find peace.

Another practice useful for living and dying is called "tonglen" in Tibetan. This practice is known by another name, "giving and receiving." It grows a compassionate heart. This is a very simple practice whereby the dying person can visualize the suffering and pain of others with the same affliction, breathe in that suffering; see it as a blackish smoke at the heart center mixing with one's own suffering and pain and on the exhale see all the karma and pain purified into a golden light, and release that healed energy into the world. I have used this practice in my life to cultivate more compassion in my own heart. Those tending to the dying can do this practice along with their loved ones.

This practice allows the person who is dying to feel connected to others who are suffering in the same manner, and helps the person to feel that her/his suffering is not in vain. This is also a practice of "exchanging self for others" in which one consciously chooses to feel what it is like to be another. If you feel you don't have enough compassion or are afraid of "taking on" the karma of others, then perhaps it would be better if your prayer could be something like "may I be able to see the suffering of others and may I be able to bring that suffering into my own and purify all the suffering together," still using the breath as the vehicle for bringing in and releasing. When you do this practice for others, be sure you see all their karma and negative conditioning purified and the release of this purified energy into the world as loving and healing.

Another kind of helpful practice is to see yourself as a loving mother whose dying child is before you. I have already touched on this, but as a practice, you might want to spend some time with yourself before entering the room of a dying person, practicing what it feels like to give unconditional love. First, practice giving it to yourself — maybe there is something you can think of that you don't like about yourself, and give yourself love and compassion around this issue, relaxing the body and loosening the constriction, particularly around the heart, that is the result of negative self-criticism. After you feel in the body the effects of this meditation, then think of a friend who might need some compassion and give some to her/him, all the while allowing the heart to expand and open. Notice what happens to any fear you might be holding.

Next, think of someone who might be a difficult person for you, and give her/him this love. See this person as a sentient being like yourself, and see at their core their Goddess nature — pure, loving and kind. Allow yourself to go beyond how you perceive the personality and let yourself feel the suffering. People who are difficult for us are sometimes in a state of suffering of which they often have no awareness. This does not make it okay for them to abuse you, and you need to set clear boundaries with people who do not take responsibility for their pain. However, you can learn to offer them love and not get entangled in and react to their dramas.

See if you can let your love surround them. Notice what happens to the dualistic beliefs you might be harboring. Pay attention to how you feel in letting go of anything that keeps you in a dynamic of separation. Before you enter the room and sit at the bedside of the dying, think of her/him as your child who is leaving this world, and give them your compassion and love. They are in a holy state, and in order to be of service to them, you must be able to be in a holy state too.

Another simple practice that can be used both in instructing the dying as well as assisting them is what is known as the "AHH" practice. It is very simple. For someone who is dying and is perhaps experiencing some anxiety, simply tell them to make the sound "AHH" on the outbreath and breathe "AHH" with them. Let the sound be slow and deliberate. Often when women are giving birth, making this kind of low sound on the outbreath helps a great deal in opening up. It is the same in death. It is not only used when anxiety is present. It can be used whenever you feel it is appropriate. For the dying, it is a very helpful way to focus on letting go. When you are breathing with the person, a certain kind of shared oneness can be experienced and together you can feel like one person.

There are many ways to be with people in their dying process. I have touched on different approaches that can be used and combined together. I think one of the most important considerations in being with the dying is to take care of the energy. Do not allow people to talk as if the person isn't there or to chat about mundane concerns. Have and maintain respect for the space and the person. They are in a holy and sacred experience. People should not be loud and insensitive. They should be instructed in being calm, open and attentive. As a mother, I knew when my children were babies, if I was okay, they were okay. If I wasn't then they would feel something to be wrong and it would bring a sense of insecurity to them.

I believe it is the same with the dying. If you are confident about being with them, and are not filled with worry and anxiety, but are calm, sensitive and joyful, they will feel a certain peace. If you are uptight and fearful, they will reflect that. One might think that it might be hard to be joyful in the face of someone's death. I believe if we have a true understanding of the death process and have shed the patriarchal fears, then perhaps it is not so difficult.

Midwifing my mother in her death taught me a great deal about this. She was able, in her letting go, to show me about very deep states of consciousness that were full of peace, expansion and spaciousness. I would have missed this had I been preoccupied with worry, fear and anxiety and the need to control. The same is true for birthing. If anxiety, resistance and fear are the primary emotional experiences of the mother and whoever else is present, then a peaceful state is not possible. What ensues is a "fix it" response — drugs, monitors, episiotomies, "let's get through this as quickly as possible." In that experience, the mother is completely absent from the event. How do you think this affects the baby? How do you think this affects their bonding? Fortunately for me, I was fully conscious, at home and was able to completely participate in giving birth. And I can tell you that peace, magic and mystery pervaded the entire experience. It was intense, uncomfortable at times, and at others, blissful — and I was there to experience the wholeness of life giving life. I think it can be the same in death.

Buddhist teachings often stress the importance of treating those we enconter throughout our lives with love and tenderness because all forms of life have, at some time, been mother to all other forms. I believe the ancients knew the depth of this understanding long before Buddhism appeared. To them, the cosmos was Mother, and so She made Herself manifest in all things as an immanent and chthonic, primordial, numinous power. There was nothing that was not Mother. Even though we descendents of the ancients have strayed a long way from the Mother Path, the Path remains. It is up to us to find our way back to Her. In honoring death as a sacred passage, with beauty, grace and love, we can create an opening to find our way home. This is, of course, true in life as well. If we treat ourselves and each other with dignity, respect and an understanding of non-duality, we would never want to hurt one another.

Rituals

Summerland, Monica Sjöö, 1996

I have had the honor and privilege to experience authentic ritual with death in various ways in which the person's life was truly celebrated. If we can learn to see life as a cycle, then we can learn to create life-honoring rituals for death. I believe a ritual to be an important marking of a life passage. In my work, I often suggest that clients "ritualize" a shift in their healing process to ground the work in physical reality. I think if we had more respect for our life passages, authentic rituals would truly help us in integrating the impermanence of life and in learning how to be with the unknown. As we move into puberty, for example, a rite of passage witnessed and supported by family and friends, as practiced in many tribal cultures, is like watering the young spirit of the person as s/he is guided by the strength of the elders. Rituals bring sacredness and meaning to life and they can do the same in death. Death rituals bring closure for the living. When loved ones can participate in caring for the dead the process of letting go is softened.

Creating rituals for the dying means allowing creativity to blossom and brings meaning to the process. Most people are terrified of what they might see and experience at the bedside of a loved one, let alone at their own death. And most people give their power away to the institutions of death — the hospital, mortuary and church. Many people think the doctor, the undertaker and the priest/minister know best — even if they haven't known the deceased. Having things conducted very businesslike keeps people from being real and from being in their feelings.

201

A dear friend of mine passed away as I was nearing the finishing of this book. She had been like a mother to me and a grandmother to my children. Her own children had been very close to me, as I was partnered with her son for about five years in my early twenties. Her funeral service was, for me, disastrous, as it was exactly a giving over to these institutions. She was not particularly christian, but her family of origin and her husband were Catholic and so, it was decided she was to have a Catholic funeral. Even though she wanted to be cremated and belonged to the Neptune Society, she was embalmed and buried in a fancy coffin. The man "performing" the services was out of his body and had no emotion. My kids asked me "is this Jesus' funeral or Lily's?" The whole experience was intellectual and empty. Lily's daughter, my good friend, asked me if I could "do something" as she wanted it to be said that they were returning their mother to the Great Mother. (She had no say, really, in the plans for her mother's funeral, as her aunt and her mother's husband already figured things out before she and her brother were able to travel to get there.) So I went to the podium and spoke directly from my heart, as I faced a room full of Catholics. I didn't know what I was going to say that would not be alienating, so I waited for the words to come. They did. I spoke of Mary, Queen of Heaven and asked people to see Lily embraced by the loving arms of the Mother. After speaking about Lily's capacity as a loving mother and about her grace, I then sang "Amazing Grace," and asked people to join me. At the end of my time, people were crying and felt much more present. However, the man-in-charge couldn't let the service end on that note. While he was mumbling "Amazing Grace" he was thumbing through his book to find something to say to take back the service from the Mother and give it once again to the father. It was quite something to witness, as I could feel his competitive demeanor and his fear of the Mother. I knew Lily knew what was authentic and what was not. And her daughter and son, and Lily's grandchildren all thanked me, as did others, to my surprise. But not the man-in-charge. He avoided me. The grandchildren, who have grown up with my children, were quite upset at the nature of the funeral, and so they were so glad to have had something spoken that brought people into their hearts. After the man-in-charge ended on an intellectual, unfeeling note, the mortuary man appeared and informed all of us we were now "dismissed" and that we could leave according to his instructions. I was sickened at how people give their power away to these institutions. Simply put, I did not feel the presence of spirit until truth was spoken about who Lily really was and until the Mother was brought into the space. Until that point, it was unbearable, and I felt it was that way for others too, even though they probably didn't know why they were shuffling their feet, sighing, shifting their bodies about and staring off into the distance. The man-in-charge was clearly the center of the show, and it was about him and his father god. In his world, it was not about Lily.

Rituals for the dying and for the dead can be as individual as anyone wants them to be. I feel it is imperative to have the presence of those who have an understanding of the process—who are good at the shamanic skills of reading energy and knowing what to do from an intuitive place and who have no need to control. Because women were the priestesses of life and death in matrifocaled cultures, I would like to see a reclaiming of this wisdom however we see fit to do so. I feel that because women's culture is vastly different from patriarchal culture, education about death and dying from this perspective is vital. When re-awakening occurs regarding the truth of women's ecstatic culture, rituals for honoring the dead will change—as will our shared quality of life on this planet. (I am not supporting an essentialist view, the judgment of which I honestly think is a way to stop women from sharing our truth, as men's actual essentialism goes completely unnoticed in this culture.) I believe the rituals should include the dying from the time they know they are facing their death. I feel they should be encouraged, if possible, to participate in the planning of the rituals and express what they want. I feel that we should not wait until we are dying to figure this out. I feel it is vitally important to share with trusted loved ones what we want in our dying, educate them in advance and write it down. Even though I agree with Sogyal Rinpoche's view that most of us are unprepared for death's arrival, I believe that women who give natural child-birth are perhaps more prepared than anyone, because we have gone to the edge of death, dying and birth all in one experience. He does not appear to be aware of this experience as the valuable teaching that it truly is. Perhaps he might want to ask his mother what she learned in giving birth to him. In my own birth-giving, I saw the oneness of death and life, and rested in a place of deep surrender and eventually, fearlessness. I could not control outcome and had to give myself over to trusting a reality from which I was birthed by my mother—the deep Mystery. Women who go through this experience are indeed the teachers of life and death. This does not mean that one automatically has incisive wisdom, but it does mean that one has been opened to the deep realms of knowing, and with the right support, that knowing can grow and help others. Certainly, in conscious mothering, this knowing grows because it has to in order to support the new life one has birthed. But so much of women's wisdom has been disregarded in patriarchy that women ourselves have a difficult time believing our own deep inner knowing.

Caring for Sedonia

Sedonia, photo by Michael Toms

Another friend of mine died as I was nearing the finishing of this book. She was a spiritual guide in my community for many people, and the women close to her found ways to reclaim their wisdom in caring for her body and in creating a ritual for her memorial. In so doing, some of them were deeply struck at the necessity of women resuming our role of priestess in midwifing death and bringing the honoring of the passage back to whole/holiness. What follows is a description of how her friends tended her body after it came back from Morocco where she died in an auto accident near the date of Candlemas in early February—like Marija Gimbutas six years before—the time of the witches' initiation.

Her best friend, Justine Toms, tells the story:

You may know that my retreat was interrupted by the death of my very best friend, Sedonia Cahill, beloved teacher of circles, vision quest guide, women's advocate, lover of poetry and the desert. She was killed instantly in a car accident as she traveled a high desert road in Morocco. She had been vacationing with her sister and her son and his wife. As she lived, she died, arms open to the Mystery, broken-hearted for the troubles of the world, laughing and grateful for the pleasures life gave her. In her enormous heart she gracefully held the exquisite paradoxes of pain and beauty, solitude and relationship, wildness and refinement. Her greatest teachers, she said, were the desert, its silence, the rocks, all the small creatures who live there and especially the wind. For 64 years she walked the earth lightly and with dazzling beauty.

Sedonia's body came home. Her close circle of women including me, went to the funeral home. We drummed and smudged and undressed the body. Sedonia was thrown from the car and her heart was impaled on some object and she died instantly. She looked quite beautiful when she arrived, natural and serene. We washed her with rose water and washed her hair, dried it and even gave it some body with curlers. We sang to her, chanted Tibetan chants as she had asked. We painted her toenails and fingernails. She had such cute toes. Because we had cut up her black tights she had on under her clothes, Jana (her oldest friend up from southern California) said, "Oh, here she can have mine." And she's pulling off her black tights. It was such a women's moment, sharing clothes. We cut out the feet in the tights so Sedonia could be barefoot and put an anklet on her ankle that she at times wore. We put a long black velvet dress on her and covered that with a special antique kimono that she had given me. I felt she had given it to me in trust because she mentioned it in her funeral notes that she left. We put a beautiful scarf on her that had 10,000 black beads hand-sewed by Egyptian women plus earrings and a simple necklace. We slipped a bar of chocolate under her kimono and made a beauty field. We ALL felt we were honoring the vehicle that carried Sedonia's spirit. But we knew her spirit was free. There was lots of laughter and sadness. The interesting part of it all was how many, many days this whole process was slowed down and that gave a chance for all her many close and extraordinary friends to come and make a contribution in some way. The circle is much stronger because of it.

We got a pine box for her and decorated it. We wrote the words of a Hafiz poem on the bottom, inside, where Sedonia rested. The miraculous existence and impermanence of form always make the illumined ones laugh and sing. Then we put soft padding and black velvet and some of her sweet little lace pillows for her head and feet and Alexandra affixed lace to the inside of the top of the box. Barbara Wild brought a huge basket of rose petals that Sedonia had been collecting for such an occasion. She covered the whole body with rose petals except for the face. Then on Friday morning, February 11, the day before Sedonia's sixty-fourth birthday, there was a cremation ceremony. There were eight women (including me) and Gray (Sedonia's son) there to drum Sedonia's body into transformation. The crematorium was in the cemetery, an old stone building about fourteen feet by fourteen feet built on the side of a hill. The oven was inside. It had an awning about twelve by twelve feet, like a carport that kept any drizzle off of us. The doors were large doors that swung open from the middle, one to the left, and one to the right.

They made us all sign a release form saying they did not recommend that we do this and that if anything happened including going crazy, they were not libel. But it wasn't anything at all like that. The pine box was lifted out of a truck and we smudged it before it went into the oven. We all watched it go into the oven. Then they closed the doors. So we could really not see anything, but it was great to be outdoors looking at the clouds, birds, grave markers, trees, and green grass. We drummed for two and half hours, which was how long it takes for the body to break down into ashes. We could look between the door and the rock wall and see the *temperature guage. It went almost up to 2000 degrees. It felt so good to drum and drum and drum together. I had Sedonia's drum and it really sang. It was so healing.*

Ani's Circle of Healing

I have just returned from a healing circle for Ani who has metatastic breast cancer. One year ago, I was walking a field in Gozo with Ani where the subject of this book came up and she was recounting a very touching story about her mother's passing. She shared how gentle and peaceful it was. Now, Ani is facing the possibility of her own death.

The circle became a healing ritual. There were perhaps about thirty-five to forty of us and we each offered her a gardenia before she lay down on the mat. She became the goddess—receiving each one of us. The aroma from the beautiful gardenias filled the air. Someone said that it is important to have aromatic flowers in sacred ritual space sometimes because the energy is transformed just by their presence. Indeed, this was so at Ani's circle. After the gift-giving of flowers and blessings, we began to chant and drum. We chanted "purify and heal us, heal us and free us" for an hour while people gathered and placed their hands on Ani's body. We raised healing heat for her. The love in the room was so transformative—and I knew it was on deep levels, including the physical. As we did our laying on of hands, I began to experience a remembrance. I could feel all the women present as ancient priestesses and the singing as a powerful sonorous, angelic sound creating a deep healing vibration. At this point, she opened her eyes and looked right at me, acknowledging she could feel the healing energy coming from my hands. Reflecting an ancient Hopi women's teaching, my hands knew just where to go. With the presence of this love, I could feel Ani's fear diminish and joy fill her heart. I mused on how our ancestors must have held one another in their dying with such grace and beauty and with a deep understanding of the cycle of life. With the presence of such love, how could fear and desperation stand a chance? I could also feel a sense of passage—a continuity from this life to the next. The veil between the worlds seemed to fade away as the actual physical warmth we generated in our hands, the sensuous aroma from the flowers and the healing sound and touch bathed Ani and the rest of us in a delicious golden aura of love and gentle calm. This is women's way of healing, grounded in the wisdom of women's culture.

Ani passed away, quietly at home, a year later.

Linda's Message

Linda, photo by Susanna Frohman

A few days ago my friend Linda died from metastatic breast cancer. She was fifty. The previous year we had been together in a Goddess retreat in an extraordinary natural setting where we shared deeply with our laughter, tears, stories and love. We had known each other over twenty years, as we had been on the Farm together. I recently looked over the photos from that event and saw such abandon and beauty on her face. Her breasts were painted with swirls and flowers and she looked radiant and lovely. I marveled how quickly things change and how impermanence is always with us. Six women friends of hers gathered in a circle of remembrance the night after she died. I had wanted to create a circle for her where she could be the recipient—which was hard for her, as she was always taking care of others—of the love of friends and family sharing with her how she had touched their lives, but it was not to be. In our circle following her death, we simply gathered in sacred space and passed around a shimmering handblown glass goddess given to me by my daughter for a "talking stick." We spread out pictures of Linda around the center of the circle. All of us present had known her for the same amount of time, and each other, as we had all been on the Farm togther. We could feel her strong presence in some very unusual ways. We were playing a CD of women's music and all of a sudden, it just stopped—just like that! It certainly got our attention! It felt like an announcement of the beginning of the circle. As we got deeper into the circle-sharing, after a "blessed be" was spoken, a candle holder on the altar burst and a triangular piece of glass shot off the altar. It was a shard that had on it the Egyptian ankh, symbol of life, which is also the symbol of woman. It was the only spot on the glass candle holder with a design. We all felt Linda was speaking directly to us! It was like she was saying "Go Girls! Be your strong woman-selves!" The circle continued into the wee hours of the morning as we shared from our hearts and realized that Linda brought us together not only in remembrance of a beautiful sister, but to facilitate healing amongst ourselves and to speak important truth about women, patriarchy, change and transformation. It was a simple ritual, but full, spontaneous and powerful. It is important to say that we shared not only the "good," but the "bad" as well, which means that we spoke not only about the joy and love in Linda's life but also about the shadow as well. I shared that I felt her early death was a casualty of patriarchy, and that until the war on women and children stops, many more casualties will sadly and grievously befall us. We spoke of how she has now entered the ancestor realm and asked her to guide us, as we spoke of wanting to make the world a better place for our children. She leaves behind three grown daughters, who must look at their future with some trepidation, knowing that both their grandmother and mother were victims of breast cancer. There is certainly more here than meets the eye as to what this kind of breast cancer is about. I believe when women speak our rage, we will see less of this kind of cancer. I believe when men learn to give and stop taking so much, then more equality will emerge and there will be less suffering on the planet.

Donna's Pre-Death Ritual

Holy Grail-St. Non's Well, Monica Sjöö, **1996**

Donna was studying with me for two years when she went in for a check-up and was told that she had a spot on her lungs. She had been a cigarette smoker for many years. Some time later, she went again, and learned that she had lung cancer. She was in her late fifties. When she knew she was going to die she shared that information, and a mutual friend from the same women's circle planned a healing ritual for Donna.

We gathered at Carol's house one evening — about eight women. Carol called in the directions and we rattled and drummed for a while as the spiraling tufts of sage smoke gently danced around us. We created an altar in the center of the space and we were all sitting on the floor. There were flowers, sacred objects and candles.

I call this a pre-death ritual because we all knew Donna was dying. She was in good spirits and wanted to fully participate. She had been a therapist for many years and now it was her turn to receive. After the drumming, rattling and burning of sage, we shared stories about Donna and shared the things we appreciated and admired about her. She quietly listened and received — something different for her. I had felt that receiving for her had been difficult, as it is for many women who are so used to giving. She was actively preparing for her moment of death. She listened, accepted and expressed gratitude. It was a simple ritual — loving, open and truthful.

The most amazing part of the evening was when we asked Donna to get in the middle of the circle and lie down. At that point, we all seemed to enter a timelessness and became the ancestors caring for her and helping her prepare for her passage. We began to sing and gently touch her, using hands-on healing and caressing her. Our hands did the talking. Our touch reassured her that she was held in love and seen for who she was. She could feel the presence of our love and felt that she could die right then and there! She said that if dying could be like that, she wasn't afraid. Sometimes it is very difficult to express in words the feelings that arise in a momentary experience such as this one. The energy in the room was extraordinarily peaceful and sparkled with a clarity that I feel arises when women gather in sacred intention. The synergy takes on a life of its own and wraps us in it, creating a deep peace and safety. I have experienced this many times in the presence of women acting as one, as the shemama who heals.

After this delicious time, Carol closed the circle, and we prepared to go home. Donna was glowing. She died several weeks later, at home, with her partner by her side.

Julia's Ceremony

I did not know Julia. I did know of her. I learned of her suicide shortly before my dear friend Carol died. Julia was fourteen. What makes a fourteen-year-old end her life is a deeply disturbing question. She was gifted, kind, loving, sensitive, and all those things that life is at precious fourteen. Placing her father's gun to her head, Julia ended her young sweet life in an instant. Her suicide is indeed a statement of the severity of the woundedness and insanity of our times. Her mother contacted me to see if I could assist her in honoring the year anniversary of Julia's passing. I felt it would be a privilege to do so, and we collaborated on finding a way to celebrate Julia's memory in sacred circle with Nancy's close friends. In learning about Julia from Nancy, I was saddened to hear that she had spent a great deal of time being raised by her very depressed father. I knew this had something to do with the pain Julia felt at the time of her death. Her father had been so depressed that he couldn't work.

So, her mother had to support the family. I think this was especially hard on Julia and her mother, and is now especially hard on her mother, who felt torn during the time her daughter was growing up. Julia didn't need to absorb her father's depression, or struggle with the attending feelings of a child who wants to heal the adult, or fix things, or make things feel better for her father, which she couldn't do. She needed her mother. It always seems to come to that in one way or another — needing the Mother. And of course, there is no blame. Julia's father was good to her as he could be, trying to be there. Nancy did the best she could do. She is a loving woman and mother. She just didn't know the depths of her daughter's suffering. No one did. Sometimes the voices in the unspoken realms are louder than those in the spoken.

Julia's ceremony was a celebration of her bright spirit. We celebrated her short life through speaking the truth, singing, remembering her and sharing food. The altar was covered with pictures of her from early childhood to adolescence. Part way into the ritual the doorbell rang, and Nancy opened it to receive flowers from another mother whose young teenage daughter had suicided a year before. The room was filled with an undeniable presence — our children are trying to tell us something. Our children are trying to tell us that life here can be too painful and hard. Why is that? What do they mean? They are our legacy. What are we leaving them that they can't take?

From my perspective as a feminist shamanic practitioner, I see the denial of the feminine as the root cause of the many and varied ills from which we all suffer. Our children are acting out in many ways trying to tell us something is deeply, grievously and hideously wrong with the way things are. With the loving presence of the Mother, abuse would be quite diminished, as is evidenced by the peacefulness of the cultures of our Neolithic ancestors. Perhaps some would say this is too simplistic of an analysis. I don't think so. What do you envision when you close your eyes and see a time and space where women and children are loved and respected? A vision where boy-children are allowed to feel, cry and be sensitive and nurturing? Do you see violence in that vision? Do you see rape, rampant abuse and war? Do you see children killing themselves and each other?

The sweetness and loving presence of this wonderful child who took her life because she couldn't heal her father's depression will stay with me as a reminder of the most precious thing we have in life — the life of our children. We must protect them and care for them, which for me, means to uncover the love and wisdom of the Goddess in order to bring that love to them in meaningful ways. When I say "we," I mean all of us — including men, whose pain is so great and whose ignorance of the feminine within them is begging to be seen and healed. This can only happen when men take responsibility for their pain and walk the difficult path of healing. It means admitting they are afraid of feeling. It means that they can say they are afraid of being vulnerable and don't know how to surrender. It means they seek the means to heal themselves, and not depend on women to do it for them, which women cannot do, though many try. This naming of this condition is not to be confused with blame. What naming does say, however, is that we pay a high price for our ignorance.

The Gift of Giving

And Her belly lit up the world, Monica Sjöö, 1996

I feel I have been blessed with some very important teachings from the dying themselves. I feel preparation for dying needs to become more of an accepted practice. As we have seen, situations can arise when you may be the one person on the spot who needs to know what is needed. With someone who is slowly dying, and is bedridden, you may still be the only person on the spot who needs to know what is needed. Depending on what that person has chosen regarding her/his death, and if you are a friend or relative, you will need to find out just what is going on and how you can be of service, without your own agenda. So, primarily, one needs to learn to simply show up and be in the moment with what is. You cannot know "what is" until you are in that moment.

This requires a simplicity of being, not of doing. This skill requires you to know how to be present — not by what you say, but by who you are. If you are ambitious about being the wonderful care-giver and "s/he who knows," you will only get in the way. I feel that a person's actions can have a strong psychic affect on the dying — even if they are not able to say so. I feel that dying people are exceptionally sensitive, and an inappropriate behavior can cause anger and fear in them. Once when a hospice assistant came to bathe my mother the day before she died, the woman washed my mother's face and my mother quietly spoke from a deep place of wisdom "she has hurt someone." I noticed the woman had a roughness about her, and reported her to hospice. My mother, in having her face washed by this energy, could feel the harm in it.

The image of a loving mother who gently tends and nurtures her child is a most powerful image to hold in working with the dying. Loving mothers just know what to do, how to be and what to give to the needs in the moment. There is no thinking or intellectualizing — there is only giving and caring. Loving mothers do not have selfish agendas nor are they judgmental. They are present with their love as an offering — as a gift. I see loving mothers as free — they are not controlled by a fear-based male religion telling them how to behave. They are grounded in the spirituality of the Great Mother, the Goddess, who informs their true nature. Where are these mothers?

I think these mothers are remembering ourselves and our ways. The mother culture is a far different culture than this patriarchal one in which we are all trying to survive. The mother culture is free from violence, domination and control. It is rooted in the earth, and is governed by the magical rhythms of the moon-mind. To remember these ways is to bring back the wisdom of our foremothers who did, indeed, midwife the dying and tended their journeys as they left this world and passed into the next. These ancestral mothers understood the secrets of life, death and rebirth and their rituals were woven with this sacred knowledge.

Midwifing someone in motherly love in their death means just that — loving them from a pure heart. You cannot go wrong with this kind of attention. Kind and loving words, soothing silent presence, gentle singing, tender touch, creation of beauty in the environment, acceptance of the process, the offering of non-invasive support, protecting their dignity, affirming their precious worthiness, giving permission to them to let go, using compassionate prayer, whatever can be given in the spirit of love and kindness are all the offerings of motherly love. While motherly love protects life, it also knows when to let go. Motherly love trusts the entire process of life on its journey and helps it to pass gently and peacefully. In this manner, this kind of love assists the dying person to meet death with a sense of surrender instead of paralyzing fear.

Perhaps in this, death then, can be a kind of celebration/initiation that can only be experienced at the time — a passage through a portal into the next world. It seems to me that if we can die without fear, we are creating for ourselves an opportunity to be open and conscious to what is as we leave this life and enter a new one. It makes sense to me that how we die — that is, what our intention is at the time of our death — affects the coming experience. We celebrate birth and new life when a baby is born. Would it be so different to celebrate the death of a person as they are born into another world? The moment of my mother's death was filled with light, awe and wonder. Though she suffered from cancer, and I believe her cancer was connected to the anger she carried all of her life, all traces of suffering seemed to disappear as she surrendered. On this side of the veil, it is hard to know, though it seems our ancestors had a strong sense of the other side as the regenerative transformative domain of the Goddess.

I believe midwifing the dying in simplicity of being and motherly love is based on giving. It is not based on exchange. When you sit with someone in their dying, you are not looking for payment or something for yourself. You are simply giving your presence. The gift of giving is its own reward, as it fills the hearts of the giver and the receiver with a warm love, communication and compassion. This gift-giving is the foundation of motherly love. Our whole society and economy are based on exchange, so how do we know what giving really is, especially in a time of need? If we don't understand the nature of giving, then we also don't understand the nature of receiving. Exchange is not about either one of these. Exchange is linear and patriarchal, based on an expectation of "getting."

Gift-giving is cyclical and circular, ushered forth from the very Earth Mother who gifts all of us. Gift-giving creates true community and communication — "muni" is Latin for "gifts." If we have lived a life in giving, then we can die in the same experience. If we have lived a life dependent on exchange, we have limited ourselves to always seeking "what's in it for me" and feeling we don't have time to give unless we get something in return. It is no wonder that we live in a death-denying society. The patriarchal mind sees death as a "there's nothing in it for me" situation. There is no sense of a giving back to the Mother in this denial. A mother gives unconditionally because she simply loves. She is capable of loving and giving. And yet, this giving does not just happen effortlessly. Any mother will tell you that nurturing requires mindfulness, great effort at times and the ability to put another's needs before one's own. This is not a blind giving away of self, as has become the condition women find ourselves in patriarchy, but rather a sharing of the self.

Another way of viewing this capacity to give is learning to exchange self for other — putting yourself in the shoes of another, or seeing them as yourself. Mothers do this naturally, all the time. Why do we have male authority figures in our religious traditions telling us how to love like a mother? Who knows best how to do this? Why when men speak of this, they are listened to, and when women do it, we are ignored? Author of **For-Giving, a Feminist Criticism of Exchange**, Genevieve Vaughn writes, "By not recognizing gift-giving as an important independent human way of behaving with its own logic, the continuity between mothering and other types of activity are lost . . . . We must become wise enough to shift paradigms towards the mothering way." ("Gift-Giving and the Goddess," Genevieve Vaughan, **Avalon**). It is self-evident that this continuity is all but lost in the current ruling paradigm. There is nothing more important to do than to re-store this continuity in our lives.

I see many people who are not able to freely love and give. And the odd thing is that all of us want to be loved and to be gifted, as well as to give love and to give our gifts. So we are desperate for the very thing our fear pushes away — fear of allowing someone to love us because they might take advantage of or hurt us, like someone may have done when we were little, fear of being visible and seen for who we really are, fear of not knowing, fear of being wrong, fear of being right, fear of fear. How can people learn to shed this fear in the face of death? How can people learn to shed this fear in life and not wait until death has arrived? Vaughan states that when we are ready to truly create a gift-based society then we will be able to create a community with the spirits of the dead forming a "practical heaven on earth." (ibid.).

I do want to speak to violent death, as it is difficult to think of death as a celebration in the face of such grievous pain. I know that many people, many women and children die horrific and violent deaths in patriarchy. I do not want to say that these deaths are celebrations. I know these deaths are very difficult for the living to accept, and to have any sense of deity when a child dies a violent death must be unspeakably difficult. And yet, while we are on this side looking at the violence that has stolen our loved one, what is happening on the other side to the one whose life was taken?

I remember when four women were murdered in Yosemite in 1999. They were: Carole, a mother, her fifteen-year-old daughter, Julie, Julie's sixteen-year-old friend, Silvina, and twenty-six year-old Joie. The crimes were particularly heinous, committed by a woman-hating man who was completely consumed by demons, though apparently appearing to many people to be "gentle." He was so manipulative that he fooled the FBI after having been questioned several times. The FBI even engaged his help in collecting possible evidence at the scene of the crime of the murders of Carole and Silvina, where he worked.

I had the opportunity to visit Joie's grave, as she was buried in the cemetery close to my home. She was the last victim he decapitated in the pristine wilderness near her rustic cabin. He left her headless body in the creek beside her home. When I sat at her graveside, I wept in bewilderment and rage. How could this loving, sweet Goddess-child, naturalist and wonderful teacher about Yosemite's environment to many children, have been taken in such a manner? I still have no answer for that question, but as I sat there, I was overcome with a sense of peace. I had told her in prayer I was going to Yosemite with a group of women to do a healing ritual to cleanse the energy where the murders had taken place and asked her if there was anything she wanted me to do.

I then had a vision of a beautiful butterfly, but instead of an insect body, it was a woman's body, wings outstretched glistening in radiant color. I knew it was Joie. She said to me "make the world safe for the children." She was not in pain, nor was she suffering. She was beautiful and at peace. As I got up to leave, a butterfly appeared and landed on the flowers marking her grave. I felt completely blessed. While her death was grotesque, I knew she was in a place of celebration. When my friend, Monica, and I talked about the death of her youngest child, who was killed by a car in 1985, she said that the look of peace on young Leif's face at the very scene of the accident gave her a sense that he was in a good place, that he had been "met" by loved ones. Her agony at his loss cannot be described, but he came to her later in a dream and said "love is all that matters." Are his words an honoring of a kind of celebration of spirit?

Though I would never ask a mother who has lost a child to regard that death as a celebration, because of her own loss and grief, I do have to wonder what is taking place on the other side for the one who has died. While I know that the Mother is not always serene and nurturing, that she is sometimes wild and fierce, mysterious and untamable, I trust She knows what is going on.

While I do not understand why certain things happen the way they do, I have felt She is there on the other side, guiding and loving. When Monica shared with me what Leif had communicated to her, I replied that he was the child of the Mother, speaking Her wisdom. We both agreed this was true. And, her pain is still her pain, as is true for Joie's mother, Silvina's mother, and the family of Carole and Julie. Sometimes I think a deep piercing of the heart opens us up to things we would not otherwise know. A mother's love for her child knows no bounds. This is a fierce kind of love that is feared in patriarchy. We need this love more than ever now as we face tremendous odds for our survival in this new millennium.

Pat's Story

Ancient Cornwall — Land of the Goddess, Monica Sjöö, 1993

Pat was a beautifully brave woman. She called me to her side because she knew what she wanted, contrary to her family's wishes. She was at home where her eighty-three-year-old mother was caring for her, along with her older sister, who was nearing seventy. Apparently the mother had been very young when she started having babies. Pat was the one in the family who sought healing — who confronted the dysfunction and abuse in her family and brought it to light. She also seemed to be the one who carried most of the family's pain. Her sensitivity and gentleness revealed this, whereas others in the family were more guarded and controlling. Even unto her dying day, she commented on how her mother just wouldn't listen to her, or see her for who she was. I never witnessed her mother shed a tear for her the entire time I was in her home.

Pat knew I was "different." She knew I was a "shemama" — a modern-day medicine woman and a priestess of the Goddess. She had wanted to take a class with me, and had been attracted to the "she-manic" path. She joked with me about how she didn't think she was going to be able to take my class after all. She didn't really care whether or not her family would like me, nor did I. However, I was prepared to be compassionate with everyone while tending to her. She had several main issues she wanted to share with me. She wanted instructions as she was dying, and leaving her body, and she wanted to plan her own memorial. She had a large empty glass mayonnaise jar on her dresser she could see from her bed, and insisted that her ashes be put in the jar. This was her way of expressing her wry sense of humor.

We spent hours together talking and getting to know each other. The time came when she wanted to gather her family together to explain to them just

219

who I was and what my function was in her process, since I had just basically shown up out of the blue. The whole family gathered in her bedroom, and she spoke eloquently about her wishes — that she wished for me to facilitate her memorial and that she wanted me there as she was passing. She was making it very clear to her family what she wanted. She told them she was paying me to do this, which I realized was her way of ensuring that she was honored, since I hadn't asked her for money. The family all acted in accord at the time — some even crying.

During the time I spent with Pat, we discussed what happens at death, so that she could be prepared. Not being one who can say for sure what happens, as I don't think anyone really can, I shared with her what I had read, and shared with her my most recent experience with my mother. She was all ears, and eager to know. I didn't feel any fear from her. She felt like a wise teacher for me, modeling the right way to die, in the midst of a painful illness. We discussed details of her memorial, and I sang Amazing Grace. She loved hearing that song and was grateful that I was going to sing it for her at her memorial. She wanted people to share about their lives with her — the good and the bad, she said. And she wanted some of her own journal to be read. She wanted her memorial outside, on the earth.

After all things were put in order, Pat began to settle into a deep state of consciousness. It felt like she found a peace, knowing that she had gotten to plan things the way she wanted, and was ready to let go. She told me that she thought I was tender and kind and also told her entire family. I felt that being treated in this manner was significant to her because she hadn't known much of that in her life. It made her cry to be treated lovingly and respectfully, and I could tell she had been hungry for this for a long time all the while enduring life the best way she knew how. I had an agreement with her sister to call me when it was time.

The call never came. I was on the phone with her sister two hours prior to her death, and didn't know she was that close. Her sister said she would call me, as she relayed to me that the hospice people had told her that it could be a while still. But when it became apparent to her sister that Pat was indeed dying, she did not honor Pat's final wish to call me. I didn't even receive a phone call after she died. The family proceeded to make the memorial service arrangements without me, picking a date without asking me, which turned out to be a time when I was going to be out of town.

They didn't honor any of her last wishes. It was astounding. The deep-seated control issues of her family came to light, and I had a feeling I understood what contributed to her having cancer. I was the target of projections of family members and decided that I would have nothing to do with them. I knew I had to honor Pat in the way I had agreed to, and so decided to have a second memorial for her in the way in which she asked. It was grievous to me that her family members were so involved with their own need to control that they couldn't honor her the way she had asked them to when she gathered them all together. Not even her children. To this day, I am still stunned that people could treat a supposed loved one in this manner. Pat was an amazing teacher for anyone paying attention. It appeared to me that no one in her family could see her even in her death. The second memorial felt like the one she had wanted. No one from her family was there. Her women friends attended it and it was truly "Pat."

In sitting with Pat just days prior to her death, I had the privilege of recording several conversations with her, with her permission, regarding her process. I had told her that I would be honored to be able to do some record-ing with her so that I could include it in the book I was writing. She was happy that maybe there would be something in our conversation that could possibly help someone else. What follows is one of the recorded conversa-tions I had with her when she was preparing to die. Even though Pat was on a morphine drip, she was able to be present with our dialogue and was able to express her authentic self.

Leslene: Today is May 31st, and since we were together last you have been to the hospital and back with a transfusion and you were feeling not so good and feeling like maybe it was time to go. And then after the transfusion you felt better. So, we have been talking about your memorial and if you could just share a little bit about how it is for you to be talking about that now, while you're still in the body and planning it and how it feels. What would you want people to know about this part of your experience?

Pat: If I don't go to sleep first! (Laughter)

Leslene: I'll poke you. (More laughter)

Pat: Alright. I can't go to sleep through this! I don't know what to say about that right now.

Leslene: A few minutes ago you said you were "tickled" about being able to plan this and to be a part of this.

Pat: Tickled about?

Lesenee: About planning.

Pat: Oh, huh-huh. Ok. Well I've always wanted to be a part of everything, and . . .

Leslene: And planning this is about your life?

Pat: Yes. And I want to be a part of this.

Leslene: And so you are.

Pat: Yes.

Leslene: And so how do you feel about it being a celebration of who you are and what you've meant to others — how does that make you feel, know-ing that's what it will be?

Pat: I think it's wonderful. I've talked with my kids in the last few days and they're tickled about it and think it's cool. I'm really surprised at my son,

John — to have it be a celebration of my life.

Leslene: That surprises you?

Pat: Yeah. Especially with John. I don't know about Patrick. But they seem to really want it to be that. I think it's growth for them.

Leslene: Good!

Pat: Yeah! They're just happy — for me. John especially is happy.

Leslene: Well, you see, what you're giving to your children is such an amazing gift because of the way you're doing this — it's very beautiful. They're seeing you're ok with this!

Pat: Yeah. Patrick said "I don't want you to go." I think that's what he said. (Giggle)

Leslene: Well of course he doesn't want you to go —

Pat: No.

Leslene: Nobody wants anybody to go. But we do go. We do go.

Pat: Yes. I'm going. So, that's that.

Leslene: That's that.

Pat: Yep.

Leslene: Ok. And you're going in a way that makes it ok for everybody, which is so amazing. Nothing has to be hidden and nobody has to deny anything. So, ok. Is there anything else you want to share at this time about your process, ups and downs or anything that you want people to know about at this point in time, besides that you're sleepy?

Pat: No. (Laughter)

Leslene: You look very comfortable.

Pat: I am very comfortable.

Leslene: That's wonderful. Well maybe that's all people need to know right now, that you're very comfortable. And that you are tickled about planning your memorial.

Pat: Ok.

Lelsene: The other day we were talking about practicing dying, remember?

Pat: Yes.

Leslene: We're going to do some of that now. I would like to read to you a death meditation from Steven Levine's book, **"Who Dies?"** Is that ok with you?

Pat: Yes.

In the Face of "Terminal" Illness

Michele's coffin, painted by family.

I do realize that in our society doctors are prone to playing "god" with their often hopeless decrees of finality regarding someone's life. No one can be sure of when someone will pass, and I don't think it is beneficial for a doctor to speak with the voice of authority regarding someone's state of health. My friend Carol who had metastatic breast cancer defied doctors all the time. She refused to believe them — and Carol was an RN. Though she did die young, she did not die within their time frame; right up until the very end they thought it was hours or days, and Carol lived for weeks. I think harmful effects are possible when one speaks with an air of authority to a sick person exclusive of that person's own divine authority — that person could believe something negative and actually be shaped by the opinion of a doctor who really doesn't know.

So, the first rule is not to give your power away to anyone — especially doctors. However, serious situations do arise in illness, and if it looks like a long life is not possible, one must then think of what comes next. Secondly, it is vitally important to not wait until one is dying to contemplate dying. However, if this is your first encounter with contemplating death, then it is extremely important to face your fears and learn whatever you can about death and dying — keeping in mind that most available material is written in male-speak.

Optimally, I would strongly recommend a spiritual practice of "death acquaintance" during one's life. I have practiced some of the Kali practices of meditating in cemeteries to learn about my responses to death and dying. I learned to accept death as an ally. I also learned a great deal about "ego death" during my training with the deva spirits of the various plant and synthetic mind-medicines I took. Even though some of the hallucinogenic substances were made in a laboratory, I believe they had helpful spirits. That was over thirty years ago. Now, with so much going on in the lab, I couldn't say, though I work with a woman who has chosen to use LSD (on her own) in her medicine work, and she experiences profound teachings. I have a great deal of respect for her process and what she is learning. She uses it in a sacred manner, and perhaps this is the key.

Ego death is tricky business for women in patriarchal society. Many women have not been allowed to develop a healthy sense of self — however, it is not this self that I am referring to in ego death. It is more of what author

223

and artist Cristina Biaggi describes as the kind of ego death one experiences in entering the sacred temples of the Goddess resulting in the "rebirth of one who is blessed by the Goddess" (Cristina Biaggi, "Temple Tombs and Sculptures in the Shape of the Body of the Goddess," **From the Realm of the Ancestors**, p. 499).

We live in a society built on the denial of death. What the white male elite has done to the native peoples of this land is a shameful unspeakable example of this denial. In my own meditations, I have seen that this denial found a foothold in my unconscious, and I needed to come to terms with it in order to really find peace about dying. This was not about becoming submissive or passive. It was about freeing myself from the constrictions and bindings of patriarchal lies I inherited from my parents, and they from theirs, and so on. Being aware of death while living allows one to be in process with it. In my medicine journeys, death was a constant companion, as I embodied a great deal of fear about being alive as well as dying.

So, learning about death in those cemeteries helped me to learn about living. The simplest practice is to go to a cemetery and just sit there. Allow whatever wants to come to you as you sit, and just be with the images and thoughts. You may find yourself thinking about the people whose names surround you. You may get messages from ancestor spirits. You may get graphic images of decomposing bodies, and see your own body decomposing. You may have some reflections on the impermanence of life. You may have insights about the nature of the immanent/transcendent Goddess. It may help you develop a sense of humor!

In my work with the terminally ill, I have experienced a range of responses from the dying. The one experience that stands out for me the most is the struggle with the lack of preparation I have seen people endure. My own mother regressed for a while to a very young helpless child when she learned she had a terminal illness. At seventy-two, she was frightened, desperate and victimized by the uncontrollable outcome of her own death. (Fortunately this didn't last the entire time, as the predominate experience, though it was always there. I do feel she was able to relax as she became more accepting, but she also relaxed because I took care of her — which gave her a sense of safety. She told me how much better she felt when I was around her.)

However, she was unable to take care of her household and possessions, though she did manage to make a living trust and will. (It took great encouragement to get her to do this, as the thought of making a will brought up her fear of her mortality.) The task of sorting out her material plane was left to her children, which I don't recommend. I like the teaching that encourages people to let go of possessions and to give them away before death, if possible. I like the idea of making a clean exit, and not leaving a trail for my kids to clean up after me.

Even though my father had an intuition that he was going to die, he had plenty of time to prepare a will and did not, and I had to do this with him as he was dying — something else I don't recommend leaving to the literal last minute. It was very difficult. Midwifing my mother and father in their deaths inspired me to want to prepare positively for my own death. In my research, I came across the story of a remarkable woman in my community who did exactly that. I will share with you some of who she was and how she took responsibility for her death as an example of what to do, when one can, in facing "terminal" illness. From my point of view, I consider Michele to be a woman who learned to mother herself in her dying process and was able not only to give that love to herself, but to give it to those who surrounded her in her last days.

I did not know Michele, though I would have liked to. She was diagnosed with pancreatic cancer at the age of fifty and died at fifty-two. I learned of her through several newspaper articles chronicling her decision to do death in her own way. From the pentacle she wore around her neck in the news photos, I knew she was involved with the Goddess, and I was deeply inspired by her story. She decided that she would die at home and made all the arrangements for her own funeral beforehand with her family and friends. She worked closely with the Natural Death Project — an organization that assists people in alternative care for the dying and after death situations.

Michele's courageous honesty about her dying and coming death taught everyone around her about life. She made all the arrangements, down to discussing the details needed for her death certificate. Her cardboard box in which she was cremated, which rested in her living room until she was ready to be placed in it, was painted in a colorful Egyptian motif and was lined with purple satin. When Michele died, she lay in state in the box for three days surrounded by mementos and sacred objects tucked in close to her side. In the months before her death, she went through her belongings and gave them away as she wished. Michele was truly living her dying. She knew how the funeral was going to be conducted, as she planned it herself, inviting special friends and family members to accept certain responsibilities, down to who was going to get the dry ice for her body.

The funeral was seen as a celebration of her soul and spirit. Her ceremony was a mixture of pagan, Buddhist and Native American flavors, with readings from the **Egyptian Book of the Dead**. Four men carried her cardboard coffin, accompanied by four candle-bearing women all following a path strewn with rose petals into the circle of wise old trees on her property. A soothing sound of flute music put her to rest in the grove until the time arrived to take her body to be cremated. A long-time neighbor had commented that she didn't think she was gong to be able to be at the ceremony and was pleasantly surprised at how "euphoric" she actually felt. She said she felt she hoped she could do her death in a similar way.

Michele's decision to take her death into her own hands empowered her in her final days. Rather than suffer in denial, she met her mortality with courage, strength and grace, giving her the opportunity to die in peace. There were no loose ends, no things left undone and people close to her were constantly involved with her process. She was not isolated in fear. While Michele's story might seem to some to be totally out of the ordinary, which it is, I can see how her story might just become more of the ordinary.

Michele knew she was going to die, and from what I gathered, she was able to say with some certainty, by paying attention to her intuition, approximately when. She thought perhaps spring, and it was that summer. My father also had an intuition, and told me he thought he was living his last year. He was right. The difference between him and Michele was that she was able to accept her death and prepare for it. My father was too frightened to have done that in advance. He did, however, consciously move into surrender the night before he died.

Michele, photo by Jane Kirn

Helen's Passage

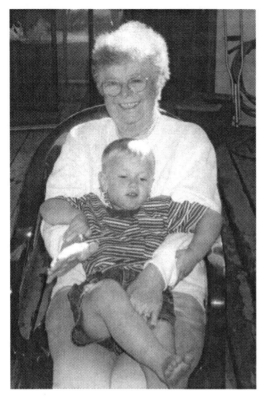

Helen with grandson Noah, photo by Beverly Walker

I was surprised during the writing of this book how many people I knew in my life passed on. Shortly before publication, yet another family friend made her passage. My daughter called me from the hospital and told me that her then boyfriend's grandmother was not doing very well. She had been in and out of the hospital many times in the last year, and told her family she was not living a quality of life and that she didn't want to live anymore. I could feel that this stay in the hospital would probably be her last. My daughter was very close to her and she felt Helen was her grandmother too. Two weeks prior to Helen's passing my youngest daughter had a prophetic dream. She was away at college, and didn't really know exactly what was going on at that time with Helen. In the dream, Helen's daughter, Bev, told Celena, my daughter, something of a very serious nature. Celena went to Bev's youngest child, Kevin and hugged him for a long time. (Since Celena was away at school, she hadn't seen Kevin for a long time, and he had entered that very changeable time of puberty. The last time she saw him, he still had a "baby face", and in her dream he was taller and thinner, which was quite accurate.) As the dream continued, Celena found herself hugging Kevin's brother, Matt, also for a long time. She was comforting both of them. At the time, Celena felt very moved by this dream, and it became quite clear to everyone why.

I went to see Helen because I felt closure would be very difficult for everyone if they didn't have help — they wanted help and asked me to go and be with her. Very few people really prepare for death — including the family and the person dying. With preparation, the experience can be much softer and truly beautiful. Helen had no problem remembering my name and who I was, which surprised me because my daughter told me she had been in and out of being lucid, and I didn't know Helen really well. But she wasn't having any trouble when my daughter, her grandson and I were there together with her. It became clear that Helen needed to talk. I think it was easier for her to talk with me because I was someone outside of her family. I could tell that she needed to speak her truth with her family, and needed them to listen to her. It had been very difficult for her family to hear in the year preceding her death that she didn't want to go on. She had numerous health issues and was in her late seventies. She was tired of going back and forth to the hospital. I felt she held on for so long because her family couldn't bear to think about her death. But this time, she was sure she was ready to die. I felt she made up her mind about what she wanted and needed support in telling her family. At one point, she turned to her grandson and said in a very calm way that she just didn't want to live anymore. When he heard her words, he began to cry, realizing that his beloved grandmother, who had been like a mother to him, was really going to die. She told him it wasn't a bad thing to want to go. At that point, my daughter, Larissa, told her that she wanted her to stay and she loved having her around. Helen, with great humor, unwavering from her decision, sweetly told Larissa, "Well, I don't hold that against you." It was such a heartfelt reply. Her resolve was undeniable.

David left the room, and Larissa went with him. I was left alone for a while with Helen. We talked about how the family would handle her death. She knew how each person would be affected. I could feel her compassion as well as her letting go of attachment, which was amazing to me, because it was just like some teachings suggest—to not be attached, neither in life nor in death. She told me that it was time for them to support her and think about her and think about themselves later. She was clear, calm and collected. Later that day, she told her daughter, Bev, David's mother, in the presence of her granddaughter, David's sister, that she had to let her go. As hard as that was for Bev to hear, she knew her mother was right. It was time to let go. The next morning, the nurse had Helen up on the commode, washed her hair and gave her a shower. Shortly afterwards, after getting back into bed, she transitioned into a state that surprised everyone, including the doctors. She simply began to die. She clearly demonstrated her power to choose. It was amazing and awesome. She received the permission from her loved ones she needed in order to let go. She was not fearful. She passed away that night, surrounded by loving family singing her favorite songs to her. Just before her last breath, she opened her eyes wide, looked at everyone, and then seemed to look past everyone, with awe in her eyes. Larissa said she could see light beaming into the room from the direction Helen was facing.

I arrived minutes after she passed, and asked everyone to gather around her bed. We held hands, and I spoke to Helen, guiding her into the after death state, telling her she just left her body and not to be afraid. We did the visualization seeing her heart merging with the heart of a great loving being in front of her, a loving motherly presence. We then bathed her body, draped her with a sheet, anointed her with lavender oil and covered her with rose petals. Larissa and David had transformed her hospital room into a beautiful sacred space, with pictures, tapestries and flowers. Serene flute music was gently playing in the background. And yes, sadness and grief were present too, but a beautiful memory was created for all those who witnessed Helen pass from this world to the next without fear. At one point, Bev felt overwhelmed. She was feeling a childhood memory when she had a frightening experience of having to go up to her father's coffin after he died. Because of this, she felt she couldn't approach her mother's body and kiss her good-bye. I gently coaxed her to come closer and reminded her that this was a different time and that it was okay. She and I together went to Helen's side and Bev kissed her mother's forehead. It was deeply healing for her, and she felt she could let her mother go in peace rather than stay contracted in fear from that earlier childhood memory.

David had some difficulty with the fact that his grandmother was in the hospital because she had wanted to come home, and he wanted to fulfill that wish. The family could not agree on bringing her home, so they brought home to her in the hospital. He struggled with leaving her body there in the hospital. This was a time when I thought how better he would have felt had there been plans in place beforehand. An organization in our town called "Final Passages" helps people plan their own funerals and assists the family in dealing with things after someone dies. They approach the whole situation with kindness and simplicity, and they keep the costs very low. People need to know that following the death of a loved one, we can take much more into our own hands than we are led to believe, such as bringing the body home from the hospital and/or bringing the body ourselves to the place of cremation. I had my mother's body at home for three days before having her cremated. I thought better for all to have her body rest at home than in a cold refrigerator. "Final Passages" educates people about how to take things more into our own hands. I would like to see such groups everywhere, assisting in midwifing death in love and compassion. All it takes is some preparation and foresight—just like life.

Grief

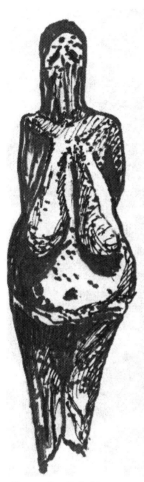

Figurine from Dolni Vestonice, Moravia, c. 26,000 BP, drawn by Melissa Meltzer

The grieving process is extremely important for those left behind. Letting go does not mean "getting over." Letting go means allowing the relationship to the deceased to change — for them and for you. If you remember from the discussion on ancestor worship, we maintain a relationship with the dead. In some traditions, a final ceremony of letting go is practiced on the fiftieth anniversary of a person's death.

If the death is sudden, and/or violent, grieving seems to be a particularly challenging process. There seems to be a burning question of "why" on the lips of loved ones who do not understand. I don't know that "why" can ever be answered. In the case of sudden and/or violent death, the truth of impermanence is glaring, reminding us that we are not in control. The tidal emotions of anger and fear come crashing down on the shore of an illusive reality. If the death is expected, we have more time to spend getting used to the idea, though, in my experience, there is no complete preparation for the finality when it arrives.

There are many cross-cultural traditions for grieving and many resources available on the grieving process, so I will not go into the whole subject of grieving here. I am interested in focusing on aspects of grief from a spiritual feminist perspective. As a Goddess devotee, I am always searching for new ways of doing and being, and since I feel we don't have the ways of the elders in this tradition so available I feel I am always trying to see things from a perspective that lives deep in my bones — the perspective of the "wild mother." I am rather constantly questioning my conditioning and the assumptions of "mainstream" patriarchal thought. The "wild mother" perspective is the "untamed" wisdom of the ancestral grandmothers. When I think of their expression of grief, I sense their embodiment of an understanding of the greater whole — that life is birthed from the Mother's love and is returned to Her in time. What would it be like if we knew this all-pervasive love in our daily lives? Because I think our patriarchal experience makes us very afraid of death, I think the experience of our grief is often colored by this fear. What is grief like without fear?

I have had several different kinds of experience with grief and the dying. When my father died, though I witnessed his surrender into a deep peaceful place, my actual experience of his "leaving" was life-altering and shattering in an unpredictable kind of way. Though I have had a rather independent life-style since my teen-age years, my identity had been of course, connected to my parents. When he died, I was faced with learning who I was without him. When my mother died, I had the same experience, but in a different way. She was in my home, and my father was not. I was with her, holding her hand, gently touching her and whispering into her ear. My father died alone, which I felt he wanted.

Nevertheless, I felt my grief to be softened with my mother since I was such a part of her dying process. Even though I had tended my father consistently as he was dying, I was still somewhat removed from it, as I had to travel back and forth to where he was and couldn't create for him the warm, safe, beautiful environment I was fortunate enough to create for my mother. And there were also overlaps as well in my experience with both of them

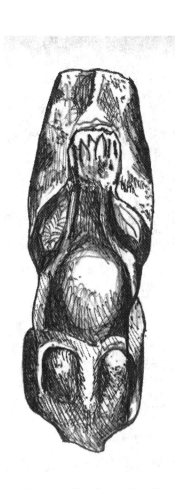

Double Goddess figurine, Grimaldi, Italy c. 28,000-20,000 BP, drawn by Melissa Meltzer

as there was a sense of pervading peace in both situations. I felt that being involved with them and involving my family changed the nature of grief for me. Though I don't know how I would have grieved had things been different, I know that having witnessed both of them surrender into peacefulness somewhat alleviated my own fear about death. Had I not had that experience, I think my fear of the unknown would have been more present in my grieving their loss.

Human grief is part of the whole continuum of life. An ancient figure from Grimaldi, Italy from the Gravettian period circa 28,000-20,000 BP profoundly illustrates this truth. Mistakenly named as the "Hermaphrodite" by phallocentric archeology, the Goddess figurine is actually, according to prehistorian James Harrod, a representation of the Double Goddess. She is a figure about five centimeters tall carved with archetypically nourishing breasts and pregnant belly. When she is turned upside down, she appears as a grieving woman holding her hands over her face. The mistaken identity was due to the detail in the thigh area of the figure that was interpreted as "dangling arms and male genitalia." Interesting assumption.

It is clear in reversing the figure that this detail is hands. This so-called scholarship deciding that this figure was hermaphroditic seems to be typical of male perception/projection. How difficult could it have been to turn the figure upside down and see the truth? This mind-set just seems to see itself everywhere, even where it is not! If women scholars attempted this kind of arrogant egocentric approach, the reproach would be phenomenal.

(As it is, Marija Gimbutas was profoundly judged when her Goddess work emerged. As long as she talked about weapons and the Bronze Age, she was considered an esteemed expert. When she changed her focus to woman-centered cultures and the Goddess, many of her peers began to feel threatened by her discoveries.) Harrod claims, "The figurine is a masterpiece depicting the Double Goddess. In its stunning and beautiful design, this figurine represents the double perspective of the Double Goddess spiritual transformation: grievous loss, abandonment and death; and pregnancy, the engendering of a creative and abundantly nourishing life." (Harrod, "The Upper Paleolithic 'Double Goddess': 'Venus' Figurines as Sacred Female Transformation Processes in the Light of a Decipherment of European Upper Paleoithic Language," **From the Realm of the Ancestors**, p. 491)

Grieving as expressed by this magnificent figure is shown to be a part of the Goddess herself. She is that which gives life and that which grieves life, and within that reality She embodies the paradoxical nature of life in incomprehensible compassion.

Another figurine representing the Double Goddess is the well-known piece from Dolni Vestonice, Moravia, dated approximately 27,000 BP. She stands eleven centimeters tall and is a full-bodied figure with pendulous nourishing breasts and possible pregnant belly. These self-nourishing characteristics are contrasted by her mask-like and perhaps death-like face, with streaming lines, probably tears, flowing from her eyes. Harrod remarks that the entire figure seems to be one of grief and loss. She is stained with red ochre, "as if to reiterate the thematics of death, grieving, and flowing, nourishing life in touch with the earth." (ibid., p. 488) The streams from her eyes flow down her chest to her breasts. Because moisture and water were sacred to the ancients, the streaming lines become a metaphor for divine tears and the eyes of the Goddess are the source of life-sustaining water as the breasts are the source of life-sustaining milk.

As emanations from Her womb, humans mirror this kind of paradoxical experience in our lives. Grief is a part of spirit/earth-flesh mind/body wholeness. To feel it deeply and openly, as many people do in various cultures, for example, by the cutting of hair, wailing and not washing for long periods of time following the death of a loved one, is to be fully present with the wholeness/holiness of life and mystery beyond our control and understanding. The patriarchal mind does not understand such abandon. It would rather have grief be hidden and controlled. For this very reason, some of my family members have not been able to grieve their losses of other family members. But I know that un-cried grief lies hidden in their souls, desperate for expression. I see in them that this hidden grief has hardened their hearts, encrusted them in anger and denial, leaving them with a paralyzing fear of intimacy. I grieve for them.

As in practicing dying to the moment while alive, I feel it is also important to learn how to grieve our losses while living as well. Acquiring this skill allows one to be open, vulnerable, soft and flexible with strong emotions and teaches one how to let things come and go. This gives us the practice of fluidity and helps us to have courage in expressing ourselves. It keeps us from stuffing these strong feelings, "grinning and bearing" and "keeping a stiff upper lip" and then projecting those unhealed and unresolved feelings, often hurting those we love. If we give ourselves permission to be vulnerable, we become more available to ourselves and to one another. In the event of a death of a loved one, we won't hear so often "he just wasn't there for me" because "he" will have been practicing how to "be there" in his life by living with the Goddess and Her way of being in self-love, humility, compassion, empathy and openness.

It is suggested in Tibetan Buddhism that it is efficacious to grieve beforehand with the dying, if possible. This teaching says that this practice allows people to share the truth together and gives people permission to be honest with one another. It also says that the grief for those left behind is lessened and the attachments one might feel to the dying are lessened at death because the grief has been shared.

In the prehistoric times of women-centered cultures, women were the priestesses to the dying. I also feel from the way in which many tribal people collectively deal with life passages, women probably grieved together and shared the grief of their losses in these ancient times. When my friend's daughter, Ellie, died at the age of twenty, Donna's world crumbled. Because Ellie was born with a rare medical condition, Donna had taken care of her since birth. Ellie lived eighteen years longer than the doctors predicted, with a "normal" quality of life. I feel it was Donna's unwavering motherly love and devotion that created this magic for Ellie — not to mention Ellie's own strength and determination. (Donna also had three other children. Ellie was the oldest.)

When Donna came to see me, I felt a deep stirring within me about how to help her through her difficult and trying time. I asked her if calling a circle of her sisters from the community we had all lived in together would be something she might want to do. (The Farm community disbanded in the early eighties as an intentional community. It is still a community, but with far less people and the agreement is quite different now. It is more like a small village. When people left, some tended to move in close proximity to each other in different areas around the country.) She agreed, and about fifteen women gathered together one night to share Donna's grief. We created an altar to Ellie, and shared stories about her. We sang songs and cried together. Donna was held in the arms of the mother — and many arms there were! The sharing of her grief with women who loved her, and who knew Ellie literally made Donna glow.

She changed before our eyes as the love from her sisters reached out to her and wrapped her in a warm blanket of telepathic communion. The circle that night felt ancient to me, as if we had all been together before, doing the same thing in some other place in time. For Donna, it was a deeply needed infusion of female compassion and empathy that helped her immensely on her own journey of rebirth. Sharing grief in this way changes the isolated feeling one can have in mourning the loss of a loved one. It's not that you mourn any less — it's just that you are fully seen and held in tenderness by the intention of the circle.

In my experience as a mother, and as a sister to my friends, I feel there is nothing like a mother's love and nothing like a mother's sorrow. Sharing these deep states together allows a kind of connection that I am convinced holds the health of the community together. Without these bonds between women, the community breaks down.

It is my experience that telling the person they are dying is beneficial. While they might appear shaken, I have witnessed that deep down they already know. I think one has to handle such honesty very delicately. If you feel the person is in extreme denial, then telling them might create more constriction, fear and resistance for them. In a case such as this, you can still do your prayer practices for them, and not be in denial yourself. I do believe it is very important to give permission to the dying to let go. Something like "It is time for you to let go now," or "it's okay for you to let go. I/we will be fine" can be very reassuring words. When my mother had a sense of her coming death, the one thing that she seemed to really think about was if her five children would be okay. I was able to reassure her that we would be fine, and she was able to relax enough to move into her process of facing her own death.

Sekhmet and Callanish Stones, Monica Sjöö, 1989

Wise Women Circle

During the writing of this book, I asked my friends, Vicki Noble and Monica Sjöö if they would gather with me to discuss death and dying from a spiritual / feminist perspective. I wanted to hear from the deep wise-woman place in each of us about this subject. They agreed, and Monica brought her friend, Nancy. We gathered together on a warm summer day in June. Somehow it felt a bit surreal to be discussing this subject in the light of day and in the heat of the sun. It seemed we should be having our discussion at night, in the dark of the moon, where we could gather close together around a fire, invoking the ancestors.

The subject was not an easy one—especially for Monica. We, of course, all knew that she was deeply pained by the losses of her two sons. She told me she was a bit afraid of our opening into this together, as no one present had any experience like hers. I had a deep respect for her feelings, and wanted to create a safe space for her to feel that she could share from her heart.

Her young son, Leify, was killed on a bright sunny August day, run over by a car in France. When we were gathering, Monica shared her trepidation, and as she did so, her heart just opened, and her tears began to flow. Her grief was timeless, as quite a few years had passed since the death of her two sons. In that moment with her, I felt the saying "time heals all wounds" was false. Monica's pain and grief were right there.

I felt in that moment that a mother does not heal from losing her child, let alone two. Such a loss is always a loss. I remembered the first time I met Monica. She came to stay with me when she was on a book tour. I had to let her know, at the right time, how grieved I was at the loss of her children. I cried, and we cried together. As a mother, I could not and cannot imagine such pain.

My friend's daughter, Lizzie, was tragically killed in a car accident the summer after we had gathered in this circle. Lizzie was a child in my extended family from the Farm and she was in a way, like a daughter to me. She was only fourteen, and she died along with two of her friends. This experience is the closest I have come to Monica's, and even at that, it is still very different.

I realized that the truth of being together in circle was not only to talk, but to experience the sharing of the very thing we were going to be talking about—the truth of women's way and holding each other in warm embrace. The Goddess opened us up immediately through Monica. We all cried together, and held Monica, sharing the grief together. I felt the presence of something very ancient. I felt how when women hold each other and share the grief together the burden of such unspeakable pain is somehow gently soothed. Vicki said that in the ten years she had known Monica, she had not touched into this deep place of sharing grief with her about the loss of her children. So there we were, with our hearts opened wide by the Goddess, not wasting any time, diving deep together into this mystery we call death.

What follows is an in-depth conversation with wise, loving, Goddess women about one of life's most profound mysteries.

Leslene: I don't even know if this is a question that can be answered. . . I'm wondering how can we as women remember and hold something like this together so that there isn't a sense of isolation, so that the grief is shared and we do it together . . .

Monica: Most of the time I've found that when a child dies, even the closest friends would be embarrassed, couldn't talk to the person, couldn't face the person . . . they felt completely isolated and there was no one to share it with; often families would break up, marriages would break up because the father particularly would totally act like it never happened, but break down later on, you know, just hiding it. But I am in a different situation. I'm in a different community.

But even then I found at the time when Leify died, I spent nights and days for weeks reading everything I could on death and dying and near-death experiences, out-of-body journeys, trying to understand where he was. And then I got involved in the spiritualist church. It is very patriarchal in many ways, but at least they do take for granted that life continues in another form and that there is communicating between the worlds. I also found in the Buddhist teachings that there is an understanding about death and dying, which helped me at the time, you know?

Leslene: Yes, I do know, having written about it . . .

Monica: In Ireland, for example, they have this tradition of the wake and the whole community shares the grief . . .but in patriarchy now people are dying in hospitals and in isolation and you're getting born in the hospital and cut off and the whole thing is totally alienated you know . . .

236

Leslene: There's been a natural birth movement, and there's been a reclaiming of that and I think that reclaiming death is as important from a feminist perspective so that we can create when we leave here, by how we leave, a space for something better to happen. I mean when we think about all these people dying in isolation with such fear that creates a deep psychic impact on the psyche, and so reclaiming the Goddess in all Her experience, including death, is vitally important. So I'm just really exploring this and wanting to know what wise women think and feel.

Monica: Well I think I've been sharing this, and it's very unusual. It makes it public.

Leslene: Yes, you have, and I think from women's hearts we have to reclaim this.

Monica: It's every woman's greatest fear, the death of a child. I had no idea. I had no idea.

Leslene: You couldn't. I can't imagine. And I know you and I've cried with you, and even when I think about it for you, I just cry.

Monica: It's like you go into the other world and don't come back.

Leslene: Yes, but I still don't know what it is . . .

Vicki: Or why — why were they taken so young.

Leslene: So in terms of women's wise view completely free of any patriarchal overlay, where do you think they are, both of your sons? Are they with the Mother, do you feel that? Do you feel they are with the Mother?

Monica: They are in the spirit world with the ancestors and in my dreams.

Leslene: So, in that sense they are okay . . .

Monica: Yes, but I can't touch them.

Leslene: Yes, you can't touch them.

Monica: It's all very well to say these things, but I can't hold my sons. I can't smell their skin and hair. It's the physical presence that I desperately need and want. It's like barrenness, like a huge gaping hole, you know?

Leslene: I hear you.

Monica: It's all very well to say they are of course close in spirit, but it's very abstract in some way.

Leslene: You're talking about the paradox of them being with the Mother but wanting their physical presence?

Monica: Of course they are present, but they aren't present the way I need them to be present. And of course they are present that way too, but it's difficult to explain in words. But you know what I mean, you like to hold your child, you want to smell their presence, you know? It's like a whole something that is properly missing in my life.

Leslene: You were talking about Caitlin Mathews and soul midwives, Nancy?

Nancy: Caitlin Mathews and a number of other women in Britain got together to meet the need as they saw it to help midwife people when they die because there wasn't that there for pagan people, when they died in hospital or hospice, wherever, and they formed themselves into this group and they publicized it in pagan circles . . . .and also went to hospice and said we're here . . . it's something that they are developing; they go on intensive retreats . . . .

Leslene: So, they're midwifing death. Vicki, you have expressed that the shaman, the birthing woman is bringing the soul from one place into another, this place. How do you see death in the soul's movement from one place to another?

Vicki: In a structural way, in a shamanistic way, I think it's like a revolving door. It's here in this world, there in that world. It's all Her world. So structurally it doesn't matter where we are—here or there. We're always coming and going through that door. It's only for us here left that it's painful to lose people through that doorway. Who knows what it's like on the other side? I have no idea.

Monica: There's a special quality about life — there's a reason why we're here. It's not just you're going through into empty space. There's very much a reason why we're here. It's a learning place. I was just going to say that after Leify died I was going to commit suicide and I was going to kill myself on Leify's birthday at the end of January or on my own birthday on New Year's Eve. But a couple of friends of mine in Bristol decided to go with me on Leify's birthday to Greenham Commons, and then to Silbury. And we were sitting up on Silbury Mound and I did bring a knife with me. I felt the Mother of Silbury took my son who died on the *Lammas* full moon, and she's the *Lammas* mound. I met Musawa (Monica's friend she met years before) on Silbury and it was the full moon, and I was with Musawa when my son died. I was afraid of the connection and I thought "you have taken my son, take me now."

My friends didn't know I had the knife, of course. And then up came this sadness and grief and I felt love from Silbury and I just felt this love from Silbury. I felt it was wrong, and I just couldn't do that, you know?

We went back home and in the night I had a dream. And I dreamt that I saw my son flying in a dark channel up through the sky, He had reddish curly hair. Then next to me there was this little girl sitting on my knee who was about four years old who had just come in. And I asked her "are you Leify?" She said "no, not really, kind of, not really." I've looked for her in my life ever since. And then I heard the words "and he looked like a beautiful red flame." That felt like such a gift on that particular night. That's what I'm talking about. I very much experienced that of course, we are born through. The birth in 1961 of my son that led to my painting "God Giving Birth," was this miraculous experience, you know? I was seeing these great masses of darkness and light alternately, which was the Goddess, but not in person you know—this incredible power of this birth. And then experiencing it the other way around with Leify's death.

And the very strange thing was after spending thirty hours at the hospital after the accident, Musawa and I were hoping and hoping against hope that somehow Leify would come back . . . I just couldn't face the possibility that he died. On this hot beautiful sunny August day, it was mockery to me . . .that sunshine . . . I couldn't stand it . . . I wanted to be eternally in the darkness . . . for years after that . . . I couldn't face the sun . . . and this whole thing, that yes, I actually flew with him into the other world, I actually flew with him. Just before, he was on this heart machine that kept his heart beating, his heart beat for thirty hours after he was brain dead, and I was lying there and got blood on my hair from his blood, and I kind of flew with him, like on great wings of light, and this presence, this life presence, and this was the truth and this is what I experienced, and not having any idea . . . and at that particular point, the words came to me "the only thing that matters is love", and I just couldn't understand any of it . . .

Leslene: You understand more now? Is it still as much of a mystery?

Monica: No, the mystery is how do you live it? How do you live that knowledge? Of course I know it's true. You can't be in that incredibly extreme situation of pain, and these words come to you, and they were not coming from me, absolutely they were not coming from me . . .

Leslene: Well, yes, because you weren't thinking that!

Monica: Absolutely not . . . not consciously thinking that, so I absolutely know it's true.

Vicki: But you know Monica, you have been living that, because you keep it present and you keep it in front of you and everyone has to deal with it. You're always a mother who lost her children, and you don't shut up about it, and it's so important.

My sister lost her child — he was seventeen, about five years ago. He was driving a car in front of a train, he and five other kids, and they all went out, boom, like that . . .and my sister and brother-in-law will never get over it.

Leslene: Of course not.

Vicki: People after a very short time were so cruel with them. Everybody wanted them to just get on with it now. There are platitudes that people say, I'm sure you've heard them. . . .

Moncia: "Life must go on." Life doesn't have to go on at all, thank you very much.

Vicki: Right, exactly. My sister was so angry that she stopped speaking to everyone. She said people are so insensitive. I just think that it's exactly what you are talking about, Leslene. We have no intact tradition of women's medicine around death anymore. We don't know how to behave, we have no idea of what really happens. Christianity teaches us nothing . . .

Leslene: A lot of fear.

Vicki: We haven't got our hands on any medicine to provide and it's overwhelming because we have such terrors about it ourselves. Terrors of being in your place like "oh my god, she lost her child." Unbearable.

Leslene: Yes, it's her children.

Vicki: But each time it happens to a woman everyone else pulls back away from it instead of coming forward because they don't know about it and so they don't know what to do. And so because we don't know what to do in our culture we don't do anything. And then it turns into this superficiality, you know, "get on with it." And so I think, Monica, that you live it.

Leslene: People pull back…peoples' fear — it sounds like the way people are afraid of illness…

Vicki: Yeah, it's unconscious, unacknowledged terror.

Nancy: I think also in our society it's because everything pulls you toward eternity and growing old is thought not to be good — it's horrible, and you become invisible. And I think when you're confronted with that you're suddenly confronted with the things you try to repress and so we've got to think about that. We've lost that rhythm and tradition. And so I think when you come across somebody like Monica or anybody who's lost a child it brings up — it's so much in your face and people cannot deal with it . . .

Vicki: Or they're forced to deal with it. My sense with Monica is that year after year you go through your changes in relation to it, but you are right there, present with wherever you are with it and everybody who deals with you has to deal with wherever you are with it and therefore, I mean for me at least, I feel like it's a form of consciousness medicine.

I can't escape the painful knowledge of the loss of your children because you don't go unconscious to it. You don't repress this and put it into denial, and so I can't either, and I'm really glad. It's a very hard gift that you give, Monica. It seems totally right that you give voice to the truth of the experience instead of some sweet lie about it — that time heals all wounds. It doesn't really. I see it bubbles up to the surface for my sister and for my brother-in-law at unexpected moments and there it is in the center of the room and it's so uncomfortable for everybody who wants things to stay normal because it's so taboo …

Leslene: Yes, it's so taboo…

Vicki: There's the sense that we have to get past this as fast as we can—we are so lame in our culture, just completely without skills or any tradition. It just seems like what we lost in the witch burnings…we lost the priestesses and lost the knowledge and customs. What do we do? How do we stay alive with it?

Leslene: Yes, I don't think the model of a man nailed up on a cross in agony is a good idea…

Monica: I do believe there are reasons why things happen but it doesn't make it easy. I have to hold onto that. In one sense I was warned. I heard something say that you are here to learn, hard lessons, and if my son died now it is because that is what he chose to do. I tell you one strange thing that happened in hospital — in the middle of all this horror and Leify lying there dead. Now and then it looked like a kind of crown of thorns on his head and I had this dream that Leify sat up in bed and took this crown of thorns off, and smiled a broad smile. It was extraordinary. I had this dream — I dreamt, and this is what made me able to survive these experiences — I dreamt that Leify was lying on the sofa in the room by the ashes — he was fifteen years old at death. He opened his eyes and screwed his face up a bit and said "I'm not very happy," complaining you know to your mother, and the next minute he was standing in front of me and he was like ten years old — he was quite small like a younger child and I was looking at him and I thought to myself, "I wonder if I can touch him?" because I was aware that he wasn't in his body —

Leslene: So in the dream you knew it?

Monica: So when you know it in your dream that the person with you is from the other world, then that's a lucid dream as far as I'm concerned . . .

Leslene: Yes.

Monica: So I was thinking to myself, "I wonder if I can touch him?" and I put my arm out to touch him and he put his arm up to touch me and we could both feel each other's bodies. Then he communicated telepathically . . . I was thinking to him . . . he was communicating to me, "I will come back later" . . . and then I communicated back, "But will you always be that young, Leify?" and he looked at himself in a quizzical way like he hadn't realized and communicated back, "I'll have to find out about that." It was only because of things like that that I didn't completely lose my mind. I also lost my second husband who drank himself to death at thirty-six. In a dream about him several years after he died, I saw him standing in a doorway with a big joint in his mouth...he looked much younger, more like when I met him, and smiled at me and said, "I'm all right now Monica. I don't need to come back again." You see, I've had these experiences since before Leify died.

Vicki: It's awesome . . . it's total shamanism . . .

Leslene: Totally. You're getting communications from beyond the veil, you know.

Monica: So I KNOW it's true

Vicki: Well you're being taught directly.

Monica: Yes.

Leslene: What you are sharing is different than what is taught in Tibetan Buddhism. I mean I do agree with you that there are some really powerful and useful teachings around death and dying, definitely. The Bardo teachings do not agree with what you are saying. When I read the Bardo teachings, the ones I have read, I feel afraid that I don't know how to die correctly, I don't know how to do this right, oh my Goddess . . .

Monica: And you have to choose the right light . . .

Leslene: And it's full of failure, if you don't do that, then you've failed to do this . . .

Monica: And the worse thing is to be reborn . . .

Leslene: Right, and so what you're speaking of is not that.

Vicki: It's shamanism.

Leslene: Oh, yes . . .and I think you were able to get those messages because in some way you were open enough through your own visionary art, or whatever . . . to receive that. Those to me are more of the teachings that I want to learn more about . . .

Monica: I should also tell you that my oldest son, Sean, was dying from cancer and he was almost transparent. Someone said he looked like a mixture between a Saxon King and a Buddhist monk . . . he was not able to walk without crutches, he was so thin. He looked like Ghandi . . . the last time he was able, just a short walk, about a week before he died, with his brother, who is now in Portugal. They'd been lying on the grass together side by side and Sean had a vision of, he was looking at the clouds, and he saw a newborn fetus in the clouds. It wasn't a cloud that looked like a newborn fetus; he saw a newborn fetus in the cloud. And he was just totally amazed. Not only that, whenever he was very close to death, he knew it because he had these really vivid dreams of the most beautiful landscapes — like he longed to go there.

He was not afraid of dying. The only thing he was afraid of was terminal pain, but he loved going to those landscapes. So he always knew when he was close . . . but the thing is, when my grandson was born on the fifth of May in Portugal, fourteen years ago, now, I was there . . . my son, Toivo, and Toivo actually doesn't want to think about this now, but when I arrived, Toivo actually did say to me that a few weeks before I came he had a dream of his brother Sean who was just two years older than him who said to him, "I'm coming back as a baby, don't you realize?" And I was there when my grandson was born, and I saw him coming out, and I thought "Hello, Sean." But they don't want to even think about this now, because the mother doesn't want to see her son as the rebirth of her partner's brother.

Ever since Leify died and Sean died I've always been looking at every child, and wondering about them reincarnating in another child, is this possible? Could this be? And the strange thing was, in the tipi village where Leify's ashes are buried, there's this tree, it's fully grown now, and of course its roots must be into his ashes in the ground. I did an image, which I call "Child of the Mother Tree" where there is this head of a child and the roots of a tree and I completely didn't think for a minute that I did it — that there is this tree and it's actually growing . . .

Leslene: I'd love to see that image . . .

Monica: There was a little boy born in the tipi village in a caravan who is like a little fairy boy, and they actually call him "Leify", without knowing this . . .

242

Vicki: Oh my goddess . . .

Monica: So what I am saying is I have all along been wondering, "Is this Leify? Are you there?" And always kind of waiting to come across some child who would come to me and recognize me . . .

Vicki: The beautiful thing about Tibetan Buddhism is their reincarnation process and how completely wise they are about these little children who remember and can make choices of their things and can go right to the person they remember and all that. It's amazing. All children must have that capacity. We just don't encourage it in any way. We don't have any forms for it.

Monica: I mean it was strange . . . a friend of mine, the grandmother is Swedish, and her daughter has this child, Maya, with a Somali man. The first time I met her, she spent the entire day sitting on top of me, clinging to me, wouldn't let me go, you know what I mean? I'd never seen her before, she normally never did this to anyone . . . actually I cried when I left . . . that was very strange . . . anyway, I shouldn't be talking so much about all this . . .

Leslene and Vicki: Yes, you should . . .

Vicki: Monica, there are really two things happening here. It's not just your personal life, and the death of your children, which is enough because it's so big . . . personally, but you're also in a training process that's really obvious when you talk about it . . . you're a shaman woman . . . your training is direct, primordial . . . right across . . . you actually are receiving the training and I don't think it means that you need to suffer to be a shaman but it must have been a handy way to get to you through your suffering that was already in place. Its like the Buddhists say things are co-arising, co-arising phenomenon, not causal.

Leslene: Two things happening in tandem — your personal suffering and the path — how could it not be, you know? And you're being trained as a shaman at the same time.

Vicki: The things you are talking about are specific shamanistic training, direct transmission.

Leslene: Yes, of course... I think that's what women used to practice together was sharing that direct transmission and taking care of life in all its passages, with that wisdom and with that connection. I really felt I needed to connect with you, Monica, for what you had been through...as a mother. Prior to writing this book, I didn't even know all the details or why I felt so strongly about connecting with you.

Vicki: But you said to me today that you wanted us to go out in the sun because you wanted us to channel and not be in our heads.

Leslene: Yes, yes.

Vicki: And to actually move into some sort of state where we could be bringing something to a different level. So you knew that.

Leslene: Yes, yes.

Vicki: You're so good you know, to come into contact with what's happening with all the dynamics and the way that your energies are starting to press up cause what are we going to do, come in here and chat about it? You know, that's impossible.

It would really be unbelievable for someone who's had the same experience but doesn't have a shaman woman to sit with her. Because nobody has any shaman woman to sit with her with death. They have Buddhists now, and you know a few radical Christians and there's a few Jewish people doing it. There's a few people trying to do alternative things, like Caitlin Mathews but there just aren't many feminist goddess, witch women... shaman women doing this...

Lelsene: No, there are not. That's why I am writing this book and facilitating this circle. Thank you for being willing to participate!

Monica: My former mother-in-law, my children's grandmother, she was in an old people's nursing home — she was dying, she couldn't speak...but her intelligence was completely there. The last time I saw her alive, she couldn't speak. And we would just sit together. One day she suddenly turned around to her daughter and spoke. Her daughter called me and I just went in to sit. We lit two candles and just sat there talking for eight hours. We never talked so much ever. My mother-in-law was in a coma in the background...and I'm sure she heard every word. Two days later she died. In a sense it was so magical, sitting in that room in the dark. The nurses would come in with hot chocolate. It was Imbolc, or Bride's Day. She couldn't die until I had come back to see her.

Leslene: See, that sounds beautiful.

Vicki: That was beautiful...

Leslene: Yes, and it opened up your hearts together when you could share like that.

Vicki: Its female magic... and the male writers write about it and they are all freaked out.

Leslene: So what is coming up for me now, is, a great sense of beauty around death, you know, I mean I am feeling that, and we are sort of going through the whole ...incredible wisdom . . .

Vicki: In the Cycladic cultures that I've been so focused on recently, the first rituals that they know about—the only ritual evidence are the platforms in the cemeteries built on top of the tombs. Big platforms, big for dance and ritual, and that's all, no temples. It's outdoors, and they were doing rituals of some kind in those cemeteries. That is the third millennium ... and in the 800-1200 CE, our time, the yoginis were doing the same thing. They were in the cemeteries doing rituals. In Tibet, the sky burials are still happening outside with the vultures, and the vultures are considered to be dakinis and the bodies are offered to the vultures — vulture priestesses, and it's not that they are death goddesses, it's that one of the functions of the shaman priestess is to midwife death, but it's not her only function.

Leslene: I think if we lived culturally with this knowledge there would be a lot less fear about death.

Monica: I think we've lost contact with reality. Strangers come and take the body and dress it up ...

Vicki: Strangers, yes, who have no feeling. My grandmother burst into tears when she saw my grandfather in an open casket all done up. She said that it didn't look like him at all. And we had to talk to her about it, "Of course not, he's not in his body anymore, it's not him."

Monica: When you aren't part of the process, it's such a shock you know. The whole process has been taken over by Christians.

Vicki: Well, it's such a shock because it's so unnatural what they do. I had an experience recently with people in the hospital. A man was in a coma. I didn't know the man but I got invited in. I went every day for two weeks and I felt really connected and got really close with the wife. The whole family was there. He was a Salvadorian man, so all the family came every day and the whole process was kind of nice. They would come in at night and sing and be together. When we finally determined that he was not going to come back out of the coma and he was fading, then it was like, get it over with, you know, and I talked to them about well, you could take him home. Then with close friends and family around one man said, "I would never advise you to do that because if you do that the death will happen in your home and then you'll always have that as the last memory of what happened..." And I thought, "well isn't that what we want to do here?"

Leslene: We had my mother at home and she died in my living room. I took her home and it was so extraordinarily beautiful, it was incredible.

Vicki: That's what I would have expected.

Leslene: So the memory is that.

Vicki: Yes, exactly, this is such an opportunity, you can all be conscious.

Leslene: The moment of her death was the same as a birth. I had training as a midwife and so I'd been around a lot of births. The energy was exactly the same. It was so beautiful. I provided a space for her to be in a loving environment where she could feel safe and so she could let go.

Vicki: Yes, because somebody else is holding the space.

Leslene: And because of that I feel like she died in a state of grace and love where she was able to transform her own karma. She had been very angry most of her life, and for good reasons. I understood her anger. It's just that she never knew how to process it or work through it and I could see in her death she let go. You were talking about that light that Leify went into, Monica, even though it sounds new agey.... One teaching is that our true essence is brighter than 10,000 suns, and I could feel that with her. Her personality completely fell away and her true essence emerged and the whole room was filled with golden light. It was just like a birth, it was truly extraordinary. I don't know about the Navaho, like you mentioned, Vicki, burning the house down after someone dies. I don't know if that is fear based, but I don't need

245

to burn my house down. The memory of her was beautiful. I kept her body for three days. My living room was transformed into a temple. All the lines in her face disappeared and she softened and looked so young.

I had been reading the **Tibetan Book of Living and Dying** to her and I stopped cause I felt like I was inducing fear through some of it. So I said, "You are returning to the Mother," and she actually at one point put her face into the pillow and rooted the way a new born baby does looking for the breast, she was going to suck. It was incredible.

Monica: One's last search for the Mother...

Vicki: And then people naturally go into a fetal position if you leave them alone...interesting, maybe there's no difference in the revolving door which way you are going in or out.

Leslene: Well, you know it was interesting with her because in a way she had missed her life, she was so angry. She pushed people away with her anger. My other siblings couldn't be around her in her dying because of that, because she would probably have been abusive. So, it's interesting because I felt like in that moment of her death she found her life.

Vicki: In that moment of her death it sounds like you weren't her daughter, you were her priestess.

Leslene: Yes, I was her priestess. She found what she had been looking for her whole life... I did have a question. When we were talking before, we were talking about the continuity and the different practices, the sky burial and the vulture goddess and the question I asked about was, what do you think that would do to the nature of fear? I also want to know what you think about the nature of grief in that cultural experience; if we lived like that, if we were raised like that, if we were that close to the cyclical nature?

Vicki: Well, judging from the amount of images of women mourning and lamenting and making sounds and making grief an expression...in the community it must have been just so raw and purging, like our moment this afternoon just being able to cry together. I've always wanted to cry with you, Monica. And it's so awkward— we don't do it. So why don't we? I can't believe that I've never cried with you, honestly, it seems bizarre. For ten years I've shared with you about this on some level and I haven't cried with you.

Leslene: Yeah, that's such a good question.

Vicki: What's wrong with us, Why isn't that normal? I think its just amazing that we can't liberate ourselves that way. We can't because we are so isolated...you know there is something about the way we don't understand the collective sharing of grief—like in a birth everyone in the group gets the kundalini.

Leslene: Yes...you do.

Vicki: So why wouldn't everybody want to share everything exactly the same way? Why wouldn't it be healing for me to cry for you, for your loss? Everything else is kind of a tight thing—holding some kind of tight thing so that I don't cry.

Leslene: The first thing I said in a letter to you, Monica, was about your loss. I just couldn't fathom it…I was writing to connect with you about your book…and there was nothing else to say to you.

Vicki: Yeah, well of course not.

Leslene: I know that sparked something that has carried itself through me in this way to where we are here now.

Vicki: Yes, we have to have workshops about everything… we don't know how to heal our bodies, we don't know how to die, we don't know how to live, we don't know how to dance. We don't know how to move—we have to have movement workshops. Like what is that about? The body knows how to move, just turn on some music and get out of the way. We know how to grieve and be with each other and we know how to give birth. We know how to do all those things, but you wouldn't think so. We are getting further and further removed…

Leslene: There is so much fear, just so much fear and it's all interwoven with the oppression of women and backlash, the aggression and facism of the radical right…

Monica: If you talk about having a workshop…you have to contain it — you have to give it space and you do grief, and that's it there …I can't just go to a workshop and say I'm going to do grief now. It's not authentic.

Leslene: I believe that in the matriarchal view those who tended to the needs of the soul were undoubtedly women…which is the original meaning of the word "therapy" from "therapeia", one who tends to the needs of the soul. It was holistic, you could go to a temple and you would be held and touched and loved and you could share.

Vicki: And you could tear your clothes, and tear your hair and paint your face black and do all of that and scratch yourself and there's all of that in the literature, everything, everything you need to hurt as much as it hurts, and to give expression to how deeply unbearable it is and then at some point you can go on. It's not because someone said to you okay it's been three months now, could you get over it now?

Leslene: It's because you actually…you actually went that deep.

Vicki: Yes went that deep. We need that so much, but we need it in everything. We need it in healing, in dying, in living.

Monica: I've always had some kind of sense of incredible mystery associated with underground waters, the dead, the blood, the dark, but I can't quite put my finger on it. Once I had this experience in France in about 1976. There was a group of lesbian women of different nationalities. It was a full moon night and we started dancing…and dancing more and more, and at one point I felt my spirit left my body. That had never happened to me before, or since. I was taken by the moon and my spirit traveled up to her. I was afraid though that I might not be able to get back to my body. That was the only time I had an inkling of perhaps what really flying was like in those ancient dances.

Leslene: Makes me think of ancient women covering themselves with special ointments and ingesting plant helpers, you know, mind-medicine, like the sacred hallucinogens for the specific purpose of flying between the worlds...A question I had was something that came up from something you were saying... about the underworld and the blood of the ancestors and so I just wanted to talk a little bit more about that, in terms of the domain of the Goddess. Because you said earlier, that it's all Her domain, so if we go through a revolving door, it's still in and out of Her domain. It's all in Her lap. I think that is so important because the patriarchal mind just totally splits death off from life. So I would like to know if we could have more conversation about the blood of the ancestors and the earth because there is so much there...the subject of death seems so taboo...

Vicki: So is blood.

Leslene: Right, so is blood. And menstrual blood.

Monica: When I did the painting **God Giving Birth**, in 1968 (see page 95), I was told how disgusting, how horrendous, how could I possibly make a painting showing such a disgusting thing in public.

Leslene: And calling it "god". So we have birth and death as taboo in patriarchy...so where does that leave us?

Vicki: And healing is demonic in patriarchy too...

Leslene: And healing is demonic and menstrual blood is taboo and un-clean.

Everything women do is. My attempt is to bring to the surface the blood and the ancestors and what's in the underworld ...bring that out a bit more into our conversation. I don't have a goal in mind. Like you've been saying, Monica, you've been thinking about this for a long time; something about the mystery...

Monica: I've seen rock-like clefts like vaginas in the Paleolithic caves, and the subterranean waters rolling over them and hearing the voices of the ancestors from the waters, and that's the sort of image I have in my mind. And then the ancient peoples being within caves because it was the ice age and cold outside. And the only way to survive was to be in the protective caverns, much warmer, inside the womb of another form of the Mother. I was reading in the north tradition about creation from a great chasm, Ginungagap, which is like the vagina or the womb of the ancient Mother. Of course the patriarchs call it the void, or chaos, but it is actually the holy hole or the holy cavern, or the holy cauldron of the Mother. And in that is like the hot spring, vitalizing you, which is called a healing kettle, and the hot rivers flow from this healing kettle. Amidst the cold and mist coming forth life is created from the meeting of ice and fire in the womb. It is all associated with the ancestors and voices of the spirits. All is big enough to hold visually.

Leslene: It's a whole picture.

Vicki: Now this is just exactly how I experience the yoginis. Sitting in the cemetery, with the corpses doing necromancy, making the voice of the spirit come through the body in some way. Having tantric sex in that context because it's so sacred. All of it is so taboo...and it's totally linked to death and life and sex and regenerative capabilities even to the point of bringing bodies back to life, at least in the mythology, that's what the women did.

Monica: I saw in Stuttgart in the forest there had been a sanctuary of the Matronae, or the Triple Mothers. They were statues with their heads knocked off by Christian desecration. Matricide. They hated the Matronae and women. The Romans called the Matronae or Triple Mothers "sorcerers of beginning times." And there is a connection between the Norns and the ancient priestesshoods. The Paleolithic women who were working out the daily calendars...it's all connected somehow from the most ancient times. And it seems like in the sanctuaries of the Matronae in Germany, the Norns, are the most important rituals in Scandinavia, long before the pagan temple. And the disir were the ancient wandering goddesses. They were the disir of the ancient Old European Scandinavian Vanir people. Ancient goddess we don't know much about or what the worship was about, but you know that the Christians said it was obscene. I even found the cross gender priest fascinating. They danced. With gyrating hips, we danced on our toes imitating the birds with outstretched arms. I've danced like this all of my life.

Vicki: In a book on the second millennium in Germany, **Gods and Heroes of the Bronze Age**, there is a reference to the discovery of four high wide-brimmed pointy gold hats that were buried for safe-keeping. I just found this at the national museum in Athens. On the front it says "the gods and heroes" and here they have a goddess picture on the front. It has amazing things like boars tusks set in jewelry, totally witches hats, and they are gold— but then they go on about how the priest kings must have worn them. Any other time they would have been called witches' hats but under these conditions, they don't mention any association here to witches. The hats were all found buried, individually, like put in the ground with the point up. So there is a chair, just like in the pictures of the Hittite priestess...There is a high priestess buried in Crete with a horse and with boars' tusks, and with her own footstool with inlay ivory.

Monica: I have read in German texts, several places, that the Matronae were/are the sun, the moon and the earth.

Vicki: You know what I saw from Lourdes? A Paleolithic Ivory horse.

Monica: Well, of course it was a sacred place before Christianity. It's a holy well and a cave, what could be more obvious?

Leslene: Such rich material. So maybe we could finish up now...

So if we can just maybe each think for a moment when its time for you to leave this life that you are going to be remaining in the lap of the Mother and that is how you regard death — that you are going through another doorway, but you are still in the lap of the Mother, so what does it elicit in you to think about that? What does it bring up for you to actually, think about that in terms of your own death, that you will be actually going into your own death, that you will be actually going into the domain of the Mother, the mysterious, but it is still Her lap? What does it bring up for you?

Vicki: It sounds like an adventure when you put it that way.

Leslene: Yeah, the next adventure.

Vicki: We don't know what will happen now, but...

Monica: For me it's not the actual death itself. . .

Vicki: I'm thinking more of the disempowerment of the women in our culture and how distracted we are by the things that don't matter. That we are asked to do and participate in, and death is such a wonderful reality check because you can have all the things pouring in but life is short and what matters?

Leslene: But we know it's in the lap and it's safe. . .it's safe, that's amazing isn't it? Some of the teachings that I have resonated with are that death lives with you all the time, and the question of what your relationship is with it in any given moment. To me, with all the wishes and wants and desires and things that I want to do and want to produce and all that, it still comes down to death is right here—it's so interesting. So how I hold it is that when it is time, I will be letting go to be with the Mother in another way. I can do that.

I think we are done so I want to thank everyone for doing this. Sharing this is not an easy thing to do, to talk about and to really share at the levels we shared today.

I closed the circle with the following prayer:

I give thanks Mother for this circle, for these sisters for the way that our hearts have been able to open and be touched. We ask that all this sharing be healing for each one of us and that it be something that goes out with us into the world and into the community. And we ask that all this sharing might be pleasing in the eyes and the sight of the ancestors—all those who watch us and love us and guide us. Blessed Be.

Our Wise Woman Circle ended with all of us singing together. We acknowledged what a blessed experience we all shared, and knew that our being together was, in itself, a magical event.

All: Singing together: "*We all come from the Goddess and to Her we shall return, like a drop of rain, flowing to the ocean.*"

Farewell to Feather

Feather, photo by Keni Meyer

I first met my friend's mother, Feather, when she was in intensive care following heart surgery. Upon release from the hospital, she had actually died in the car on her way home. Her husband gave her CPR and brought her back to the hospital, from which she should never have been released, and wouldn't have been released had there not been insurance issues. I saw her after she had been revived. She was connected to many tubes and could only blink her eyes. Keni and I sat with her for a while and Keni shared with me that she felt her mother appreciated us being there, and that appreciation had been difficult for her mother to express, that she had closed her eyes when other people talked to her, but blinked to acknowledge us. What follows is Keni's account of her mother's passing, and the deep healing she was able to find in the experience.

Most people who knew my mother thought she was a sweet, kind, gentle woman; however, being a child at her mercy I knew differently. I believe she would suffer bouts of severe depression when I was very young. During these depressive episodes she would become unpredictable, enraged and abusive towards me. My father was gone at work, sometimes for weeks and I had no siblings living at home. This would leave us alone for extended periods of time where I would receive the full force of her abuse. I remember these times with my mother as torture sessions. Her unpredictable rages would escalate into full-scale beatings that left me in terror and on the brink of unconsciousness. The beatings were not often but her onslaught of verbal abuse was daily; she had no mercy on the sweet little girl that I used to be. She left nothing in my psyche unscathed. The only relief was when my father came home or when I escaped to school.

Thirty years later it was recommended my mother have open-heart surgery because her heart had calcified or in other words, turned to stone. I was not upset; after years of therapy and trying to heal from her abusiveness it seemed to me that perhaps only death could provide transformation for our relationship. I expressed this to her one day while driving her home and added that if she wanted to die that this operation might be the time to do it. I'll never forget her expression; she got very pale and quiet and was apparently seriously considering this as an option.

My mother had her operation; the doctors said things went well, though it soon became obvious that they had not. She spent seven days in the hospital. She couldn't remember her name or anyone else's; she was hallucinating, recalling names of long

251

dead dogs. Her defiant attitude was wearing thin on the hospital staff. Even though her heartbeat was not stable and the head nurse was very reluctant to let her go home, the doctors sent her home anyway.

My father picked her up and within five minutes from the hospital she had stopped breathing. He tried to administer CPR as he drove back. By the time they got to the hospital she was in complete cardiac arrest. The hospital staff worked on her for an hour and got her heart restarted but she couldn't breath on her own and was hooked to a respirator.

After a two-day fight with the hospital we decided to take my mother off the respirator. I wanted her to have the most conscious death that she could and asked that they not give her the morphine that the doctors recommended. The nurse said she had to follow doctor's orders and had to give my mother the morphine. She said it would help prevent convulsions. The nurse injected her through a catheter that went directly into a main vein; as she pushed the syringe of morphine into my mother, the syringe froze and the catheter became plugged. I felt my mother also wanted a conscious death and would not let the morphine into her body.

My mother's family stood around her bed as we began taking the respirator tubes out of her mouth. She started to turn blue and gasp for breath. As she began to struggle more, her eyes suddenly became alive and she looked around the room as if looking for instruction on what to do and deal with what was happening. I had never seen such a present look in her eyes as in that moment.

Leslene was there to facilitate her passing. As my mother was looking around, Leslene started to talk softly to her, making eye contact with her and assuring her that it was okay to let go. She continued to talk to my mother in soft assuring tones, and told her that everything she was experiencing was normal. My mother was obviously deeply comforted by Leslene's sweet comforting words. She became very relaxed as she slowly stopped breathing and her heart stopped beating. Leslene instructed us to give my mom a few minutes of space after her heart stopped beating. We then started a meditation that I consider to be the main vehicle of transformation for my mom. We all — my whole family — visualized my mother's heart merging with the heart of the Great Mother, seeing both hearts meeting and becoming one. As we did this meditation a deep peacefulness permeated the hospital room. I could feel for the first time my mother was at peace. I felt that through all of the fear and hatred that had consumed my mother almost her entire life she had finally found what I considered to be the true love of the Goddess.

My mother had been stuck in a very constricted state of being, void of any love. When we all gathered and did this meditation I felt her soul start to expand. I had a sense that it was the first time in a long time — lifetimes — that this had happened for her.

Several hours after she passed, while I was on my way home, I started having visions and actual physical sensations of my mother. I felt a strong sense of my mother in the car and experienced an incredible warm sensation of milk running down my throat. I, for the first time in my life, felt she was there for me and that *she had immediately migrated back to me with some type of insight or recognition of the fact that she had been less than an adequate provider for me. I felt that she was trying to give me what she hadn't in her lifetime.*

The visions and sensations continued for days. I actually physically felt her hold me in a loving embrace (something she never did when she was alive). I felt her everywhere — I could feel her rage in the wind and see her beauty in the shimmering ocean. I had dreams of her sitting in a circle with other women, bare-breasted, expressing her thoughts and sensual nature, connecting to something she had been without for a long time. It was strange to suddenly, at thirty-six, feel like I had a mother.

The day after her death I went for a bike ride and came upon a newborn baby deer that had just been hit by a car, so freshly hit that her body was still soft and warm. As I picked her up, she folded back into fetal position at my breast. I had the strangest feeling that in that moment my mother had been reborn into this tiny body just to let me hold and feel her vulnerability. A few days after her death I was feeling deeply moved but felt that my mother still had not taken responsibility for the abuse she had inflicted onto me as a child. Her attempts to give me back the energy that she had taken from me were deeply healing but I needed to hear that she was sorry for the scars that I still contend with. I had been listening to music on the radio which is very unusual for me. Just as I was having these thoughts and feelings of needing an, "I'm sorry," a song came on called "I'm Sorry," by Tracy Chapman. I new then that my mother was really sincere about cleaning things up with me.

I feel that by doing a visualization (the phowa practice) and bringing the Goddess to her at her time of passing was the truest possible answer for her searching soul. Even the strongest invocation of "God" couldn't have connected my mother to her ancient female roots. What my mother had been looking for was the Goddess and finding Her was not only transformational for my mother, but was for me also. Since her death I have felt for the first time in my life that I have a mother, which is quite an extraordinary transformation to make after years of dealing with the horrendous abuse that I suffered at her hand. Now, at times, I cannot distinguish between the Goddess, Herself, and my mother. I believe they reside closely together. I still deal with the abuse she inflicted on me but even during my worst moments I can still feel support and love and that somehow, throughout the horror, we have both truly found the Goddess.

Epilogue

Author and daughters.

From time to time, in the back of my mind, I wondered what led me to this deep interest in death and dying. That reason surfaced when I faced a near-death experience myself.

I had been experiencing, over time, heavy menstrual bleeding. I thought it was just menopausal flooding, which I'm sure it was, to an extent. However, it was much more than that. I didn't know that I had become extremely anemic over time. There were no symptoms. I had my work schedule and family life, traveled and just maintained a kind of high-paced life. Then, I experienced some tightness in my chest upon exertion and felt that I might be anemic and that I should get checked out.

Not only was I anemic, but extremely so. The doctors could not believe I was doing all that I was. My blood counts were near transfusion level. I had a fibroid tumor that had aggravated the bleeding. So, I was put on birth control pills to stop the bleeding, which they did. I did not have time to research how synthetic birth control pills would affect me. I now feel I was not cared for properly by a patriarchal system of "medicine," which I do not equate with healing, and that to give me a high dose of estrogen without checking my hormone levels was wrong, as it almost killed me. I developed a blood clot in my leg at which point I had to be put on blood thinners and taken off the birth control pills.

I knew that the bleeding would start again, and that I didn't know what would happen. I was also informed that if a part of the clot broke off and traveled to my lung I could die. I also knew I could die from bleeding, and that if the bleeding didn't stop, I would need surgery. I was admitted to the hospital. My doctors were not sure what to do, and had to discuss several options. The first one was to give me a D & C and pack my uterus to see if the bleeding would stop. So, into the operating room I went. It didn't work. I bled all night long. The next day, I was to have an emergency hysterectomy. But, because of the blood clot, I was at risk. My doctors were trying to decide if I needed to be transported to another hospital for a special procedure to have a filter inserted in my leg in case the blood clot traveled during surgery. But they decided I was not in stable enough condition to travel.

Prior to surgery they did a cat scan on my leg and saw that the clot was not there — they thought it had dissolved, which was a green light for surgery. At this time, I was administered a third pint of blood, and was prepared for the operation. My two daughters came to see me in the pre-op room, and we did a simple ritual for the removal of my female organs. I cried and said my womb was their first home and they cried with me. My youngest daughter then said, "Yes, mom, but we're here now." It reminded me how precious they are, how alive and beautiful, and how grateful I am for being given the opportunity to birth them. I felt that I was now giving my womb back to the great Mother, in order that my life be spared. I surrendered to the Mother. I asked a nurse to witness my grief as I lay on the gurney preparing myself to enter into the unknown. I had never been in a hospital before for anything, with the exception of my own birth.

I was then taken into the operating room, again. At this time, I began my prayer to Tara, "Om Tara, tutare, ture, soha" — asking for protection and the dispelling of fear. I also created a sacred circle by invoking the ancestors and grandmother spirits I work with as well as the energies of the directions of the sacred wheel. And I called upon my power animals. I had in the right pocket of the hospital gown two fetishes of my animal totems tucked away, nestled close to my heart. And then the mask was placed over my face. I came to in recovery, hearing distant voices telling me I had had a complete hysterectomy, and that I was a "real trooper." I was given morphine, which I didn't like, and asked that no more be administered to me. I preferred consciousness.

I was then taken to my hospital room, and my children came to see me a little while later. They stayed with me for a while, mostly in silence and in that deep kind of witnessing energy, as I was not into talking much. I asked them to gather around my bed and hold up their hands, palms facing me, and instructed them in channeling green healing light through their hands, directing healing energy to my body, and to the incision site. There was a sweet peacefulness and calm pervading the space. I was not in fear, which gave permission for my kids to be more relaxed. I had been surrendering over and over for two days, as the gravity of my situation kept revealing itself. I had to find that place of inner peace, and knew that fear would only cause difficulty, both in the odds of surviving as well as in healing.

While I certainly felt fear, I had to let it go, and asked the Goddess to hold me in Her arms and protect me. I heard a voice from time to time telling me I would be ok. I trusted that. Everything I believe in was tested to the maximum. I was able to have peaceful nights, sleeping fairly well. I was only taking half the amount of prescribed pain meds. I still preferred to be as conscious as possible, and realized that consciousness aids healing. The more conscious I could be, the more present I was for myself. The more prayer I could do, the more I could have a watchful eye on my own care — which I needed.

There were several times when meds were going to be administered, and I knew they weren't supposed to be given, as they were orders for my pre-surgery condition, not my post-op condition. The day after surgery, a cat scan was ordered to check my lungs, just in case the clot didn't totally dissolve, and went to my lungs. Usually one has symptoms of a pulmonary emoblism such as difficulty in breathing. Very often the condition is fatal. The scan revealed that I indeed had a clot in my lung, and I was asymptomatic. It was in the right lung over which I had placed my animal totem fetishes during surgery.

The doctors were amazed and told me I had dodged a bullet. It was hard to know when the clot traveled to my lung — perhaps it was already there during the surgery. I will never know that. What I know is that I survived. They put me back on the blood thinners, which put me at risk for internal bleeding. Just when I thought my ordeal was over, I had another hurdle to jump, and again had to surrender. I prayed for my tissues and muscles to heal and placed my hands over the incision frequently, giving myself healing energy, so that there would be no internal bleeding. Fortunately, there was none. The doctors had told me that even with all the blood I was given in transfusions, I bled the least amount they had ever seen in that kind of surgical procedure.

I chose to have no visitors, except for my kids, and a couple of friends at the end of my stay. I did not want anyone pulling on my energy in any way. During my six-day stay, I had two surgical procedures, three blood transfusions, cat scans, IV's and hovered at the edge of life and death several times. For someone who had never been in the hospital before and was used to being strong, it was quite humbling. The doctors told me on several occasions that I was quite healthy, even given all the trauma my body had experienced. That was good news.

The experience was indeed a shamanic death and rebirth. When I came home, I was pink and glowing, and people over and over told me how good I looked. I felt reborn. The meaning of it all is still making itself known, but I know that the Goddess was there at every turn, and I was able to be courageous and strong because of my faith in Her.

Following this life-altering event, I had two life-affirming experiences that reminded me of my connectedness to all of life.

One day I went to the beach. For some reason, there were very few people out that day, and for sometime I was the only one there. I walked down the beach and saw three vultures standing in the sand. I walked very slowly and watched them for a while. I had never seen vultures on the beach before, let alone three of them hanging out, unperturbed by my presence. I found a spot to lie down and so I rested for a while under the warmth of the sun. Fairly soon, I noticed that the vultures were flying overhead, circling me. At first, I was frightened. What did this mean? What kind of omen was this? As I watched them flying, I realized that they were the Triple Goddess — maiden, mother and crone — and were also the Black Dakini. They were letting me know that I had been reborn, and I felt welcomed by them. After circling me for a while, they flew off, soaring, as they do, into the blue of the spacious sky.

This experience reminded me of the matrix of life all living beings share, and that the synchronicity in our lives is a rich and vibrant affirmation of our being. Feeling that connectedness to the sacred, in a slight incident in one's day can be deeply empowering, if one is able to recognize it. I felt gratitude to be alive and that the yoniverse was affirming and celebrating my new aliveness with me.

Not long after this experience, I had another one of mysterious origin. I was driving and spontaneously decided to go the cemetery where I had some plaques engraved with the names of my parents. Once there, I noticed a couple with a child looking at the many plaques of names. I didn't really think much about their presence, and began to look for my parents' names. I was having a hard time finding them. So, this couple came up to me and asked me if I needed help, and I said that would be nice. I told them the name I was looking for was "Reid." The man responded by saying that was his mother's maiden name, spelled the same way. We all continued to look, and then I told them my father's name was Ralph, and my mother's was Barbara. They looked at me, and then at each other, and then said those were their names. At that moment, I felt my parents were present, witnessing my rebirth. It was amazing. We all just looked at each other, and realized what an incredible circumstance it was. I then found my parents' plaques. We parted ways, all sharing the same sense of the presence of the Mystery that cannot be explained.

I felt held by the Mother in my new awakening, and was so glad I just happened to decide to go there that day, at that moment. It was awesome, and again, generated within me a deep feeling of gratitude. I could feel the love of the Mother all around me.

A friend recently shared with me a story. She is a pre-school teacher and was sitting out in the yard with a four-year-old girl. They were appreciating the burst of spring in the beautiful flowers and ornamental trees. The little

girl said "Mother nature must be so proud!" What a wonderful observation
— the kind that a beautiful innocent child would make. That is how I felt
in the cemetery that day. The Cosmic Mother must feel so proud of me that
I survived a difficult near-death experience and I believe She found a way to
communicate that to me.

Re-Storing, Re-Kindling, Regenerating

In Memory of Shakes, Monica Sjöö, 1992

The beings in these stories that have been told have all shared in the love of the Mother in one form or another. The Goddess was a part of their dying process — for the humans, some more so than others, depending on spiritual orientation. For me, as midwife, I brought the Goddess in any way I could, knowing that it was Her guidance that would sustain me. Even in my father's death, though I did not consciously know the Goddess, I feel She was there, guiding me in how to be with him.

For others, I respectfully invoked Her in non-traditional ways that resonated with what was hapening in the moment. Covered over though She may be, She is at the core of every spiritual tradition. In Her presence, I feel that love, laughter, humor, grief, sadness, joy and selfless surrender can all be present. The burning compulsion to control can be dissolved, as people feel safer and more loving. Of course, this is a process, and not all people are able to rise to the occasion, as we have seen, but Goddess love provides an opening into something wonderful and sacred — something I feel most humans have forgotten yet nevertheless have a deep longing for.

While we are indeed, at this point in time, experiencing a collective near-death global tragedy, we cannot lose hope. As some of the aboriginal peoples of this land lived their lives with the axiom of making decisions according to the effects on seven succeeding generations, we must begin to do the same. If we cannot intelligently figure out how to dispose of nuclear waste, then we shouldn't use it. If using finite resources will deplete the earth, as is true, then we must create renewable resources. If hating women and our wise blood and fearing the Goddess do not promote life, then this behavior must be seen for what it is and transformed. If we are slowly killing ourselves and our children through war, abuse and greed, which we are, then we must find a way to end this destruction. There are over 2,000 children in Rwanda living parentless and homeless as a result of the civil war that took place there several years ago. They eat, if they are lucky, out of garbage dumps, and are parenting themselves. This is unspeakably hideous. How can we expect the survival of our species if this is what we do here on this planet to our children?

It is not possible to return to the past. However, it is possible to awaken to the remembrance of our ancestors and really begin to practice some of their wisdom in the present. It is deeply significant that humanity has lived longer in peace than we have in war — this memory is in our cells. We must tap that memory, and act on it. We must find the Goddess in all our current spiritual traditions, and make Her visible. This does not mean that one has to give up her/his chosen spiritual path. It does mean, however, that male-dominated internal and external hierarchical structures must be de-structured and transformed into loving, egalitarian circles and spirals.

It means that we must re-connect with the female origins of life and begin to repay the long overdue respect and attention to this fact. It means that men will need to learn to let go of their need to dominate and control, and women will need to come into right relationship with the deep menstrual moon-mind that lives in the "wildzone" of our foremothers and uncover the solely/souly female wisdom necessary to sustain life. Women will need to understand how we have been "colonized" by the patriarchal mind. Men will have to surrender their need to colonize and possess and their fear of not "being on top." They will need to connect to the Sacred Feminine within. We will all have to surrender aggressive competition and embrace peaceful cooperation. We will have to learn to trust each other, the greater cycles in which we live and the interconnectedness of the web of life and come to understand that we are simultaneously the dreamer and the dreamed.

Bibliography

Barham, Penny, "Baubo and Women's Sexuality," *Goddessing Magazine*, 1997.

Biaggi, Cristina, *Habitations of the Great Goddess*, Knowledge Ideas & Trends, Manchester, 1994.

Birnbaum, Lucia Chiavola , *dark mother*, Authors Choice Press, Lincoln, 2001.

Brener, Ann, *Mourning and Mitzvah*, Jewish Lights Publishers, Woodstock, 2nd ed., 2001.

Campbell, June, *Traveller in Space, In Search of Female Identity in Tibetan Buddhism*, George Braziller, New York, 1996.

Chesler, Phyllis, *Women and Madness*, Avon, New York, 1972.

Chokyi Nyima Rinpoche, *The Bardo Guidebook*, Rangjung Yeshe Publications, Nepal, Hong Kong, 1991.

Dalai Lama, *Illuminating the Path to Enlightenment*, Thubten Dhargye Ling Publications, Boston, 2002.

Dashu, Max, *Suppressed History Archives*, Oakland, CA, 2003.

_____*Streams of Wisdom*, Oakland, CA, 2000.

Drolma, Dawa, *Delog*, Padma Publishing, Junction City, 1995.

Eadie, Betty J., *Embraced by the Light*, Gold Leaf Press, Placerville, 1992.

Eisler, Riane, *Sacred Pleasure, Sex, Myth and the Politics of the Body, New Paths to Power and Love*, HarperSanFrancisco, 1995.

Eliade, Mircea, *Shamanism-Archaic Techniques of Ecstasy*, Routledge and Kegan Paul, London, 1964.

Gadon, Elinore, *Once and Future Goddess*, Harper and Row, San Francisco, 1989.

Grahn, Judy, *Blood, Bread and Roses: How Menstruation Created the World*, Beacon Press, Boston, 1993.

Gimbutas, Marija, *The Language of the Goddess*, HarperSan Francisco, San Francisco, 1989.

_____ *The Civilization of the Goddess*, The World of Old Europe, HarperSanFrancisco, San Francisco. 1991.

Göttner-Abendroth, Heide, *The Dancing Goddess: Principles of a Matriarchal Aesthetic*, Beacon Press, Boston, 1982.

Halifax, Joan, *Fruitful Darkness, Reconnecting with the Body of the Earth*, HarperSanFrancisco, 1993.

Harding, M. Esther, *Woman's Mysteries, Ancient and Modern*, Bantam, 1971.

Harner, Michael, *The Way of the Shaman: A Guide to Power and Healing*, Bantam, New York, 1980.

Harrod, James, The Upper Paleolithic "Double Goddess": "Venus" Figurines as Sacred Female Transformation Processes in the Light of a Decipherment of European Upper Paleolithic Language, from *The Realm of the Ancestors*, Marler (ed.), Knowledge, Ideas & Trends, Inc., Manchester, 1997.

James, E.O., *The Cult of the Mother Goddess*, Thames & Hudson, London, 1959.

Jeffries, Rosalind, Image of Woman in African Cave Art, *Black Women in Antiquity*, Transaction Publishers, New Brunswick, 1988.

Johnson, Buffie, *Lady of the Beasts: Ancient Images of the Great Goddess and Her Sacred Animals*, Harper & Row, New York, 1988.

Kalweit, Holger, *Dreamtime and Inner Space: The World of the Shaman*, Shambhala, Boston & London, 1988.

La Monte, Willow, *Black Madonna Sampler*, Goddessing Magazine, 1997

Leadbetter, C.W., *The Masters and the Path*, Theosophical Publishing House, Adyar, Madras, India, 1965 [1925].

Leake, Jonathan, *Britain Sunday Times*, January 30, 2005.

Levy, Gertrude, *Religious Conceptions of the Stone Age*, Harper Row, New York, 1963.

Macy, Joanna, *World as Lover, World as Self*, Parallax Press, Berkeley, 1991.

Marler, Joan, (ed.) *From the Realm of the Ancestors, An Anthology in Honor of Marija Gimbutas*, Knowledge, Ideas & Trends, Inc., Manchester, 1997.

Mithen, Stephen, *Britain Sunday Times*, January 30, 2005.

Mindell, Arnold, *The Shaman's Body*, HarperSanFrancisco, 1993.

Mountainwater, Shekhinah, *Ariadne's Thread, A Workbook of Goddess Magic*, The Crossing Press, Freedom, 1991.

Nicholson, Shirley, *Shamanism*, Theosophical Publishing House, Wheaton, 1987.

Noble, Vicki, *The Double Goddess, Women Sharing Power*, Inner Traditions, Rochester, 2003.

Paul, R.A., *The Tibetan Symbolic World*, University of Chicago Press, Chicago, 1982.

Reis, Patricia, *Through the Goddess, A Woman's Way of Healing*, Continuum, New York, 1996.

Rowan, John, *The Horned God, Feminism and Men as Wounding and Healing*, Routledge, London, New York, 1987.

Sanday, Peggy Reeves, *Women at the Center, Life in a Modern Matriarchy*, Cornell University Press, Ithaca, London, 2002.

Sjöö, Monica, *Return of the Dark/Light Mother*, Plain View Press, Austin, 1999.

_____with Mor, Barbara, *The Great Cosmic Mother*, Harper and Row, San Francisco, 1987.

Skafte, Dianne, *Listening to the Oracle, The Ancient Art of Finding Guidance* in the Signs and Symbols All Around Us, HarperSanFrancisco, 1997.

Sogyal Rinpoche, *Tibetan Book of Living and Dying*, HarperSanFrancisco, 1992.

Stein, Diane, *Psychic Healing with Spirits Guides and Angels*, Crossing Press, Freedom, 1996.

Streep, Peg, *Sanctuaries of the Goddess, The Sacred Landscapes and Objects*, Little, Brown and Company, Boston, New York, Toronto, London, 1994.

Tolle, Eckhart, *Power of Now*, New World Library, Novato, 1999.

VanPraagh, James, *Talking to Heaven*, Dutton, New York, 1997.

Van Sertima, Ivan, *Black Women in Antiquity*, Transaction Publishers, New Brunswick, 1988.

Vaughn, Genevieve, "Gift-Giving and the Goddess," *Avalon Magazine*, Spring, 1999.

Veen, Veronica, *The Goddess of Malta, The Lady of the Waters and the Earth*, Innana-Fia, Haarlem, Holland, 1992.

von Cles-Reden, Sibylle, *The Realm of the Great Goddess*, Prentice Hall, Englewood Cliffs, 1962.

Walker, Barbara, *The Crone, Woman of Age, Wisdom and Power*, HarperSanFrancisco, 1985.

_____*The Woman's Encyclopedia of Myths and Secrets*, Harper and Row, San Francisco, 1983.

Leslene, photo by Miriam

About the Author

Leslene della-Madre has studied shamanism (she-moon-ism) for over thirty-five years. She is founder of *Winged Woman Return*, a center for shamanic healing in Sebastopol, California. She has served as spiritual adjunct to the medical and therapeutic communities for many years, assisting the dying and their families as well as offering spiritual guidance for healing of mind, body and spirit. She holds sacred healing space for individuals, couples and families and facilitates sacred circles, rituals and retreats for women. She has taught women's spirituality for many years and has synthesized her studies of different spiritual traditions into a practice of the loving Mother presence. Leslene is the mother to two daughters, a foster son and a step-son. She is a fierce lover of life and holds a vision of bountiful love, peace, justice and beauty for all.

About the Artist

Monica Sjöö was a radical anarcho/eco-feminist and Goddess artist, writer and thinker involved in Earth Mysteries. Born in the north of Sweden in 1938, she lived mostly in Britain since the late 1950s, and was active in the Women's Liberation Movement since the 60s. Her paintings were inspired by journeys to, and experiences at, the Neolithic sacred sites of the ancient Great Mother, and have been exhibited throughout northern Europe and in the USA.

She was the co-author, with Barbara Mor, of the influential *The Great Cosmic Mother: Rediscovering the Religion of the Earth* (Harper and Row, San Francisco, 1987, new edition 1991). She believed in political direct action to protect Mother Earth.

(Author's Note) Monica Sjöö passed into the arms of the ancient Mother on August 8, 2005. She wanted very much to see this book in print before making her passage. I went to be with her in England when I heard she was leaving this world, carrying with me the galley to show her what the book would look like in print. She gave her approval. The first printed copy, a proof, arrived at her home in Bristol in the morning of the day she died! Though she was not conscious, I knew she was seeing it in the way she needed to.

I spent several days with Monica during her passage, and helped create a Lammas ritual for her where her friends and family gave blessings at her bedside, each offering her a flower and heartfelt words. Monica held in her hands a bouquet of blessings at the end of the ritual. All who were present gave permission to her to leave, and she ended the ritual saying, "I want to die, I want to fly." And so she did, one week later, resting next to the very same painting of the horse goddess, Rhiannon, above.

Photo by Susan Bright of Monica in her study in Bristol, in the UK.

LaVergne, TN USA
07 December 2009
166159LV00001BA/12/A